NMLFF

D1454675

Please return
You can renew at. norlink.norfolk.gov.uk
or by telephone: **0344 800 8006**
Please have your library card & PIN ready.

NORFOLK LIBRARY
AND INFORMATION SERVICE
NORFOLK ITEM

30129 070 566 68

JOHN EDMUNDS holds a first-class degree in French from the University of Wales and a PhD in English from the Shakespeare Institute of the University of Birmingham. After a varied career as an actor, schoolmaster and broadcaster, he relinquished his post as a BBC TV national newsreader to return to his alma mater at Aberystwyth and become the founder-director of what is now the university's department of Theatre, Film and Television Studies. There he taught French seventeenth-century drama using his own translations, which have been produced on the professional stage and on BBC Radio 3. He has taught at the University of California and the University of the Americas in Mexico. Also a translator of Spanish, he has published *Four Major Plays* of Lorca in the Oxford World's Classics series.

JOSEPH HARRIS, a graduate of Trinity Hall, Cambridge, where he was subsequently awarded a PhD, is currently Senior Lecturer at Royal Holloway, University of London. Author of *Hidden Agendas: Cross-Dressing in Seventeenth-Century France* (2005), he has published widely on gender and theatre in early modern France. His latest monograph is entitled *Inventing the Spectator: Subjectivity and the Theatrical Experience in Early Modern France* (Oxford University Press, forthcoming), and he is also embarking on a project on death and murder in the works of Corneille.

Four French Plays: Cinna, The Misanthrope, Andromache, Phaedra

Translated with Notes by
JOHN EDMUNDS

Introduced by
JOSEPH HARRIS

PENGUIN BOOKS

PENGUIN CLASSICS

Published by the Penguin Group
Penguin Books Ltd, 80 Strand, London WC2R ORL, England
Penguin Group (USA) Inc., 375 Hudson Street, New York, New York 10014, USA
Penguin Group (Canada), 90 Eglinton Avenue East, Suite 700, Toronto, Ontario, Canada M4P 2Y3
(a division of Pearson Penguin Canada Inc.)
Penguin Ireland, 25 St Stephen's Green, Dublin 2, Ireland (a division of Penguin Books Ltd)
Penguin Group (Australia), 707 Collins Street,
Melbourne, Victoria 3008, Australia (a division of Pearson Australia Group Pty Ltd)
Penguin Books India Pvt Ltd, 11 Community Centre, Panchsheel Park,
New Delhi – 110 017, India
Penguin Group (NZ), 67 Apollo Drive, Rosedale, Auckland 0632, New Zealand
(a division of Pearson New Zealand Ltd)
Penguin Books (South Africa) (Pty) Ltd, Block D, Rosebank Office Park, 181 Jan Smuts Avenue,
Parktown North, Gauteng 2193, South Africa

Penguin Books Ltd, Registered Offices: 80 Strand, London WC2R ORL, England

www.penguin.com

These translations first published in Great Britain by Penguin Classics 2013
001

Translations and Notes copyright © John Edmunds, 2013
Introduction, Chronology and Further Reading copyright © Joseph Harris, 2013
All rights reserved

The moral right of the translator and the introducer has been asserted

All applications for a licence to use these translations in performance must be made to
Penguin Books, c/o Permissions, 80 Strand, London WC2R ORL.
No performance may take place unless a licence has been obtained.

Set in 10.25/12.25 PostScript Adobe Sabon
Typeset by Dinah Drazin
Printed in Great Britain by Clays Ltd, St Ives plc

Except in the United States of America, this book is sold subject
to the condition that it shall not, by way of trade or otherwise, be lent,
re-sold, hired out, or otherwise circulated without the publisher's
prior consent in any form of binding or cover other than that in
which it is published and without a similar condition including this
condition being imposed on the subsequent purchaser

ISBN: 978-0-141-39208-0

www.greenpenguin.co.uk

MIX
Paper from
responsible sources
FSC
www.fsc.org   FSC™ C018179

Penguin Books is committed to a sustainable
future for our business, our readers and our planet
This book is made from Forest Stewardship
Council™ certified paper.

ALWAYS LEARNING   **PEARSON**

Contents

Chronology

Especially before the mid seventeenth century, the date of a play's first performance is sometimes difficult to establish; the dates given below are therefore approximate. Plays are categorized as 'C' (comedy), 'CB' (comedy-ballet), 'T' (tragedy) and 'TC' (tragicomedy); the names of other genres are given in full. Many of the plays have never been translated into English; only the translated titles of major works have been included in brackets here.

1606 Birth of Pierre Corneille in Rouen.

1610 After the assassination of his father, Henri IV, Louis XIII becomes king of France.

1615–22 The young Corneille studies with the Jesuits.

1622 Birth of Molière, as Jean (later Jean-Baptiste) Poquelin, in Paris.

1624 Corneille starts his legal training in Rouen.

1629 Corneille's first play, *Mélite* (C). Moves to Paris following the success of *Mélite*.

1630 Corneille, *Clitandre* (TC).

1631 Corneille, *La Veuve* (C) and *La Galerie du Palais* (C).

1632 Corneille, *La Suivante* (C).

1633 Corneille, *La Place Royale* (C).
    Molière starts his studies with the Jesuits at the Collège de Clermont in Paris.

1634 Jean Mairet writes *Sophonisbe* (T), often regarded as France's first 'regular' tragedy.

1635 Foundation of the Académie Française.
    Corneille, *Médée* (*Medea*) (T).

1636 Corneille, *L'Illusion comique* (*The Theatrical Illusion*) (C).

1637 Corneille, *Le Cid* (*The Cid*) (TC). Prompts a heated literary debate known as the 'querelle du *Cid*' ('quarrel of *The Cid*').

1638 Birth of the future Louis XIV.

1639 Birth of Jean Racine at La Ferté-Milon, in Picardy.

1640 Corneille, *Horace* (T) and *Cinna* (T). Marries Marie Lampérière.

1642 Death of Cardinal Richelieu, chief minister to Louis XIII. He is succeeded by Cardinal Mazarin.
    Corneille, *Polyeucte* (T).
    Molière starts his legal training in Orléans.

1643 Death of Louis XIII. Start of regency of Anne of Austria.
    Corneille, *La Mort de Pompée* (T) and *Le Menteur* (*The Liar*) (C). First meeting of Corneille and Molière, in Normandy.
    Molière founds the 'Illustre Théâtre' troupe.

1644 Corneille, *La Suite du Menteur* (C) and *Rodogune* (T).
    Jean-Baptiste Poquelin first adopts the pseudonym 'Molière' and becomes director of his troupe.

1645 Molière is briefly imprisoned for debt.

1646 Corneille, *Théodore, vierge et martyre* (T).

1647 Corneille, *Héraclius* (T). Corneille becomes member of the Académie Française.

1648 Start of the 'Fronde', a period of civil war in France.
    Corneille publishes a revised version of *Le Cid* as a tragedy.

1649 The young Racine moves to Port-Royal convent with his grandmother.

1650 Corneille, *Andromède* ('machine tragedy' – a new genre making use of impressive and elaborate stage machinery) and *Don Sanche d'Aragon* (heroic comedy).

1651 Corneille, *Nicomède* (T) and *Pertharite* (T). Corneille retires from the stage after the failure of *Pertharite*, which receives only one performance.

1653 End of the Fronde.

Racine studies at the Collège de Beauvais in Paris.

1655 Molière's first full-length play, *L'Étourdi* (C).

1656 Thomas Corneille (Pierre's younger brother) offers *Timocrate* (T), arguably the most popular tragedy of the century.

Corneille, translation of Thomas à Kempis, *Imitation of Christ*.

Molière, *Dépit amoureux* (C).

1657 François Hédelin, abbé d'Aubignac, publishes *La Pratique du théâtre* (started *c.* 1640), a key text of seventeenth-century dramatic theory.

1658 Molière's troupe settles in Paris under protection of 'Monsieur', the king's brother.

1659 Corneille returns to the stage with *Oedipe*.

Molière, *Les Précieuses ridicules* (*Such Preposterously Precious Ladies*) (C).

1660 Corneille publishes a complete edition of his plays to date, accompanied with three *Discours sur le poème dramatique* (*Discourses on the Dramatic Poem*) and an 'Examen' on each play.

Molière, *Sganarelle, ou le Cocu imaginaire* (C).

1661 Death of Cardinal Mazarin and start of Louis XIV's personal reign.

Corneille, *La Toison d'Or* (machine tragedy).

Molière, *Dom Garcie de Navarre* (C) and *L'École des maris* (C).

1662 Corneille, *Sertorius* (T). The play is heavily criticized by d'Aubignac, who will attack two more of Corneille's plays in a succession of irate pamphlets.

Molière, *L'École des femmes* (*The School for Wives*) (C). Marries Armande Béjart.

1663 Corneille, *Sophonisbe* (T).

Heated literary debate about *L'École des femmes*, to which Molière contributes two meta-theatrical plays, *La Critique de l'École des femmes* (C) and *L'Impromptu de Versailles* (C).

1664 Corneille, *Othon* (T).

Molière, *Le Mariage forcé* (CB) and *La Princesse d'Élide*

(CB). The first version of *Tartuffe* (C) is banned after its first performance. Birth and death of Molière's first son, who has Louis XIV as godfather.

Racine's first surviving play, *La Thébaïde, ou les Frères ennemis* (T), performed by Molière's troupe.

1665 Molière, *Dom Juan* (*Don Juan*) (C); the play is soon banned for supposed impiety. Molière's troupe becomes the king's official troupe.

Racine, *Alexandre le Grand* (T); the play is initially performed by Molière's troupe before Racine withdraws it.

1666 Corneille, *Agésilas* (T).

Molière, *Le Misanthrope* (*The Misanthrope*) (C), *Le Médecin malgré lui* (C), *Mélicerte* (C), *Pastorale comique* (C) and *Le Sicilien* (C).

Racine replies harshly to Pierre Nicole's condemnation of the theatre in his 'Lettre à l'auteur des "Hérésies imaginaires"' ('Letter to the Author of the "Imaginary Heresies"')

1667 Corneille, *Attila* (T).

Molière, second performance of *Tartuffe*; this version is also banned.

Racine, *Andromaque* (*Andromache*) (T).

1668 Molière, *Amphitryon* (C), *George Dandin* (C) and *L'Avare* (*The Miser*) (C).

Racine, *Les Plaideurs* (C).

1669 The ban on Molière's *Tartuffe* is finally lifted. Molière, *Monsieur de Pourceaugnac* (C).

Racine, *Britannicus* (T).

1670 Corneille and Racine both produce plays on the same dramatic subject: Corneille's *Tite et Bérénice* (heroic comedy) and Racine's *Bérénice* (T).

Molière, *Les Amants magnifiques* (C) and *Le Bourgeois gentilhomme* (C).

1671 Corneille, Molière, playwright Philippe Quinault and composer Jean-Baptiste Lully collaborate on *Psyché* (tragedy-ballet).

Molière, *Les Fourberies de Scapin* (C) and *La Comtesse d'Escarbagnas* (C).

1672 Corneille, *Pulchérie* (heroic comedy).

Molière, *Les Femmes savantes* (*Those Learned Ladies*) (C).

Racine, *Bajazet* (T).

1673 Molière's last play, *Le Malade imaginaire* (*The Imaginary Invalid*) (C). Death of Molière.

Racine, *Mithridate* (T). Becomes member of the Académie Française.

1674 Corneille's last play, *Suréna* (*Surena*) (T).

Racine, *Iphigénie en Aulide* (*Iphigenia in Aulis*) (T).

1677 Racine, *Phèdre* (*Phaedra*), his last secular play. Appointed king's official historiographer. Marries Catherine de Romanet.

1682 Corneille publishes a complete edition of his plays.

1684 Death of Corneille.

1689 Racine returns to the stage with *Esther* (T), a religious drama written at the request of Madame de Maintenon, Louis XIV's second wife.

1691 Racine's last play, *Athalie* (*Athaliah*) (T), another religious drama.

1699 Death of Racine.

Joseph Harris 2013

Introduction

Given the rich and varied corpus of French theatre from its medieval origins to the present day, it might seem perverse to give the title 'Four French Plays' to a handful of works not even spanning four decades. Yet in many respects the thirty-seven years that separated Corneille's *Cinna* (1640) from Racine's *Phaedra* (*Phèdre*, 1677) were the defining period of French theatre. Not only was it one of the most fertile in French dramatic history, but the plays that emerged provided standards and models with which later writers had to contend. This was also the period whose theatre came to be recognized across Europe as somehow typically French. When critics such as Dryden (in seventeenth-century England) or Lessing (in eighteenth-century Germany) spoke of 'French theatre', what they meant was the drama of Corneille, Molière and Racine. So if one wants an introduction to French theatre, the seventeenth century is an obvious – and very rewarding – place to start.

And yet labels such as 'seventeenth-century French theatre' can be as restrictive as they are helpful. By stressing the historical and (for most English-speakers) geographical gulf that separates us from the works themselves, such labels draw our attention to what makes these works different and risk pigeonholing them in ways that constrain their power to move and affect us. This is not to say that these plays are therefore somehow 'timeless' or 'universal' either. They each bear the unmistakable stamp of their birthplace, and a sensitive engagement with them – whether as reader, spectator, actor or director – involves steering a middle course between treating them as historical curiosities and unfairly expecting them to conform to our own expectations, tastes and values. The aim of this introduction is to equip readers with enough information about the context and conventions of seventeenth-century French theatre to encourage and enrich their appreciation of the four plays featured here. The first three sections provide a general introduction to French theatre of this period, drawing examples wherever appropriate from the four texts in this volume; the subsequent sections then focus in turn on each of the authors and their plays.

Seventeenth-century French theatre has never quite escaped the image of clichéd inflexibility it acquired during the early nineteenth century. Rebelling against what they regarded as the stultifying dictates of 'classicism', Romantic polemicists such as Hugo and Stendhal were swift to condemn the theatre of Racine and his contemporaries as unnecessarily rigid and formalized, especially in comparison with the works of their own dramatic hero, Shakespeare. This image of a grand but impersonal classicism has proved an abiding one, even for admirers of the period; indeed, some have revered these plays for the very qualities that others reject and condemn. Yet both critics and devotees of the period risk perpetuating very similar basic stereotypes of a theatre whose grandeur supposedly lies in its stateliness, seriousness and dignified restraint. Such clichés are not always helped by some well-meaning modern directors, who either adopt a tone of supposedly authentic solemnity (even in comedy) or artificially enliven plays deemed insufficiently dramatic on their own terms.

As I hope to suggest here, it is not through such clichés as these that we should approach a theatre that was conceived throughout in terms of performance. Seventeenth-century French playwrights sought to produce powerful and irresistible emotional effects in their audiences, and the printed page can scarcely do justice to the richness of dramatic performance. Molière clearly acknowledges this when he recommends one of his plays 'only to those with eyes to find, in reading, all the performance of the stage'.[1] Part of the purpose of this introduction is to help readers develop such 'eyes' for themselves – to shake off preconceptions and to embrace these plays as, above all, engaging pieces of theatre. Of course, Molière was writing for his contemporaries, not for future generations, and so some understanding of the cultural and aesthetic context is needed to let these plays speak to us as they did to their first audiences. We should never forget that a play script is both the residue of a long-lost performance and the template or dramatic 'score' for future productions. Appreciating the theatre of different historical periods certainly means adopting a different mindset, but this mindset does not have to be one of po-faced reverence or pre-emptive, a priori respect.

BETWEEN 'CLASSICISM' AND MODERNITY

The three playwrights featured in this collection – Corneille, Molière and Racine – have long been regarded as the figureheads of a certain French 'classicism'. Used loosely, the term has certain advantages in reflecting some general aesthetic tendencies that developed in France across the century – most notably, an appreciation of order, restraint, harmony, balance and reason. Yet such labels can also skew our understanding of a period, leading us both to perceive what is not present, and to overlook or misjudge what is. With its connotations of formal architecture and statuary, the term 'classicism' can impose a misleading homogeneity and apparent stasis on to a period that was characterized, as much as any other, by diversity and experimentation. At least in the theatre, a more appropriate term would perhaps be 'neo-classicism', in that seventeenth-century dramatists frequently sought inspiration in classical antiquity, while attempting to update ancient material for modern audiences. The use of classical content is most evident in tragedy, where plots and characters were largely taken from ancient history or Graeco-Roman mythology, but the classical influence can also be found in some of the plots and characters of comedy. In all cases, though, a key concern was the creative transformation of ancient sources and models. The ancient world often had a coarseness and savagery that sat uneasily with the refined, delicate sensibility upon which French high society increasingly prided itself. As his first preface to *Andromache* suggests (p. 140), Racine discovered this, to his cost, when King Pyrrhus, in the playwright's already diluted depiction of him, was nonetheless criticized for ungallant behaviour towards his beloved Andromache.

As this example suggests, one of the greatest divergences between modern and ancient theatre was the new importance given to romantic love and appropriate behaviour in courtship. Love plots were integrated into ancient material with varying success. Although the gallant discussions of love that Corneille introduced into his own version of the Oedipus myth (*Oedipe*, 1659) seem perverse against the horrifying backdrop of plague and incest, the love element in the plays featured here is integrated far more successfully. Much of the dramatic and ethical intensity of *Cinna*, for example, derives from Corneille's introduction of a love affair between Cinna and the largely invented Emilia. It is this love that transforms the original historical conspiracy from a purely political matter into a far more ambiguous and dramatically engaging affair, where personal motives and interests jostle with and often undermine nobler ideals.

DRAMATIC PRACTICE
AND 'THE RULES'

The love plot in *Cinna* – as, indeed, in the other plays featured here – is not an extraneous element tagged on for popular appeal, but rather belongs organically to the play as a whole. The need for each play to work as a fully integrated whole also reflects a certain classical influence: that of the Greek philosopher Aristotle, whose *Poetics* (c. 335 BC) was regarded as the main authority on dramatic matters. Perhaps the most familiar, but also the least well understood, characteristic of 'classical' theatre was its adoption of the 'three unities' of time, place and action. Although interpretations of all three differed widely, the 'unities' were typically summed up as stipulating that a play should have one main plot (action) that takes place in one location (place) and lasts no longer than a single day (time).

Yet French playwrights did not just embrace the unities out of misplaced deference to ancient models. While these conventions might strike modern (or Romantic) spectators as unnecessary restrictions on the dramatist's creative freedom, they made perfect sense to theatre theorists and practitioners of the day. Indeed, the unities began in the 1630s to be justified in terms of the spectator's experience. Obliged to remain stationary for two or three hours, the audience, it was argued, would have difficulty following plays in which the action leaped around between different times and locations, since such changes would break the continuity of their own experience. Maintaining a unity of action – that is, having one main plot with no unrelated subplots – likewise helped to retain the spectator's attention throughout the play. The ideal was thus, in effect, to produce a compelling dramatic fiction that would not overly tax an audience's capacity for attention or imagination. Spectators – or so the theory went – should be given the impression of being present, not just at a faithful representation of a genuine historical event, but at that event itself. This is, of course, a very naïve notion of theatrical representation, and one which must have been counteracted in practice by numerous anti-illusionistic elements of the period – the stylized acting modes, use of verse, frequent monologues and (in tragedy at least) strange composite costumes combining modern and pseudo-ancient dress.

It is perhaps the plays themselves that let us best appreciate the true dramatic significance of the unities: namely, that they concentrate the dramatic action to levels of intensity that are hard to attain otherwise. For example, playwrights from alternative traditions can start their dramatic narrative at whatever point they please. A Shakespeare or a Marlowe, say, might have started *The Misanthrope* or *Phaedra* with the moment in which the protagonist first sets eyes on the object of his or her ill-starred love, and then traced the gradual development of this passion in a succession of loosely connected episodes. Seventeenth-century French dramatists, by contrast, are compelled to home in on the one day in which the plot's most decisive events happen. The actions of the whole narrative are not, therefore, implausibly condensed into a single day (although many of Marivaux's comedies in the early eighteenth century would trace the birth and blossoming of love in a drastically foreshortened time period). Rather, the day chosen marks a point of climax after an accumulation of events and pressures whose origins may date back years. Emotions such as Emilia's desire for vengeance (in *Cinna*) or Phaedra's love for Hippolytus (in *Phaedra*) have long simmered under the surface but are now ready to burst out, with potentially lethal consequences. So, although these plays take place in a single day, the past continues to exert pressure on the present. Were we shown the plot from its very inception we might be distracted by the possibility of alternative outcomes; as it is, the basic situation is given to us from the start as something fixed and unchangeable.

These formal restrictions thus promote the sense that the range of options open to the characters is severely limited. When watching seventeenth-century French theatre, we know that there will be no drastic change of location, and that the action will not suddenly skip ahead to some later point that might put the present situation into perspective. Similarly, we know that we will not get distracted by side-plots that might grant us some brief respite from the main action – and still less, in tragedies, by any sudden moments of comic relief. The stage starts to resemble a pressure-cooker with no release valve; the pressure mounts steadily throughout, leading towards an often explosive conclusion that can seem inevitable. Because the stage's metaphorical 'camera' is focused inexorably on one action as it draws towards its conclusion, it is easy as a spectator to feel that the conclusion itself is therefore just as inexorable. Perhaps mistakenly, we let the conditions of the theatrical performance inform our experience of the fictional plot, and attribute to the fictional world a fatalism that may derive ultimately from the demands and conventions of the dramatic genre itself.

Skilfully handled, then, the unities can produce a dramatic sense of intensity, entrapment and even fatality. Familiarity with the period's conventions also helps to throw into relief dramatic features that might otherwise pass us by, especially as readers. In the curious opening lines of Racine's *Phaedra*, for example, Hippolytus informs us that he is leaving. Now, Racine's audience knows that he cannot truly do this, since if he is to be a major character – and the unity of action demands that nothing onstage be irrelevant – then the play would have to follow his movements and thus break the unity of place. Throughout the play Hippolytus repeats his desire to flee, but a succession of events prevents him from leaving. The tragic irony is that once he finally does leave the palace – by now as a shameful banishment rather an escape to freedom – his fate has been irrevocably sealed; his wish to leave is finally granted, but only once he has lingered long enough for everything to go horribly wrong. A comparable structure underlies *The Misanthrope*, albeit in a more comic mode. Throughout Molière's play, Alceste hopes to compel Célimène to forsake her various suitors, but events – above all, ironically, the arrival of various romantic rivals – repeatedly detain him in Célimène's house and defer the confrontation he seeks.

POETIC LANGUAGE AND DRAMATIC POETRY

In a sense, the unities are only the most obvious examples of a far more general drive towards concentration of dramatic effect. Half a century ago, the critic Odette de Mourgues referred to Racine's theatre as the 'triumph of relevance',[2] and her formulation holds for much of Corneille's and Molière's work too. This 'pared-down' approach can be seen in the *dramatis personae* for the plays in this volume. Leaving aside non-speaking roles, *Cinna* features nine characters, *The Misanthrope* eleven, *Andromache* and *Phaedra* eight each – in comparison with some twenty or more in many of Shakespeare's plays. Yet it is not only the cast list that is pared down. Ideals of appropriate diction and clarity of expression meant that the vocabulary on offer to dramatists was considerably restricted, with a particular emphasis on abstract nouns. It has been estimated that, in the original French, Racine uses a total of 800 different words across his entire corpus, while estimates of Shakespeare's vocabulary often reach into the tens of thousands.

What this restriction brings in effect is a drastic increase in poetic intensity. Through reuse in different contexts, even the most familiar of words can build up across a single play an impressive richness of poetic, dramatic and psychological connotation. Take an everyday word like 'blood' (*sang*), for example. Even if dramatic conventions prohibited the depiction of bloodshed onstage, blood features heavily in the tragedies – whether literally, as in Augustus' violent past or Hippolytus' tragic demise, or more metaphorically, in the sense of the family bloodline. The same word can thus connote both death and the continuation of life, and these connotations can come into conflict when, as so often in tragedy, family is turned against itself. Cinna, for example, cites 'The son still dripping with his father's blood' (l. 201) as a sign of Augustus' brutality, while Phaedra's appeals to Theseus not to kill his own son are more evocative still:

> Spare your own blood, I make bold to implore you.
> Let me not quake to hear its tortured cry;
> Do not store up for me the endless pain
> Of causing it to spill by a father's hand.
>
> (ll. 1171–4)

Phaedra's emotional plea combines literal blood (the bloodshed she wants to prevent) with more figurative meanings. Technically, the 'tortured cry' she imagines hearing is that of Hippolytus, but she attributes it rhetorically to the blood itself

– that is, to Theseus' own blood, crying out in horror at the unnatural act of father murdering son. Although, needless to say, this poetic density is very hard to achieve in translation, the translations here steer a masterly course between fidelity, depth and comprehensibility.

Indeed, although all three playwrights are great poets, it would be artificial to distinguish the poet from the dramatist. At its best, poetic theatre harmonizes the poetic and the dramatic, such that each builds on – and feeds off – the other. On the one hand, the verse gains incomparably in richness when bodily metaphors and images such as the 'blood' motif are set against a literal situation being acted out by living, breathing actors. Yet, as a brief reflection on the conditions of dramatic performance will suggest, poetic evocations of the characters' bodies can be dramatically and psychologically significant in other ways too. For most of the seventeenth century, France did not have purpose-built public theatres, but tended instead to use converted real-tennis courts with a stage at one end. Seated spectators would line the two longer walls, while the 'pit' (*parterre*) would be filled with standing spectators. The poor lighting, awkward angles and sometimes considerable distance between stage and spectator meant that there was no guarantee that the audience could see every gesture or facial expression of the actors onstage. As a result, dramatists would frequently have characters make explicit reference to their or others' bodily movements or facial expressions, not only as implicit stage directions for actors – actual stage directions being very rare in this theatre – but also as clues for spectators who might not be able to follow the performers' physical movements closely enough. Seventeenth-century French drama texts thus offer a wealth of clues about performance that can easily be overlooked on a cursory reading. Perhaps the masterpiece in this regard is the final scene of Racine's *Andromache*, in which Orestes has terrible hallucinations of sudden darkness, rivers of blood, and the apparition of the murdered Pyrrhus and Hermione, followed by the monstrous Furies, deities of vengeance. Clues about Orestes' frenzied movements – looking for an escape, attempting to attack his ghostly rival and finally offering himself up to the Furies and to his beloved – are all implicit within the script.

What the general avoidance of stage directions thus means is that the physical body is, as it were, rendered or doubled in language, embedded in the verse itself and hence worked into the overall poetic fabric of the play. Significantly, although there are numerous indications about the subtleties of gesture and expression, French theatre of the period contains very little physical action of any real import. Increasingly strict conventions of decorum and propriety restricted, in effect, the depiction of anything too bodily onstage, be this violent (bloodshed) or sexual (for example, kissing). What this means, of course, is that whatever action we do witness onstage – Cinna kneeling in supplication before Augustus, or Phaedra simply sitting down as her legs give way – gains inordinately in significance and can express complex states of mind, body or soul. Particularly in tragedy, the convention against bloodshed onstage meant that the stage space is preserved as something of a 'no-man's-land', where physical action is almost precluded and where all conflicts are conducted on a verbal level. Yet such conflicts do not forfeit any of their ferocity or intensity for all that; this is a theatre in which, as one of the foremost dramatic theoreticians of the time put it, 'to speak is to act'.[3] Language has a special status in this theatre. Words do not just refer to actions that take place elsewhere (although they can certainly do so); rather, they comprise the dramatic action itself. The traditional example to cite here is that of Phaedra, whose love only becomes harmful to others once she breaks her self-imposed silence, but there are many other examples too. In *The Misanthrope*, for example, Célimène initially woos her suitors through her mastery of language, but is undone when her letters pass into the wrong hands. Indeed, the dramatic action of all these plays is carried largely through the characters' words – words which retain their awesome power to affect, touch, seduce, shock or move us even today.

PIERRE CORNEILLE

Perhaps paradoxically, the supposed 'father of French tragedy', Pierre Corneille (1606–84), retained throughout his career a certain discomfort with tragedy as a genre. He started out primarily as a writer of comedies depicting the conversations of refined, urbane individuals known as *honnêtes gens* ('decent people'). In contrast to the crude farces of his day and the long and somewhat clumsy high comedies of his Renaissance predecessors, Corneille's witty plays showed a great sophistication of language, and interesting psychological observation that never stood in the way of an entertaining plot. In initially favouring comedy, Corneille was also swimming against the popular taste for the highly irregular, heroically 'unclassical' composite genre known as tragicomedy. The playwright himself wrote only two tragicomedies – his rather sprawling early work *Clitandre* (1630), and the play that really made his name, *The Cid* (*Le Cid*, 1637). *The Cid* marks the tipping-point both in Corneille's career and in the history of French theatre. On one level, the play pushed tragicomedy to its very limits, investing it with a psychological depth and moral seriousness that brought it closer to tragedy. Yet it was still formally 'irregular' enough to attract swift and harsh criticism from various self-appointed experts (often rival playwrights), and the ensuing debate or *querelle* played a formative role in the development of French dramatic doctrine.

Corneille's response to this debate was profound but complex. Although he continued to seek popular approval as the touchstone of a play's success, he also attempted to reconcile his plays more closely with dramatic orthodoxy, submitting drafts of subsequent plays to others for critical approval and later remodelling *The Cid* as a tragedy. Profoundly marked by the *Cid* debate, the later Corneille nonetheless seems to have relished the challenge of placating the experts without losing the common touch. Above all, he remained attracted to the sorts of dramatically impressive, magnanimous, larger-than-life heroes that tragicomedies like *The Cid* had offered.

He was particularly dissatisfied with Aristotle's insistence that tragedy should invariably depict the downfall of a flawed or 'middling' hero, insisting instead that what made a tragedy was the severity of the threat rather than the play's actual outcome. Indeed, Corneille is a contradictory figure, torn between innovation and convention. His long dramatic career, from his early comedies to his swan-song, the tragedy *Surena* (*Suréna*, 1674), shows a constant drive towards experimentation and the exploitation of the resources of the stage. This drive, though, jostles with a certain natural taste and respect for dramatic regularity, and a desire to be acknowledged by (and even to supplant) the self-appointed legislators of dramatic orthodoxy.

Corneille's idiosyncratic interpretation of tragedy and his consequent willingness to take up dramatic challenges perhaps help to explain the power of his great Roman tragedy *Cinna* (1640). Reduced to its bare bones, the basic plot of *Cinna* is sparse indeed. Cinna and Emilia conspire against the emperor Augustus; their assassination is thwarted. Augustus learns of the conspiracy; he refrains from exacting justice. This basic narrative, in which someone seeks to kill another but fails to do so, had been specifically condemned by Aristotle as the weakest and least tragic of all plots – and so on this count *Cinna* twice flies in the face of dramatic orthodoxy. Yet Corneille somehow manages to create out of this basic (non-)plot a compelling and moving piece of drama, thus anticipating Racine's definition a few decades later of poetic invention as the art of 'making something out of nothing'.[4] How does he manage to do so? Corneille fleshes out the bones of his source material in various different ways. For a start, the play gives him ample opportunity to exercise his considerable powers of political oratory. Corneille had been trained as a lawyer, and was well versed in rhetoric, even if, according to tradition, his one appearance in court was something of a failure. *Cinna* features some of the lengthiest scenes and speeches in all his plays, such as Cinna's account of his meeting with the other conspirators in the first act and Augustus' protracted interview with Cinna and Maximus in the next. This latter debate, which takes up almost all of the second act, clearly supports the claim of one of his eighteenth-century admirers, Diderot, that Corneille is so persuasive that one can break off his dialogues at any point, and it is always the person currently speaking who seems to be in the right.

Yet the interest of such scenes does not lie simply in the political debates. Rather, Corneille constantly reminds us that behind even the most convincing rhetorical displays can hide a wealth of conflicted personal motivations and emotions. Ostensibly reflecting a political desire to free Rome from tyranny, the conspiracy is in fact motivated (and later undone) by personal passions: love, vengeance, ambition, envy. Duty-bound to his beloved Emilia, Cinna is compelled to seek vengeance on Augustus for the murder of her father, despite his growing respect for Augustus and his horror at what is tantamount to regicide. In contrast, the conspirator Maximus' initially genuine political motivations are promptly discarded when, upon learning that Cinna is his romantic rival, he exposes the conspiracy and fakes his own death. This tension between the personal and the political profoundly shapes our engagement with the different characters. This is particularly the case with the Emperor himself, whose honest expressions of uncertainty and doubt increasingly throw into relief the overblown rhetorical bluster of the more naïve conspirators. *Cinna* also demonstrates how Corneille's tendency to spare his heroes' lives does not mean that his tragedies necessarily end happily. Many of his heroes actively welcome death as a way to preserve their *gloire* or glorious reputation, and even though Cinna and Emilia are in several respects rather less mature than many of Corneille's other dramatic heroes, something of this attitude underlies their defiant tone in the play's final act. Survival, then, is not necessarily the reward or reprieve that it might at first seem; indeed, Cinna's tragedy, such as it is, is to suffer the humiliation of his intended victim's clemency and forgiveness. The play does end on a positive note, with the triumph of Augustus' magnanimity and the evocation of his later apotheosis, but this all serves to throw into relief the lingering sense of unworthiness that seems to beset the play's title character.

MOLIÈRE

Of the three dramatists in this volume, Molière (1622–73, real name Jean-Baptiste Poquelin) is no doubt the most familiar in the English-speaking world. In many respects, Molière's brand of laughter and mockery appears far more accessible to us than the rarefied and stylized world of tragedy, even if his own period insisted that tragedy was far more universal than the more culturally specific genre of comedy. And even though the playwright does hold up for public mockery various aspects of his culture whose relevance to modern society is indirect at best (the venality of doctors, for example, or the vogue for refined language known as *préciosité* or 'preciousness'), even here Molière's comedy transcends the specific satirical focus of the original plays. The laughter typically remains even when the original targets are long gone.

Surprising as it might sound, Molière was revolutionary in insisting on comedy's need to be funny. Before his time, laughter had largely been regarded as an optional extra in a genre essentially defined in distinction to tragedy. That said, Molière did not always seek to produce belly-laughs; across his plays, indeed, he shows a mastery of numerous comic techniques, including wordplay, bathos, surprise, satire and slapstick, producing responses that range from outright hilarity to what one of his contemporaries described as 'laughter in the soul'.[5] Molière's tendency to juxtapose different comic modes was not uncontroversial; for example, his early five-act play *The School for Wives* (*L'École des femmes*, 1662) was condemned, among other things, for introducing knockabout humour and slapstick stage antics deemed appropriate only to farce into what was otherwise high comedy. Importantly, Molière was (unlike Corneille and Racine) an actor as well as a playwright, and although his attempts to introduce a more naturalistic acting style into tragedy met with little success, in comedy he swiftly became known for his impressive command of physical humour. He invariably performed the main comic parts in his repertoire, typically taking the subservient role when two characters vied for this position – the servant Sganarelle in *Don Juan* (*Dom Juan*, 1665), the credulous Orgon in *Tartuffe* (1664) and the hen-pecked Chrysale in *Those Learned Ladies* (*Les Femmes savantes*, 1672). In *The Misanthrope* (*Le Misanthrope*, 1666), unsurprisingly, he took the role of Alceste.

Although he produced a wide range of plays (from farce to 'comedy-ballet', from heroic comedy to comedies of intrigue), Molière is best known for what we might call his 'comedies of character'. He was certainly not the originator of this genre – Corneille's Spanish-inspired *The Liar* (*Le Menteur*, 1643) offers an obvious precursor – but his most successful examples achieve great psychological subtlety without forfeiting comic effect. Between the early 1660s and his death in 1673, Molière created a host of memorable figures, each dominated by one overriding passion, such as avarice, misplaced learning, gullibility, social pretensions, hypochondria or – in Alceste's case – a deep-seated hatred for the hypocrisies of modern society. Officially, Molière subscribed to the standard claim that comedy should be morally improving. His plays themselves, however, tell a rather different story, one in which character flaws are inherent and individuals stubbornly resistant to any correction.

Often recognized as his masterpiece, *The Misanthrope* is in some respects an oddity in the Molière canon. Although the cantankerous Alceste takes pride of place among the playwright's 'monomaniac' comic characters, the play as a whole is atypical of his major plays for not being concerned with the family unit. Many of Molière's obsessives are father-figures whose guiding passions bring chaos and misfortune on their households, but the only real victim of the bachelor Alceste's *idée fixe* is Alceste himself. This change marks a profound difference in terms of dramatic structure. Most of Molière's main plays set up clear narrative stakes: will the father's obsessions be brought under control long enough to let the young heroes marry? In comparison, little is obviously at stake in *The Misanthrope*. Indeed, Alceste's values allow him to face the threat of public humiliation and the failure of a legal trial with a haughty, self-righteous indignation that is as impervious in its own way as stoicism, if not necessarily as dignified. Yet it is precisely the play's looser narrative structure that allows deeper and more troubling questions to rise insistently to the surface. The play's different scenes offer variations on its dominant theme – the various hypocrisies of society – in ways that, if anything, justify Alceste's own jaundiced position. Society is shown to be duplicitous and backbiting, and the dominant urbane ethos known as *honnêteté* is often at odds with true honesty. In contrast, the moderate, conciliatory stance of Alceste's friend Philinte essentially evades, and hence remains complicit with, the more complex issues of social hypocrisy.

In this and many other respects, Alceste proves to be a deeply problematic comic figure. On its own terms, his desire for authenticity and sincerity is reasonable and even noble. Many of the characters express respect for him, and their comments often have a ring of sincerity about them since they are not always uttered to his face. Even so, as Molière amply demonstrates, one can have right on one's side and still be ridiculous. For a start, the play does not necessarily advocate Alceste's overblown response to social hypocrisy. Perhaps more importantly, Molière is – not unlike his contemporary, the moralist La Rochefoucauld – a master of exposing the base urges and self-interest that underlie even the noblest of sentiments. As the play makes clear from the start, Alceste's high-minded embrace of sincerity is grounded in his own desire to stand out from the common herd; he wishes others to be sincere so that he can believe their flattery of him. Furthermore, Alceste is exposed as being comically unable, or unwilling, to live up in practice to the values he preaches in theory. After forcefully outlining his principles in the opening scene, Alceste finds his commitment to them swiftly put to the test when he is asked to judge a poem by the courtier Oronte. The circuitously indirect routes that the supposed crusader for frankness follows in his criticism of the poem reveal quite how implicated he remains in social practices.

Much of the humour of the play, then, comes not from a clash between Alceste and society, but from clashes within

Alceste himself, between his desire for honesty and his complicity with the society he supposedly abhors. The most interesting example of this tension can be seen in his passion for the coquettish Célimène, whose flirtatious intimations of love to her various suitors embody everything he loathes and fears about society's duplicity. On the face of it, Alceste's feelings for her appear anomalous given his values and temperament. In fact, though, a certain self-interested logic underlies his curious infatuation with Célimène, precisely because of her privileged social position. If he truly can secure the love of society's darling for himself, then he has won a certain victory over his rivals and the values they embody. As the play's final act makes ironically clear, however, Alceste's insistence that Célimène definitively make up her mind ultimately renders him no different from her numerous other suitors. Although Alceste is an exceptional comic character, Molière's play as a whole repeatedly reveals how the boundaries between the exception and the norm are rarely as stable or as watertight as we might like to think.

JEAN RACINE

Compared to the writings of Corneille and Molière, the relatively slender dramatic output of Jean Racine (1639–99) is noticeably more coherent and focused, and it is his name that has been most tenaciously tagged with the label 'classical'. Certainly, Racine tends to follow quite a strict interpretation of 'the rules' with apparently effortless ease. Yet he was also an innovator, and throughout his career tried out a considerable range of styles and dramatic modes. Even leaving aside his one foray into comedy, *The Litigants* (*Les Plaideurs*, 1668) and a couple of youthful tragicomedies (now lost), Racine's plays range from the brutality of *The Theban Saga, or The Enemy Brothers* (*La Thébaïde, ou les Frères ennemis*, 1664) and *Bajazet* (1672) to the pseudo-Cornelian heroism of *Alexander the Great* (*Alexandre le Grand*, 1665), from the sombre political machinations of *Britannicus* (1669) to the elegiac laments of *Berenice* (*Bérénice*, 1670) – not to mention the jubilatory optimism that surfaces in his two final religious plays, *Esther* (1689) and *Athaliah* (*Athalie*, 1691).

In many respects, Racine was an unlikely playwright. Brought up at the convent of Port-Royal within the strict Catholic movement known as Jansenism, he initially sought an ecclesiastical career. Like much of the mainstream Catholic Church, the Jansenists harshly condemned the theatre as a dangerous distraction from spiritual matters. Although Racine turned his back on the movement at the start of his dramatic career, his work bears the imprint of his Jansenist upbringing. His extensive training in classical Greek (rather than just Latin) allowed him an almost unrivalled familiarity with Greek tragedy among practising playwrights. And while it is easy to take such analogies too far, many commentators have found echoes of the Jansenists' rigorous pessimism about the individual's power to achieve salvation in the tragic order we find in Racine's plays.

For whatever reason or reasons, Aristotle's notion of the flawed tragic hero certainly suited Racine's disposition. Indeed, the playwright excels at depicting characters morally ambivalent enough to have a hand in their downfall while still attracting sympathy from readers and spectators. Perhaps what characterizes Racine's tragedies above all is their ambivalence. Although 'classicism' is habitually associated with principles of reason and clarity, Racine's tragedies prove surprisingly resistant to any straightforward explanations or accounts, and what initially appears simple often turns out to be far more troubled and troubling than it looks. Even his most virtuous characters make choices whose morality is at the very least debatable. In one of the two plays included here, the Trojan queen Andromache's eventual moral victory ultimately rests on the sacrifice of an innocent child (in place of her son Astyanax) and a plan involving entrusting her own son to the guardianship of the man whose father killed Astyanax's father. In the second play, meanwhile, the tragic death of the supposedly guiltless Hippolytus is hastened by his puritanical horror at Phaedra's passion, his own mistaken belief that the gods will recognize and spare his innocence, and his passive silence at those very points when he could counter Phaedra's accusations against him.

And if Racine's tragic characters are morally ambivalent, the same is all the more true of the mysterious forces that seem to guide or shape their lives. In keeping with the Aristotelian schema, Racine's heroes make mistakes and miscalculations that lead to their downfall. But despite the ruthlessly rigorous sequence of cause and effect in Racine's tightly wrought plots, the punishments the heroes finally receive invariably appear out of all proportion to their original mistakes. With occasional exceptions such as *Iphigenia in Aulis* (*Iphigénie en Aulide*, 1674), Racine often leaves it profoundly uncertain just how much of a role the gods or fate play in his plots. His heroes certainly invoke the gods, or lament their fate, but we should be wary of taking at face value the claims of such wilfully self-deceiving characters. Racine's plays can conjure up a strong impression of fate at work, especially in performance, but proof of this fate tends to disappear as soon as we look for it directly. Similarly, gods and goddesses play a key role within the mythological and poetic fabric of these two plays (especially *Phaedra*), but Racine never lets the supernatural element fully override their essentially human focus and appeal.

Racine's third tragedy, *Andromache* (*Andromaque*, 1667), was its author's first major dramatic success, even rivalling that of Corneille's *The Cid* a generation earlier. The play is set in the aftermath of the Trojan War, an event that weighs heavily on the minds of all characters. Like *Cinna*, *Andromache* demonstrates how political affairs can be threatened and undermined by personal passions, but here the political matters take on international dimensions. Although the Greeks and their allies defeated Troy a year before the curtain rises, this victory is yet to be secured. Above all, the Epiran king Pyrrhus' love for his Trojan captive Andromache (rather than for his betrothed, Hermione) threatens the precarious alliance between his own state and Greece. The Greeks in turn fear that Andromache's son Astyanax represents the dangerous rebirth of the Trojan cause, a possibility that the play's ending leaves open. Yet on to this complex political backdrop Racine curiously imposes a plot structure more familiar from comedy and pastoral (a genre traditionally depicting the romantic affairs of shepherds) than tragedy. The basic plot famously concerns a chain of lovers: Orestes loves Hermione, who loves Pyrrhus, who loves Andromache, who remains devoted to her dead husband Hector and to their young son Astyanax. In comedies, such a plot could be resolved relatively easily with a judicious change of heart from one or more characters. Although Racine's tragedy of course shuns such easy solutions, the playwright sporadically taunts both audience and characters with the prospect that such changes of heart might be possible. Under pressure from Phoenix, Pyrrhus almost cedes in his duty to marry Hermione; Hermione offers Orestes her hand in payment for Pyrrhus' murder; and, most decisively, Andromache finally agrees to marry Pyrrhus in order to safeguard her son. Each of these decisions sends ripples through the rest of the chain.

The play does veer unsettlingly towards comedy in other respects too, not least in the undignified lengths to which the main characters' overwhelming self-interest sometimes leads them. The scene in which Pyrrhus and Andromache conduct pointed conversations with their confidants in earshot of each other, for example, attempts to recast a traditionally comic technique in tragic mould, and only partly succeeds – this scene allegedly met with scornful laughter among its first audiences. More generally, there is something grotesque in the awkward hyperbole that characters sometimes adopt in their attempts to evoke pity or admiration. When Pyrrhus describes his despair at being rejected by Andromache, he finds an analogy in the very destruction of her homeland that he orchestrated:

> I'm suffering all the ills I wreaked at Troy:
> Defeated, chained, consumed with fierce regret,
> Burning with more fires than I started there...
>
> (ll. 318–20)

On one level, Racine is here reinvigorating stock poetic imagery (the 'fire' and 'flames' of love) through allusion to a literal reference-point (the sack of Troy). Yet the disproportion between the 'tenor' and the 'vehicle' of Pyrrhus' guiding metaphor – his frustration at being romantically rejected and the brutal destruction of his beloved's homeland – is profoundly tasteless. The context, however, prevents claims such as these from becoming comic; Pyrrhus is, after all, king, and however ill-judged this expression of his self-pity, it is too extreme, and he too powerful, to be easily dismissed.

Such speeches as these hold the audience in an ambiguous position. When the powerful rhetorical flourishes of the language are set in tension with the brutal reality, the spectator cannot be sure which to pay greater attention to. Indeed, *Andromache* makes great use of contrasts, not only between images and their referents, but also between different modes of language. Pyrrhus' overblown rhetoric here contrasts starkly with Andromache's dignified evocation of the fall of Troy and of her first impressions of her bloodied captor, in Act III, Scene viii. Andromache's speech is one of the most poignant in the play, and in Racine's theatre as a whole. Yet when Andromache concludes that she could therefore never marry her captor, her poetic *tour de force* is brutally punctured with her confidante Cephisa's matter-of-fact reply: 'Well then! Let's go and see your son die' (l. 1012). As here, this play frequently suggests a tragic disjuncture between the lofty rhetoric of the characters and the more brutal or debased reality – a disjuncture that Racine often highlights with a bold, sudden swing to a far more unadorned and simple register. He uses this technique most famously and to devastating effect in the final act: when Orestes, charged by Hermione with assassinating Pyrrhus, triumphantly announces the assassination to her, she rejects him in a tirade that ends with the brutally simple 'Who told you to?' (l. 1543).

In this play filled with misunderstandings and miscommunication, language seems to seduce its speakers more often than it persuades its listeners. Characters repeatedly fall – if only momentarily – for the lures of their own rhetoric, in ways that keep the audience in an awkward position between empathy and distance. In an impressive feat of self-serving logic, for example, Orestes manages to persuade himself in Act III that the gods require him to kidnap Hermione in order to justify the punishment that they have already been inflicting on him. All the characters of *Andromache* are so trapped in their own self-justifying perspectives that true communication is almost impossible – a fact which finds its most poignant dramatic symbol right at the end when the maddened Orestes, beset by his own horrifying hallucinations, is simply unaware of the presence of his companions.

Although now widely recognized as his masterpiece, *Phaedra*, Racine's last secular play, was not as immediate a success as *Andromache*. This was partly, no doubt, because early performances at the Hôtel de Bourgogne had to compete against a rival version at the Guénégaud Theatre, *Phaedra and Hippolytus* (*Phèdre et Hippolyte*, 1677) by Nicolas Pradon. Probably with the support of a theatrical cabal – Racine's success and difficult personality had earned him many rivals – Pradon's version certainly won out in the short term. It did not take long, however, for audiences and critics to appreciate the depth and complexity of Racine's work. *Phaedra* was also the last tragedy that he wrote before being reconciled with his former teachers at Port-Royal. Perhaps reflecting his newfound religious sense, both the play and its preface are saturated with a degree of moral awareness that is unprecedented in Racine's earlier work. The preface ends with the hope that plays such as his might help to reconcile religious authorities to the theatre. Racine insists that, whatever its aesthetic qualities, *Phaedra*'s stark presentation of virtue and vice makes it the most moral of all his tragedies. Vice, he claims, 'is everywhere portrayed in colours which cause its ugliness to be known for what it is and abhorred' (p. 205).

This moral focus is replicated within the play itself. Almost alone among Racine's characters, Phaedra is endowed with an acute moral sense. Most of the characters in *Andromache*, for example, act out of pure self-interest, realizing the wrongness of their deeds only when events compel them to, and only when it is too late. In contrast, Phaedra is a far more complex being, tormented from the start by a raging conscience that battles vainly with her illicit passion. She has done all she can to combat her desires, first making offerings to placate the goddess of love, then banishing Hippolytus, and finally starving herself so that she can take her terrible secret to the grave. Yet it is precisely Phaedra's problematic moral sense that undermines Racine's confident assurance that the play depicts vice and virtue so clearly; as he also admits, Phaedra is – in true Aristotelian fashion – neither entirely good nor entirely wicked. Complicating the moral issue still further is the character of Oenone, Phaedra's nursemaid. She is that most problematic of dramatic figures, a confidante who does not remain in her subordinate role but almost rises to tragic levels herself. Oenone's most destructive trait is her utter devotion to her mistress – or rather her misplaced desperation to keep her alive whatever the moral cost. Yet her involvement does not let Phaedra off the moral hook. Phaedra's passive complicity means that guilt and responsibility are shared awkwardly between mistress and servant – a fact which Phaedra herself is loath to acknowledge. Despite her own deep self-disgust, she consistently regards herself as an innocent victim of other forces throughout. Even in her moving, poetic final speech she points the finger at the gods for awakening her passion and at Oenone for doing '[w]hat followed' (l. 1626).

A further reason that Racine offers for the supposed morality of this work is that 'the slightest misdemeanour is severely punished' (p. 205). Here he appears to be thinking of Hippolytus, the young man who is eventually brought to his death by Phaedra's slanderous accusations. Hippolytus' most obvious 'crime' is his forbidden – and mythologically unattested – love for Aricia, the only remaining daughter of an enemy line. Yet even though the moral culpability of this love is thus at best debatable (since the law it transgresses is itself morally dubious), Racine takes care to stress how it nonetheless causally underlies Hippolytus' downfall in various indirect ways. For a start, love leads Hippolytus to neglect his horses, a neglect that proves his undoing when they drag him to his death after he defeats the sea-monster sent by Neptune. Similarly, in a moment of intense dramatic irony in Act IV, it is her inadvertent discovery of Hippolytus' love for Aricia that stops a repentant Phaedra from confessing all to her husband and perhaps sparing Hippolytus' life. These two examples further demonstrate Racine's mastery of dramatic ambivalence – that is, his capacity to artfully reconcile conflicting moral, causal or psychological viewpoints, or at least to juxtapose them to create intense dramatic irony. In the first case, he couples the supernatural context of the mythological Hippolytus' death with a far more naturalistic explanation of events (his neglect of his horses); in the second, the apparently naturalistic or psychological explanation (Phaedra's sudden jealousy) is triggered by a chance discovery, a moment of bad timing that seems to imply that higher forces are at work. On this level it matters little whether we regard Hippolytus' passion as criminal or not; within the poetic fabric of the play his love plays a crucial causal role in his downfall. In other words, while we might agree with Racine that the 'slightest misdemeanour' is indeed punished in this play, we might well disagree about whether this makes the play as neatly moral as he suggests. Rather, we might suspect, Racine's plays – like those of Molière and Corneille – derive their strength, depth and compelling power precisely from their resistance to any straightforward or reductive explanation or account.

Joseph Harris 2013

NOTES

1.   Molière, 'Préface' to *L'Amour médecin*, in *Oeuvres complètes*, ed. Georges Forestier with Claude Bourqui and others, 2 vols. (Paris: Gallimard, 2010), vol. 1, p. 603 (my translation, as are quotations from the French works cited in subsequent notes).

2.   Odette de Mourgues, *Racine, or The Triumph of Relevance* (Cambridge: Cambridge University Press, 1967).

3. François Hédelin, abbé d'Aubignac, *La Pratique du théâtre*, ed. Hélène Baby (Paris: Champion, 2001), p. 407.

4. Racine, 'Préface' to *Bérénice*, in *Théâtre complet*, ed. Jacques Morel and Alain Viala (Paris: Garnier, 1980), p. 325.

5. Jean Donneau de Visé, in Molière, *Oeuvres complètes*, vol. 1, p. 643.

Note on the Translation

My somewhat obsessive wrestling with the challenge of rendering French seventeenth-century drama into English began over forty years ago. While queuing with a colleague to see a French film in Hampstead, I remarked that *Phèdre* was never seen on the English stage because there were no actable translations. 'Well,' he said, 'you're an actor and a French scholar, why don't you plug the gap?' I started the next day on Act I, Scene iii and was hooked. Three months later, my finished effort having been approved by Martin Esslin, the erudite Head of BBC Radio Drama, Phaedra was played by Barbara Jefford on Radio 3 in a cast that included Timothy West and Prunella Scales. The critics were kind and Harold Pinter wrote flatteringly, asking for a copy of the script. I had found a satisfying hobby, and ever since I have been beavering away in my spare time at putting these fascinating plays into an English guise.

The translator of a play that has its roots in a different age and culture has to plump for one of two distinct objectives: to offer the new audience an experience as close as possible to that contained in the original work; or to adapt the original to suit the taste and expectations of the new audience. The latter approach is the one that has been most frequently adopted in presenting the French neo-classical dramatists on the English stage. Molière has usually been so coarsened that the discerning English speaker wonders why he is so celebrated; and a recent National Theatre production that called itself Racine's *Phaedra* used a cavalier text, introduced cheap comedy and actually cut the most moving speech in the play, the highest peak of the tragedy – presumably because stark despair was considered beyond the scope of British sensibilities. Let me state unequivocally that the aim of these translations, whether reached or not, is to offer the English-speaking public a true and authentic appreciation of French seventeenth-century drama, not only of its content, but also of its dramatic and emotional force. So what were the problems to be addressed, and how, for better or worse, were they resolved?

A translation intended for performance not only must be immediately intelligible to the listening ear, but ideally, I have always thought, should be capable of delivery by a putative bilingual cast in precisely the same way in either version. Like musical scores these verse-dramas have their crescendos, staccatos and rallentandos: in the new medium they need to be preserved. This can be achieved only by maintaining the sentence-structure so that the actor's breathing-pattern is reproduced, because the pulsation of the performer's vocal energy is the life of the play. And, clearly, the action has to flow at the same pace as the original. This necessitates a line-by-line rendering.

A play written in verse is truly recreated in another language only when it has the formality of disciplined verse-structure. Which form to employ? Rhyming alexandrines evolved in France because they suit the lightly stressed language: separated by twelve syllables containing a caesura, the rhymes are no more than a discreet, elegant echo which gives shape to the verse. But in English the alexandrine, 'that like a wounded snake drags its slow length along', as Pope ingeniously put it, is too stately for drama; and the rhythmic beat of our heavily stressed language does not need rhyme to create form. Besides, rhyming couplets inevitably sound jokey to the British playgoer reared on pantomime. Used continuously in dramatic dialogue they obtrude and alienate, as they do not in French: Dryden rightly found them unfitted for the English stage. So the chosen form has to be Shakespearian blank verse, which has a driving impetus and the rhythm of colloquial speech. Rhyme may be used judiciously to round off each act and to create a special effect, as in the visionary conclusion to *Cinna* and in Molière's passages of stichomythia, where two characters dispute in alternate lines, scoring points off each other.

The style of French tragedy is deliberately elevated, eschewing vulgar words and maintaining a grave tone. While broadening the narrow vocabulary of the original texts to exploit the richness of the English lexicon, I have tried to sustain diction that is dignified and timeless. Even in Molière's fundamentally serious comedies it seems right to avoid aggressively modern or colloquial turns of phrase: after all, when he chose to write in verse he was consciously creating a polished literary work. Just as in tragedy, his characters exist in a rarefied atmosphere: they scarcely mention, let alone handle, commonplace objects; they stand or sit in a minimalist setting and argue, often at unnatural length, in a refined, highly articulate manner. It seems to me unjust to the author and patronizing to the English-speaking audience to simplify their beautifully constructed speeches and lower the tone to that of a soap opera.

Unsurprisingly, the most challenging of the four plays here printed was *Phaedra* because it is surely the greatest play written in French, the most profound, the most poetic and the most moving. Of the three playwrights Racine is the only one to deploy pure poetry in creating the world of his drama. Certain lines are vital to Phaedra's tragedy in that they evoke a mysterious immanence, suggesting the existence of powers above and beyond human apprehension. One can only do one's best to evoke a sense of mystery by using resources such as the slow, heavy spondee, alliteration of ambivalent consonants like *w* and the assonance of long vowels, as in 'The whole world works to wound and weary me' (l. 161).

Balancing the obvious losses, there can be certain gains, I venture to suggest, in approaching an old masterpiece in modern translation. Over the centuries words change their meaning or lose their strength: for present-day French audiences the text does not mean quite what it did to their seventeenth-century predecessors. For example, *gêner* now means 'to inflict mild discomfort or inconvenience', whereas for Corneille and Racine it meant 'to torture'. If the translator has done his work competently, he will have restored the original significance of the text and clarified what time has rendered obscure.

During every production since that Radio 3 broadcast, in 1969, this translation of *Phaedra* has been chipped at and honed with frustrated doggedness: a labour of love and ever-deepening admiration for the poet. *Andromache* and *The Misanthrope* have been produced professionally, as well as by amateurs and drama students, and like any new script they were modified during rehearsals. Will someone now be bold enough to stage *Cinna*? Its themes have a contemporary resonance.

For one who enjoys playing with words but has no talent for original work, it is a pleasure and privilege to become involved so intimately as a translator with the creative process of supremely gifted authors. And to see audiences moved and students excited by the pastiche of great works that one has painstakingly put together when the real thing is inaccessible to them, that is the reward.

John Edmunds 2013

To access an audio production of John Edmunds' translation of Phèdre, *together with the text and audio productions of other seventeenth-century French plays translated by him, go to: www.FrenchPlaysinEnglish.co.uk*

Further Reading

The following is a list of English-language works that should be of interest to general readers. Although originally written some time ago, the 'Critical Guides to French Texts' series published by Grant & Cutler and the University of Glasgow's 'Introductory Guides to French Literature' remain in print and are particularly recommended as sound introductions to the plays for anyone coming to them for the first time. Readers, especially those with some command of French, are also strongly encouraged to consult the excellent Bristol Classical Press editions of Molière's *Le Misanthrope* (edited by Jonathan Mallinson, 1996) and Racine's *Phèdre* (edited by Richard Parish, 1989). Both of these editions offer extensive commentaries (in English) that will enrich understanding and appreciation of the plays, even for readers working with translations.

GENERAL

Auchincloss, Louis, *'La Gloire': The Roman Empire of Corneille and Racine* (Columbia: University of South Carolina Press, 1996).

Hawcroft, Michael, 'Tragedy: Mid to Late Seventeenth Century', John D. Lyons, 'Tragedy: Early to Mid Seventeenth Century', and Larry F. Norman, 'Seventeenth-Century Comedy', in *The Cambridge History of French Literature*, ed. William Burgwinkle, Nicholas Hammond and Emma Wilson (Cambridge: Cambridge University Press, 2011), pp. 262–73, 253–61 and 274–83.

Lyons, John D., *Kingdom of Disorder: The Theory of Tragedy in Classical France* (West Lafayette: Purdue University Press, 1999).

Worth-Stylianou, Valérie, *Confidential Strategies: The Evolving Role of the Confident in French Tragic Drama (1635–1677)* (Geneva: Droz, 1999).

CORNEILLE

Baker, Susan Read, 'Strategies of Seduction in *Cinna*', in *Homage to Paul Bénichou*, ed. Sylvie Romanowski and Monique Bilezikian (Birmingham, AL: Summa, 1994), pp. 75–91.

Ekstein, Nina, *Corneille's Irony* (Charlottesville: Rookwood Press, 2007).

Gossip, C. J., *Corneille: 'Cinna'* (London: Grant & Cutler, 1998).

Greenberg, Mitchell, *Corneille, Classicism, and the Ruses of Symmetry* (Cambridge: Cambridge University Press, 1986).

Hubert, Judd D., *Corneille's Performative Metaphors* (Charlottesville: Rookwood, 1997).

Lyons, John D., *The Tragedy of Origins: Pierre Corneille and Historical Perspective* (Stanford, CA: Stanford University Press, 1996).

Schmidt, Josephine A., *If There Are No More Heroes, There Are Heroines: A Feminist Critique of Corneille's Heroines, 1637–1643* (Lanham and London: University Press of America, 1987).

MOLIÈRE

Bradby, David, and Calder, Andrew, *The Cambridge Companion to Molière* (Cambridge: Cambridge University Press, 2006).

Broome, J. H., *Molière: 'L'Ecole des Femmes' and 'Le Misanthrope'* (London: Grant & Cutler, 1982).

Gaines, James F. (ed.), *The Molière Encyclopedia* (Westport, CT: Greenwood Press, 2002).

Hawcroft, Michael, *Molière: Reasoning with Fools* (Oxford: Oxford University Press, 2007).

Norman, Larry F., *The Public Mirror: Molière and the Social Commerce of Depiction* (Chicago and London: University of Chicago Press, 1999).

Riggs, Larry W., *Molière and Modernity: Absent Mothers and Masculine Births* (Charlottesville: Rookwood Press, 2005).

Scott, Virginia, *Molière: A Theatrical Life* (Cambridge: Cambridge University Press, 2000).

Whitton, David, *Molière: 'Le Misanthrope'* (Glasgow: University of Glasgow, French and German Publications, 1991).

RACINE

Caldicott, C. E. J., and Conroy, Derval (eds.), *Racine: The Power and the Pleasure* (Dublin: University College Dublin Press, 2001).

France, Peter, *Racine: 'Andromaque'* (Glasgow: University of Glasgow, French and German Publications, 1989).

Greenberg, Mitchell, *Racine: From Ancient Myth to Tragic Modernity* (Minneapolis and London: University of Minnesota Press, 2010).

Hawcroft, Michael, *Word as Action: Racine, Rhetoric, and Theatrical Language* (Oxford: Oxford University Press, 1992).

James, Edward, and Jondorf, Gillian, *Racine: 'Phèdre'* (Cambridge: Cambridge University Press, 1994).

Maskell, David, *Racine: A Theatrical Reading* (Oxford: Clarendon Press, 1991).

Parish, Richard, *Racine: The Limits of Tragedy* (Paris, Seattle and Tübingen: Gunter Narr Verlag, 1993).

Phillips, Henry, *Racine: Language and Theatre* (Durham: University of Durham Press, 1994).

Reilly, Mary, *Racine: Language, Violence and Power* (Oxford and New York: Peter Lang, 2005).

Short, J. P., *Racine: 'Phèdre'*, 2nd edn. (London: Grant & Cutler, 1998).

Joseph Harris 2013

CORNEILLE

CINNA

A Tragedy

CINNA

Tragédie

*First performed in Paris at the Marais Theatre
in the winter of 1640–41*

CHARACTERS

OCTAVIUS CAESAR AUGUSTUS, emperor of Rome, great-
  nephew and adopted son of Julius Caesar
LIVIA, empress
CINNA, maternal grandson of Pompey; leader of the
  conspiracy against Augustus
MAXIMUS, friend of Cinna and co-leader of the conspiracy
EMILIA, daughter of C. Toranius, tutor to Octavius Caesar,
  who proscribed and killed him during the Triumvirate
FULVIA, confidante to Emilia
POLYCLETUS, freedman of Augustus
EVANDER, freedman of Cinna
EUPHORBUS, freedman of Maximus
GUARDS, COURTIERS

*The action takes place in Rome, in the imperial
palace, partly in the apartment of Augustus
and partly in that of Emilia*

ACT I

EMILIA (*alone*)

O you, my yearnings for a glorious
Revenge, impetuous children born of my
Resentful anger at my father's death,
Whom I hug blindly in my frantic grief,
Your hold upon my will is stifling me.
Let me breathe freely, pause, consider well
What I've embarked upon, the goal I seek
And what, in seeking it, I stand to lose.

   When I look on Augustus in his splendour,
And you confront me with the sad remembrance   10
That the first step that raised him to his throne*
Was my dead father, slaughtered by his hand;
When you confront me with that blood-soaked scene,
Sprung from his rage, and from which springs my hate,
I give rein to your fury: for that one death
I feel I owe him death a thousand times.

   Yet in my righteous anger I know well
That more than I hate Augustus I love Cinna:
I feel my seething purpose cool, if to
Pursue it I must gamble with his life.   20
Yes, Cinna, I loathe myself when I recall
The danger into which I'm thrusting you.
To do my will you cast out fear, and yet
In asking blood of you, I risk your blood:
Those who'd bring down the mighty from their seat
Draw on their heads ten thousand thunderbolts;
Success is dubious, but the danger sure.
A false accomplice may betray your purpose;
The plan mismanaged or the moment botched,
The project may recoil on its inventor   30
And strike you with the blow you aimed at him;

Or, as he sinks, he may entangle you,
So that your love for me attains my goal,
But, as Augustus falls, he crushes you.
Ah, draw back from such peril! If I lose
You in my vengeance, I am not avenged.
Too cruel is the heart which takes delight
In sweetness that is soured by bitter tears.
It must be judged a self-inflicted curse
40   To buy an enemy's death with so much grief.
        But how can one regret a father's vengeance?
To achieve that goal is any loss too dear?
If I can destroy my father's murderer,
Should I consider what that death may cost?
No more, vain fear; no more, weak tenderness,
Shall you pervade my heart with cowardice.
And you, love, cause of this unworthy weakness,
Give way to duty, fight with it no more;
Your glory is to lose, your shame to win;
50   Show greatness by submitting to its strength;
The more you give it, the more it will give you:
When duty triumphs, love finds its reward.

[I.ii]   *Enter* FULVIA.

EMILIA (*continues*)
    Fulvia, I've sworn it, and I swear again:
    Though I love Cinna, though I worship him,
    I won't be his unless he kills Augustus.
    Only with Caesar's head can I be won:
    What duty asks of me, I ask of him.

FULVIA
    The retribution that you seek is just:
    Your noble purpose stamps you as a daughter
60   Worthy of him whose vengeance you desire;
    But once more let me tell you that the flames
    Of your just fury you'd be wise to smother.
    The daily favours that Augustus grants you
    Seem amply to repair the wrong he's done you;
    His special kindness to you is so marked
    That in his palace you hold pride of place;

On bended knee his foremost courtiers beg you
To intercede with him on their behalf.

EMILIA

His kindness does not give me back my father;
No matter that I may have pride of place,   70
Abound in wealth, wield power and influence,
I'm still the daughter of a man proscribed.*
Favours don't always work as you suppose:
Bestowed by hated hands they are resented;
To shower them upon an enemy
Is to give arms to a potential traitor.
His daily favours leave my heart unchanged;
I'm what I was, but now I can do more:
I use the gold he pours into my hands
To buy more Roman opposition to him.   80
I'd let him give me Livia's place beside him
To have a surer means of killing him.
To avenge a father any wrong is right;
To yield to favours is to sell one's blood.

FULVIA

But why must you display your bitterness?
Why can't you hate and keep your hate concealed?
Others enough there are who've not forgotten
The atrocities that raised him to the throne.
All those brave Romans, all those high-born victims
He cruelly sacrificed to his ambition   90
Have left their children sorrows sharp enough
To avenge your loss in avenging their own wrongs.
Many have tried and many more will follow:
He can't live long whom everyone reviles.
Leave them to battle for the common cause,
And aid them only with your secret prayers.

EMILIA

Hate him, you say, and make no move to harm him?
Leave it to chance that he may be destroyed?
Discharge an obligation so compelling
By hatred hidden and by feeble prayers?   100
His wished-for death would savour sour to me

Achieved for someone other than my father.
I'd weep at Caesar's funeral if he'd
Been killed and left my father unavenged.
It's base to let others right those public wrongs
That tangle with our private injuries:
Let me combine the joy of private vengeance
With the renown of punishing a tyrant,
So that it be proclaimed throughout the land:
110 'Rome owes her freedom to Emilia;
Her heart was won, her soul was touched, and yet
At that price only would she grant her love.'

FULVIA

Your love at that price is a poisoned chalice,
A prize that will destroy the man who claims it.
Emilia, look more closely at the danger,
The reef on which so many have been dashed;
Don't close your eyes when Cinna's death is sure.

EMILIA

Ah, now you stab where most I feel the pain.
To think what perils he must face for me
120 I almost die of fear that he may die.
In disarray my mind wars with itself:
I will and will not, I burn and freeze with fright;
And my bewildered duty staggers, crushed
By the resistance of my stubborn heart.
Be still, my stormy passion, hold your fire;
You see the risk, it's great, but be it so:
Cinna in danger is not Cinna dead.
However many legions guard Augustus,
However sure and ordered his defence,
130 The man who scorns his life controls its fate.
The greater the danger, the sweeter is the fruit;
We're spurred by honour, fame is the reward.
Whether it be Augustus dies or Cinna,
I owe my father's shade this sacrifice;
I pledged my love to Cinna for this deed,
And by this deed alone can I be his.
Besides, the time for wavering is past:

Today they meet, today they're laying plans,
When, where, whose hand, it's being decided now.
All I can do is die if he should die.   140
He's here.

   Enter CINNA.   [I.iii]

EMILIA (*continues*)

         Your comrades, Cinna, do they not
Betray some fear of the danger they must face?
When you look in their eyes, do you believe
That they will do what they have promised you?

CINNA

Never did any plot against a tyrant
Hold such a solid prospect of success;
No death was ever pledged so fervently;
Conspirators were never bound so close.
Intense joy spurs them on, as if, like me,
They strove to please the woman they adored;   150
And they're aflame with rage, as if, like you,
They were wreaking vengeance for a father's death.

EMILIA

I knew well that for such an enterprise
Cinna would choose courageous men and true,
And not entrust to doubtful hands a cause
So dear to Rome and to Emilia's heart.

CINNA

If only you yourself had seen the zeal
With which those men embraced the glorious deed.
The mere words, Caesar, Augustus, Emperor,
Kindled a blazing passion in their eyes;   160
Their faces, signalling opposed emotions,
Now paled with horror and now burned with rage.
  'My friends,' I said, 'the happy day has come
When our great purpose must be realized.
Heaven has consigned to us the fate of Rome
And her salvation hangs on one man's death,
If man he is who lacks humanity,
That tiger with a thirst for Roman blood.
To spill that blood what dark intrigues he's spun,

170 What shifts he's made of party and alliance,
     Now friend to Antony, now enemy,
     And always cruel, always arrogant!'
        Then, by recounting all the sufferings
     Our fathers bore while we were children still,
     Using those memories to refuel their hatred,
     I stoked their burning urge to punish him.
     I painted for them those grim battles where
     Rome ripped her entrails out with her own hands,
     Where eagle mowed down eagle as our legions*
180 Fought each to demolish their own liberty;
     Where our most valiant officers and men
     Vied for the glory of becoming slaves;
     Where, to shore up the shame of their own bondage,
     They strove to bind the world in their own chains;
     Where, for the soiled honour of enslaving it,
     They grew to love the squalid name of traitor;
     Where Roman fought Roman, kinsman slaughtered
            kinsman,
     Just to decide which tyrant should oppress them.
        I painted for them next the lurid scene
190 Of those three tyrants' grim, unholy pact,
     The doom of decent citizens, of rich men
     And of the Senate: their triumvirate;
     But I could not find colours dark enough
     To recreate their foul atrocities.
     I showed them vying in exultant murder,
     Rome all awash in her own children's blood,
     Some on the public scaffold hacked to death,
     Some in the sanctity of their own homes;
     The vicious paid to indulge in villainy,
200 The husband's throat slit by his wife in bed,
     The son still dripping with his father's blood
     Proffering the head to claim his due reward:
     Yet with those grisly strokes I'd traced no more
     Than a pale outline of their blood-soaked truce.
        Shall I recount which great men's deaths I painted
     To fan the fury in my comrades' hearts,

Those illustrious men proscribed, those demi-gods
Upon the very altars sacrificed?
But how could I convey to you the quivering
Eagerness, the violent emotion   210
That those foul murders which I feebly sketched
Provoked in all of our confederates?
I lost no time, but, seeing them crazed with rage,
Beyond fear, fit to tackle anything,
I added swiftly:
     'Those abominations,
Our lost possessions, our lost liberty,
The ravaged countryside, the pillaged towns,
The civil wars and the proscriptions are
The steps of blood by which Augustus chose
To mount the throne and lord it over us.   220
But we can change our miserable fate:
Of those three tyrants only he remains;
To reign alone he toppled his vile peers
And stripped himself of all support. His death
Will leave him no avenger, us no master.
With regained freedom Rome will be reborn,
And we'll deserve to be acclaimed true Romans
When our hands smash the yoke that's crushing her.
Let's seize our moment while it smiles upon us:
Tomorrow in the Capitol he makes   230
A sacrifice; make him the victim and
Before the gods do justice to all men.
There we shall almost be his sole attendants;
From me he'll take the incense and the cup;
Then let the signal be my giving him
Not incense but a dagger in his breast.
So shall the blow that strikes the victim down
Confirm that Pompey's blood runs in my veins.
Follow my lead: confirm that you are worth
The glorious ancestry that gave you birth.'   240
 When I'd concluded, each one swore an oath,
Renewing his commitment to our cause.
They approved the plan, but each one sought the honour

Of striking the first blow, which I had claimed;
Reason at length restrained their surging hearts.
With Maximus half of them will guard the door;
The rest will follow me; they'll crowd round Caesar,
And at my subtle signal hem him in.
    That, dear Emilia, is how we stand.
250   Tomorrow I shall be honoured or reviled,
A liberator or a murderer,
And Caesar will be a king or a usurper.
To those who try to end a harsh regime
Success brings glory, failure brings disgrace.
The people have a shifting view of tyrants:
They love them while they live, and curse them dead.
But whether Heaven smiles or frowns on me,
Whether my lot is fame or a cruel death,
Whether we reap Rome's praise or blame, if I
260   Must die, I'll find it sweet to die for you.

EMILIA
The outcome cannot soil your memory:*
Success or failure keeps your honour safe;
In such an enterprise ill-luck may put
Your life in danger, never your good name.
Brutus and Cassius, think what fate they suffered,
But has that dimmed the splendour of their names?
Do they and what they died for not live still?
Are they not thought of as the last true Romans?
Their memory in Rome is treasured, while
270   Octavius, the survivor, is abhorred.
Their vanquisher may rule, but they are mourned,
And all Rome longs to see their like again.
Walk in their path where honour bids you go:
But don't neglect to cherish your own life;
Remember that we burn with a sacred flame,
That glory will be yours, your prize Emilia,
That you are mine, that my caress awaits you,
And that on your dear life my days depend.
Evander? What can have brought him here?

[I.iv]   *Enter* EVANDER.

EVANDER

                               My lord,

  Augustus has sent for you and Maximus.   280

CINNA

  Maximus too? Evander, are you sure?

EVANDER

  His messenger is waiting at your house
  And would have come with me to look for you,
  If I had not been quick enough to stop him:
  I didn't want you taken by surprise.
  The matter's urgent.

EMILIA

                   The two leaders summoned!
  The two of you! Together! You're discovered!

CINNA

  We must hope not.

EMILIA

                 Ah! Cinna, I must lose you!
  The gods will not allow Rome to be free:
  Some traitor they have placed among your friends.   290
  No doubt of it: Augustus has been warned.
  Both of you! When the plans have just been laid!

CINNA

  I'm shaken by this summons, I confess;
  But I am often called to speak with Caesar,
  And he trusts Maximus as he trusts me.
  Perhaps our fears are needless and unwise.

EMILIA

  Cinna, don't be so ready to deceive
  Yourself; don't overburden me with grief.
  Since now you cannot give me my revenge,
  At least protect your life from this dire threat: 300
  Flee from the ruthless anger of Augustus.
  My father's death draws from me tears enough;
  Do not add further torment to my pain
  By forcing me to mourn as well for you.

CINNA

  What's this? You want me in blind panic to

Betray your cause and the well-being of Rome?
To accuse myself by taking to my heels,
Give up, when what's required is fortitude?
If you are wrong, what happens to our friends?

EMILIA

310 But if the plot's discovered, what of you?

CINNA

If I've been miserably betrayed, at least
My courage won't betray me too: you'll see
It shining on the brink of the abyss
In death-defying glory, blazing forth,
Making Augustus envy my spilt blood
And quake with terror as he takes my life.
I must go now, or else arouse suspicion.
Farewell, Emilia: bolster my resolve.
If I must suffer a harsh destiny,
320 In dying I shall be both blessed and cursed:
Blessed that in serving you I'm sacrificed;
Cursed that I die and leave you unavenged.

EMILIA

Yes, go: don't let yourself be swayed by me.
I'm calmer now; my reason has returned.
Forgive my love for you its shameful weakness.
It would be futile to attempt to flee:
If all is known, Augustus will have blocked
All possibility of your escaping.
Show him this steadfast confidence and courage,
330 Worthy our love and worthy of your birth.
Die, if you must, as a Roman citizen,
And crown a noble aim with a noble end.
Be sure that nothing in this life will hold me:
In dying you will draw my soul to yours,
And my heart, struck by that same blow as you—

CINNA

No! Let me, when I'm dead, live on in you;
And, dying, let me hope that you will seek
Revenge both for your father and for me.
Have no fear for yourself: our friends know nothing

Of what you planned, or what you promised me.   340
When I recalled to them Rome's sufferings,
I spoke no word of vengeance for your father,
Lest, talking of your loss, my feelings should
Betray the secrets of our perfect love.
Only Evander and your Fulvia know.

EMILIA

Then I shall go less fearfully to Livia:
For you in your great peril I shall try
To bring to bear her influence and mine;
But if my interest there fails to protect you,
You must not hope that I shall wish to live.   350
I govern my fate by your destiny:
Either I save your life, or die with you.

CINNA

Don't heap such anguish on yourself, I pray.

EMILIA

Never forget my love for you: away.

ACT II

Augustus' apartment
AUGUSTUS, CINNA, MAXIMUS,
a throng of COURTIERS   [II.i]

AUGUSTUS

Go, all of you, and leave us undisturbed.
You, Cinna, stay, and Maximus, you too.
    Exeunt COURTIERS.

AUGUSTUS (*continues*)

This absolute power I wield by land and sea,
This sovereign mastery of all the world,
This boundless might and this illustrious rank
Which cost me so much blood and toil to win,   360
Everything in my lofty state, I say,
That tedious, flattering courtiers idolize
Is worth no more than those lush, dazzling beauties
Whom, once enjoyed, one ceases to adore.

Ambition palls, when sated; its desire
Converts into a contrary desire:
Our eager spirit, till we breathe our last,
Must always strive to reach some kind of goal;
When none remains, it turns back on itself
370   And, having reached the peak, aspires to fall.
I wanted power, and I achieved it, but,
While wanting it, I knew not what it was.
Possessing it, I found its only charms
To be horrific troubles, ceaseless fears,
Veiled enemies and death at every turn,
No joy without unease, and never rest.

  This supreme power has been held by Sulla
And my adoptive father, Julius Caesar;
So different were their attitudes towards it
380   That one stepped down, the other clung to it;
But Sulla, who had been a vicious tyrant,
Died peacefully, a well-loved citizen,
While Caesar, who was gracious, kind and good,
Was slaughtered in the Senate by assassins.
From these examples I might profit, if
Examples were reliable as guides:
One smiles at me, the other chills my blood.
But examples can be mirrors that distort;
The plan of destiny, that plagues our will,
390   Can't always be deduced from past events.
The selfsame rocks wreck one, and save another:
What kills one man preserves another's life.

  That, my dear friends, is what's tormenting me.
I discussed it with Agrippa and Maecenas;*
Stand now for them, unravel this dilemma
And wield the power they had to sway my mind.
Forget the might and grandeur which the Romans
Detest and I myself find burdensome;
Speak to me as your friend and not your sovereign.
400   Augustus, Rome, the State are in your hands:
You shall make Europe, Asia and Africa
Either a monarchy or a republic.

Your counsel shall decide if I'm to be
An emperor or a simple citizen.

CINNA

We're stunned by this, my lord, but I'll obey you,
Unworthy as I am, without restraint,
Surmounting the respect which might prevent me
From combating the view you seem to hold.
Indulge my deep concern for your good name,
Which you will tarnish with too black a stain   410
If you permit these thoughts to weigh with you
So far as to condemn all you've achieved.

　　Legitimate power is never thrown away;
If justly won, it's kept without remorse;
To yield it is to judge it wrongly gained,
The more so the more precious it appears.
Don't brand with guilt and shame, my lord, those rare
Strong qualities that made you emperor.
Your absolute rule is just: you changed the form
Of government without assassination.   420
Rome bows to your command by right of war,
The right by which the whole world bows to Rome;
You took her by armed conquest: conquerors
Usurp; that does not make them tyrants. Once
They have subdued a state, if their regime
Is just, their sovereignty is justified.
So Caesar judged: now you must do as he,
Or abdicate and soil his memory.
If you now say that absolute power is wrong,
Then Caesar was a tyrant, justly killed,   430
And you should pay for all the blood you shed
In avenging him to seize his sovereign sway.

　　My lord, you need not fear his sombre fate;
Your guardian spirit has more power than his.
Ten times your life has been assailed in vain:
Those who wished Caesar dead killed him at once.
In your case plots are laid, but none succeeds;
There are would-be assassins, but no Brutus:
And even if you were to fall like Caesar,

440   How fine to die as master of the world!
            Boldly, my lord, I've offered my advice,
        And I suspect that Maximus agrees.
MAXIMUS
        Yes, I agree that Augustus has the right
        To keep the power his valour won for him,
        And that his conquest of the State, for which
        He paid with blood and risked his life, was just;
        But that his honour will be stained, if he
        Lays down the burden which has wearied him,
        And that he will be branding Caesar as
450   A tyrant, justly killed, that I refute.
            Rome, sir, is yours, the empire is your chattel;
        Each man is free to dispose of what is his:
        He may elect to keep it or discard it.
        If that choice were denied to you alone,
        You would have subjugated the whole world
        Only to be a slave to your own greatness!
        Possess it, my lord, don't be possessed by it;
        Don't let it master you, make it obey you;
        Proclaim that you, Augustus, stand above
460   The rank, the powers and titles you have won.
        Rome gave you birth, she now belongs to you;
        You wish to give her your omnipotence,
        And Cinna calls this generosity
        To your native land a capital offence!
        Patriotism he calls penitence!
        So moral courage stains a man's good name,
        And we should view it with contempt, since those
        Who show it are dishonoured for their pains!
        I will concede that such a noble act
470   Gives Rome much more than she has given you,
        But is it such a heinous crime to show
        Gratitude that outweighs the gift received?
        Be guided by the voice of Heaven, my lord:
        Enhance your fame by spurning sovereignty.
        Posterity will honour you much less
        For seizing power than for surrendering it.

Greatness may be achieved by chance alone:
Renouncing it requires a righteous heart.
That noble mind is rare that can acquire
A crown, and scorn the joy of wearing it.   480
   Remember too that it is Rome you rule,
Where, whatsoever name your Court may give you,
Monarchs are hated; the title 'emperor'
Is 'king' disguised, and stirs as much revulsion.
Whoever masters Rome is judged a tyrant,
His friends are traitors, his supporters slaves.
Those who submit to him are weak, soft, tame;
To free oneself by any means is good.
My lord, you have undoubted proofs of that:
Ten vain attempts upon your life; it may   490
Be that the eleventh is imminent, and that
This impulse which has seized you is no less
Than a secret warning sent to you by Heaven,
Which has no other way of saving you.
Expose yourself no longer to such threats:
It's fine to die as master of the world,
But we're diminished by the finest death
If we might have lived to win still greater fame.

CINNA

My lord, if patriotism is the prime
Concern, you have to do what's best for Rome,   500
And in the case of Rome her vaunted freedom
Is only an imaginary good:
Its benefits are far outweighed by those
A wise sovereign brings the country that he rules.
Honours he grants with fairness and good sense,
Rewards and punishes judiciously,
And, tenured in his office, he's not pressed
To act with haste before he is replaced.
But when the people rule, confusion reigns:
No one consults the voice of reason; honours   510
Are sold to the ambitious; authority
Entrusted to seditious magistrates.
Consuls, those petty monarchs for a year,

Seeing their power so short-lived, take good care
To abort the finest policies, so that
The fruit might not be reaped by their successors.
Owning so little of the wealth they manage,
They raid the public coffers for themselves,
Knowing their colleagues will forgive them so
520   That they will be forgiven in their turn.
The worst of regimes is democracy.

AUGUSTUS

Yet Rome is not content with any other.
The hatred of kings, which for five hundred years
Her children have imbibed with their mother's milk,
Is too deep-seated to be rooted out.

MAXIMUS

That's true: Rome has long wallowed in her sickness;
Her people relish it, and won't be cured.
Custom, not reason, is their guiding force;
And that false creed they worship, and which Cinna
530   Would like to shatter, has been so propitious
That by it they have conquered the whole world
And trampled on the heads of countless kings,
Filling the public coffers with their tribute.
How could the best of sovereigns give them more?
    Sir, I submit that no form of government
Is universally appropriate;
Each people has the one that suits its nature,
Which without detriment it cannot change.
Such is the law of Heaven, which, wise and just,
540   Sows this diversity throughout the world.
The Macedonians like monarchy,
The rest of Greece must have democracy;
The Parthians and the Persians love their kings;
And only consuls satisfy the Romans.

CINNA

It's true that Heaven with boundless foresight gives
Each people its distinctive character;
But it is no less true that these decrees
Of Heaven change with time as well as place.

Kings first gave birth to Rome and raised her walls;
She owes to consuls her great power and glory;*   550
And from your unique gifts she now receives
The crowning peak of her prosperity.
Under your rule no civil wars exhaust her:
You've closed the Janus-gates in peace, which only
Once was seen when her consuls ruled, and which,
Like them, the second of her kings achieved.*

MAXIMUS
When forms of government are changed by Heaven,
No blood is shed, no murder blights the State.

CINNA
The gods have an inexorable law:
They make us pay for blessings we receive.   560
Even the Tarquins' exile cost us blood,*
And we paid for our first consulships with wars.

MAXIMUS
So Pompey your ancestor defied the gods
In fighting Caesar to preserve our freedom?

CINNA
If Heaven had not willed that Rome should lose it,
Pompey's defence of it would have succeeded.
Heaven sacrificed him as a worthy monument
To that auspicious change of government:
His name is glorious because his death
Delivered Rome from liberty. That word   570
Has long served to delude her: Rome is barred
From true democracy by her own greatness.
    When she became the mistress of the world,
Her splendid conquests and vast wealth created
A privileged elite of citizens
With greater power than kings. By buying votes
They worked their will and dominated those
Their so-called masters, who were paid by them
And who, in chains of gold, received their laws
Thinking the lawgivers were they themselves.   580
Those great ones' mutual envy formed cabals
Which their ambition turned to murderous factions.

So jealousy made Sulla turn on Marius,*
Caesar on Pompey, Mark Antony on you:
It's clear that what's called freedom only serves
To unleash the bitter rage of civil war.
Freedom is anarchy in which one man
Accepts no master, another man no peer.
Sir, Rome's salvation lies in being united
590 Under a leader firmly in command.
If you still care for her, keep closed to her
The road that always leads to civil strife.
Sulla's annulment of his stable rule
Left Caesar and Pompey free to fight each other;
Those troubled times would not have ravaged us
If he'd installed hereditary rule.
What was achieved by Caesar's cruel murder?
Only that Antony and Lepidus
Fought you. There would have been no civil war
600 If Caesar had named you as his successor.
By stepping down, you'll simply plunge Rome back
Into those ills from which she's scarce drawn breath;
And from her flanks, my lord, another war
Will drain away her last reserves of blood.
    Be moved by love for your country, by compassion;
Through me your Rome is begging you to stay.
Recall the price she paid to be ruled by you;
Not that she would consider it too high:
The peace you've brought rewards her suffering.
610 But a just terror fills her soul with dread:
If, weary of power and for her so-called good,
You give her back that freedom she must lose
In yet more strife to buy another master,
If you don't rank her interest before
Your own, but with that deadly blessing break
Her heart, I dare not tell what I foresee.
Be constant to yourself, my lord: let Rome
Enjoy true happiness beneath your rule;
And make the common good still more secure
620 By naming an heir who's worthy to succeed you.

AUGUSTUS
Enough: you urged compassion; that prevails.
My rest is dear to me, but Rome means more;
Whatever ill I bear in consequence,
To save her I will sacrifice myself.
Vainly my heart cries out for ease: your counsel,
Cinna, persuades me to retain my power.
But both of you shall have a share in it;
I see that you are speaking from the heart,
And that in offering me advice your sole
Concern is for the State and for my good.   630
Your differences spring from your love for me,
And you shall both receive your due reward.
    Maximus, you shall govern Sicily:
Go forth and rule for me that fertile land.
Remember that you govern in my name,
And I shall answer for what you decree.
    Cinna, I give you as your wife Emilia.
You know she takes my daughter Julia's place,*
And if necessity and our misfortunes
Compelled me to deal harshly with her father,   640
The wealth I've since bestowed on her must surely
Have soothed the bitterness of losing him.
Visit her with my blessing; try to win her.
You're not a man she's likely to reject:
She'll be delighted by your declaration.
Farewell: I must convey this news to Livia.
    Exit AUGUSTUS.   [II.ii]
MAXIMUS
Such stirring words! So what's your purpose now?
CINNA
Exactly what it was and always will be.
MAXIMUS
An assassin praises the tyrant he means to kill?
CINNA
An assassin wants to grant him a reprieve?   650
MAXIMUS
I want to set Rome free.

CINNA
                              And you can see
    I want to avenge her when I set her free.
    You'd have Octavius sate his frenzied lusts,
    Pillage our altars, sacrifice our lives,
    Ravage the countryside, strew Rome with corpses,
    And be forgiven for quitting in remorse!
    When we are urged by Heaven to punish him,
    You'd let him go scot-free for saying sorry!
    A fine example! If we show him mercy,
660 We tempt more tyrants down the path he trod.
    No: let's avenge our fellow-Romans: kill him,
    And strike with terror those who crave the crown.
    An end to tyrants: if Sulla had been punished,
    Caesar would not have dared to go so far.

MAXIMUS
    But Caesar's death, which you find just, served as
    A pretext for the harshness of Augustus.
    Brutus should not have punished Caesar; then
    Augustus would not have dared to go so far.

CINNA
    Cassius it was who failed: his panicking*
670 Was what thrust Rome beneath fresh tyranny.
    But misadventures such as those will not
    Occur when Rome is led by wiser men.

MAXIMUS
    As yet we've given little sign that we
    Would organize ourselves with greater wisdom.
    It's hardly wise to spurn the liberty
    For which we're all prepared to risk our lives.

CINNA
    It's much less wise to think that one can cure
    So grave an ill as Rome's and leave the root
    Intact. A gentle remedy will close
680 The wound while festering poison lurks beneath.

MAXIMUS
    The bloody cure you want may not succeed.

CINNA
  The painless cure you want is laced with shame.
MAXIMUS
  It's never shameful to escape from chains.
CINNA
  Escape without a fight is cowardly.
MAXIMUS
  Freedom has an allure that never fades;
  For Rome it's always been a priceless gift.
CINNA
  A gift she'd scorn if it were thrown to her
  By one grown weary of oppressing her;
  Her great heart would not prize the leavings of
  A tyrant who had gorged his fill on her;   690
  And every honourable man in Rome
  Hates him too bitterly to love his gifts.
MAXIMUS
  Emilia must be hateful to you then?
CINNA
  To take her at his hands would wring my heart.
  But in avenging all the wrongs of Rome
  I shall outface him to the mouth of hell.
  Yes, when I've won her by destroying him,
  I'll join my bloodstained hand with hers; I'll marry
  Her on his ashes; so the tyrant's gift
  Shall be my recompense for killing him.   700
MAXIMUS
  My friend, how can you win her, spattered with
  The blood of him she loves like her own father?
  For you are not the man to force her will.
CINNA
  These walls have ears, my friend, we may be heard.
  We should perhaps be prudent and not speak
  Our minds in such an inappropriate place.
  Come where in safety you may understand
  That there's no obstacle to what I've planned.

ACT III

Emilia's apartment

MAXIMUS, EUPHORBUS

MAXIMUS

He told me himself: their love is mutual;
710   He loves Emilia and she loves him.
But to possess her he must avenge her father.
That's why he's leading the conspiracy.

EUPHORBUS

I see now why he argued with such force,
Urging Augustus to retain his power:
If he stepped down, the plot would come to nothing
And his assassins would become his friends.

MAXIMUS

They're pledged to serve a man who's acting for
Himself and not for Rome, as he pretends.
And bitterly I find that I'm not serving
720   My country but my rival's interest.

EUPHORBUS

Your rival?

MAXIMUS

                          Yes: I love Emilia too.
But I've been careful to conceal my feelings:
Before declaring them, I wished to prove
By some great deed that I was worthy of her.
But Cinna's using me to snatch her from me;
His plan, which I'm fulfilling, will destroy me;
I expect to die for what I do tomorrow:
I'm lending him my arm with which to kill me.
Friendship has trapped me in a cruel snare.

EUPHORBUS

730   Escape is easy: do now what's best for you.
Abort the plot that you feel sure will kill you;
Denounce your rival and secure the lady:
When you have saved Augustus' life, he'll have
No option but to let you have Emilia.

MAXIMUS
  Betray my friend!
EUPHORBUS
                    Love knows no loyalty;
  Friendship means nothing to a man in love.
  And is it not justice to betray a traitor
  Who dares betray his master for his mistress?
  Past favours he forgets: forget past friendship.
MAXIMUS
  Bad models should be shunned, not replicated.   740
EUPHORBUS
  To combat evil every means is just:
  There is no crime in punishing a crime.
MAXIMUS
  A crime by which Rome gains her liberty!
EUPHORBUS
  Don't trust a man who's so despicable.
  His country's good is not what motivates him;
  Self-interest, not honour, is his spur.
  If he were not in love, he'd love Augustus:
  There's nothing noble in ingratitude.
  Do you believe you've seen into his soul?
  He used the good of Rome to hide from you   750
  The secret of his passion; that in turn
  May hide the secret vice of his ambition.
  After Augustus' death perhaps he means
  Not to free Rome, but make her kneel to him;
  Perhaps he sees you as a future subject,
  Or counts upon your death to reach his goal.
MAXIMUS
  But how can I name him and not the others?
  All the conspirators would meet their death,
  And those like us, who only seek the good
  Of Rome, would be most shamefully betrayed.   760
  To damn so many innocent men in order
  To punish one who's guilty! It's too vile.
  I'll fight him boldly, but I fear for them.

EUPHORBUS

    Augustus has grown tired of harsh repression;
    He's sickened by executions; now he pardons
    Accomplices and punishes the leaders.
    But if on their behalf you fear his anger,
    Tell him that you're the spokesman for them all.

MAXIMUS

    No more: it's madness to believe I can
770   Obtain Emilia by destroying Cinna;
    It's hardly the best way to gain her favour
    To kill what she loves best in all the world.
    To take her as Augustus' gift means nothing:
    It's not her person but her heart I crave,
    To make her mine would give me no content
    If I had gained no share in her affection.
    How can a triple wrong win her devotion?
    If I betray her lover, thwart her vengeance,
    And save the man whose death she most desires,
780   What hope have I that she will cherish me?

EUPHORBUS

    It's tricky, that I must confess; but there
    Some stratagem may serve your turn. We must
    By some ruse mask the truth from her, and trust
    To time to smooth the artifice away.

MAXIMUS

    But Cinna might plead that she incited him.
    If she is punished with him, how can I
    Request Augustus to reward me with
    The one who caused us both to plot his death?

EUPHORBUS

    So many hurdles are conceivable
790   That you'd need miracles to jump them all;
    But still, I hope we might devise some way—

MAXIMUS

    Go now, Euphorbus: soon I'll seek you out.
    Here's Cinna; there's something I must learn from him
    Before I can decide what I shall do.

[III.ii]   *Exit* EUPHORBUS. *Enter* CINNA.

MAXIMUS
    You're thoughtful.
CINNA
                        I have much to think about.
MAXIMUS
    May I know what it is that troubles you?
CINNA
    Emilia and Augustus: both torment me.
    He seems too virtuous, and she too cruel.
    Would to the gods that he'd contrived to make
    Her love him more, or that he loved me less: 800
    That her heart had been softened by his bounty
    As mine is captivated by her beauty!
    Deep in my soul I'm tortured by remorse
    That won't let me forget his kindness to me.
    That warm affection, now so ill-repaid,
    Is killing me with merciless reproaches.
    I'm haunted most of all by his entrusting
    His sovereignty to us, his heeding our
    Advice, his praising me and saying: 'Your counsel,
    Cinna, persuades me to retain my power,   810
    But both of you shall have a share in it.'
    And I'm to plunge a dagger in his breast!
    Ah, rather . . . But Emilia is my life;
    A monstrous oath binds me to share her hatred;
    Since she abhors him, I must hate him too.
    I stain my honour if I kill my friend,
    But to break my solemn oath is sacrilege.
    I must be false to him or false to her.
MAXIMUS
    You were not troubled in this way before;
    You seemed more resolute in your intention;   820
    Your heart felt no reproaches or remorse.
CINNA
    They are not felt until the blow draws near;
    One does not see such crimes for what they are
    Until one's hand is raised to make them real.
    Till then, the soul is spellbound by its purpose

And blindly clings to its first notion, but
Who does not falter when the moment comes?
Who is not shaken, overwhelmed and crushed?
Even the mighty Brutus, I suspect,
830   Longed sometimes to abandon his design;
Before he struck, he must have many times
Repented in his soul and felt remorse.

MAXIMUS
He was too valiant to be so distressed;
He never thought himself to be ungrateful;
The more the tyrant smothered him with love,
The more he smouldered with resentful hate.
Since he's to be your model, do as he,
And find a better reason for remorse:
Regret the vile advice you gave, which choked
840   The joyous rebirth of our liberty.
Today, you, you alone, have snatched it from us;
Brutus would have accepted it from Caesar;
He'd never have allowed it to be threatened
By trivial interests like love or vengeance.
Stop listening to the friendly tyrant who
Desires to share his supreme power with you,
And hear the voice of Rome imploring you:
'Cinna, restore what you have stolen from me;
Today you put Emilia first before me:
850   Don't put my cruel oppressor before me now.'

CINNA
My friend, don't heap more anguish on a man
Whose purpose is both honourable and base.
I know the wrong I've done to Rome, and soon
I shall restore what I have snatched from her.
Forgive the pity I must feel for my
Old friendship for Augustus as it dies.
I beg you, while I'm waiting for Emilia,
Leave me to plumb the depths of my despair.
My sorrow burdens you, and to resolve
860   So many torments I need solitude.

MAXIMUS

You wish to share your doubts with your Emilia:
The kindness of Augustus and your weakness.
Lovers should meet in perfect secrecy;
Ever the discreet confidant, I'll leave you.

    Exit MAXIMUS.   [III.iii]

CINNA (*alone*)

Weakness is not the name for that glorious surge
Of noble feeling from my better self
Which honour sets against the shameful murder
Conceived in haste by my ingratitude.
And yet it is weak when confronted by
Emilia's strength: it either panders to   870
The love it ought to quash, or fights against it
Yet draws back from completely conquering it.
Conflicting duties: which one should prevail?
Which calls more loudly? Which should I obey?
How hard for an upright man to fall from grace!
Whatever I may gain from playing false –
The joys of love, the sweetness of revenge,
The glory of releasing Rome from bondage –
My reason is not duped: it's poisoned fruit
If it must be acquired by treachery,   880
If I must pierce that noble heart, the man
Who holds my unworthy self in such esteem,
Who honours me, and whose resolve to keep
His power is swayed by my advice alone.
So vile a betrayal! No man should sink so low!
Let Rome remain enslaved for evermore,
Let my love perish, perish all my hopes,
Before my hand commits so foul a wrong!
Is he not making me a present of
What love drives me to purchase with his blood?   890
To enjoy his free gift must I murder him?
Must I prise from him what he wants to give?

    But I am bound by you, my reckless oath,
By Emilia's hate, by her father's memory.

My word, my heart, my arm are ruled by you;
I'm powerless to act without your leave;
You only can decide what I must do.
Emilia, only you can save Augustus;
Your will alone controls his destiny
900   And by my hand awards him life or death.
O gods, who made her, like you, to be worshipped,
Make her, like you, responsive to my prayers;
Since I can't free myself from her command,
Grant me the power to mould her will to mine.
She's here: harsh and unyielding, but still loved.

[III.iv]   *Enter* EMILIA *with* FULVIA.

EMILIA
Cinna, the gods be thanked, my fears were groundless:
None of your friends has broken faith with you.
I had no need to plead for you: Augustus,
While I was there, told Livia everything.
910   What he revealed to her restored my life.

CINNA
Will you deny his offer? And defer
The sweet fulfilment of his gift to me?

EMILIA
Fulfilment lies in your hands.

CINNA
                                    No, in yours.

EMILIA
I am still myself; my heart remains unchanged;
There is no gift in offering me to you:
It's giving you what you already have.

CINNA
But you could . . . Heaven! I fear to say the word . . .

EMILIA
What could I do? What do you fear?

CINNA
                                          I feel
Both fear and sorrow, and I see that, if
920   We felt as one, you'd understand my pain;
And so I know that I shall anger you.

I dare not speak, and cannot hold my peace.

EMILIA

Do not torment me: speak.

CINNA

                            I must obey you.
So I shall anger you, and you will hate me.
Emilia, I love you; Heaven strike me down
If all my joy does not lie in that love,
Or if it falls below what's due to you,
The worthy treasure of a mighty heart!
But at what cost you offer me yourself:
To win you, I must act despicably;   930
Augustus' kindness—

EMILIA

                  Stop. I understand.
I see your wavering faith, your weak remorse:
The tyrant's favours outweigh your promises;
His smile can melt your love and your sworn oath.
Naïvely you dare think that he, the man
Who can do all things, can dispose of me.
You want me at his hand, and not my own,
But never in that way will I be yours.
Though he may rock the earth beneath his feet,
Unseat kings, make a gift of their domains,   940
By his proscriptions redden land and sea,
And change at will the pattern of the world,
Emilia's heart is not his to command.

CINNA

That's why I want it only at your hand.
I am still myself, my faith is still intact;
The pity I feel does not make me forsworn:
I'm yours, beyond what my oath may require,
I share your feelings, want what you desire.
As you must know, I could have saved Augustus
Without committing perjury or crime: 950
If he'd renounced his power, he would
Have left us no excuse for killing him;
The plot would have been jettisoned, your purpose

Foiled, your hate frustrated. I alone
Revived his dying will to govern Rome;
To make him your victim, I restored his crown.

EMILIA

My victim! And now, you viper, you want me
To restrain your hand, to let him live, and love him!
To be your prize for sparing him, the spoils
960   You gain for persuading him to keep his crown!

CINNA

Do not revile me: I have served you well:
Without me, he would now be safe from you.
In letting you decide his fate I put
My love for you before my debt to him.
My sworn oath proves my constancy to you:
Indulge the gratitude I show him now
In trying to soothe the unworthy rage you feel
And help you love the man as he loves you.
A noble soul seeks to avoid the shame
970   Of being charged with thankless treachery,
Disdains to benefit by squalid means,
And will accept no prize that honour scorns.

EMILIA

I glory in that shame: base treachery
Is noble when it strikes at tyranny;
Where harsh oppression is destroyed, the most
Ungrateful are the most magnanimous.

CINNA

You're seeing virtues where it suits your hatred.

EMILIA

I'm seeing virtues worthy of a Roman.

CINNA

A truly Roman heart—

EMILIA

                              Will stop at nothing
980   To kill a loathsome tyrant, choosing death
Before the shame of living as a slave.

CINNA

One can take pride in being Augustus' slave:

We see great kings kneel down to us and plead
For slaves like us to shield them from their foes;
He prostrates at our feet grand potentates
And gives us power over their great might;
He makes us rich with tribute seized from them,
And binds them with a chain that makes us free.

EMILIA

What piffling aspirations fire your heart!
You think it's something to surpass a king!   990
Would one in all the world dare boast that he
Was equal to a Roman citizen?
Antony loved a queen: that stained his honour*
And so we hated him. If great Attalus,
That venerable king who called himself
A freedman of the Romans, had become*
The lord of Asia, he'd have prized above
His throne the rank of Roman citizen.
Think of your name, uphold its dignity;
Assume the great soul of a Roman: see   1000
That every one of us by Heaven's decree
Was born to master kings and to live free.

CINNA

History plainly shows that Heaven abhors
Assassins and punishes ingratitude.
Yes, we can slaughter, but when Heaven has raised
A throne, it will avenge its overthrow;
It favours rulers it has placed in power:
If they're cut down, the wound is slow to heal,
And, when Heaven wills that they deserve to fall,
Its thunderbolt alone may wipe them out.   1010

EMILIA

Say that you favour them yourself, since you
Rely on thunderbolts to punish tyrants.
I'll say no more: bow down to tyranny;
Indulge the natural baseness of your soul.
To calm your troubled mind you'd best forget
Your noble birth and the reward you're promised.
Without employing you to serve my anger

I'll free my country and avenge my father.
That glorious honour would by now be mine,
1020   If love for you had not restrained my hand.
My love for you enslaved me to your will
And for your sake made me preserve my life.
I should have faced the tyrant all alone,
Destroyed him, and been slaughtered by his guards.
But so I'd have been lost to you; and, since
Love wills that I should live for you alone,
I tried, and failed, to save my life for you,
And let you prove that you deserved my hand.
Great gods, forgive me if I was mistaken
1030   In thinking Pompey's grandson had my love,
If a mere semblance planted in his place
Deceived me into falling for a slave.
Whichever you may be, I love you still.
When I ask treachery of you, you baulk,
But many would vie to fulfil that condition
If, like you, they could win me at that price.
But no one else shall have me, never fear.
Live still for your dear tyrant, while I die
Still yours: soon he and I will be at rest,
1040   Since you are not man enough to merit me.
Be there and see me die, bathed in his blood
And mine, with no accomplice but my courage,
And hear me say contentedly: 'Do not
Denounce my destiny for this: this is your doing;
You it was who condemned me to the tomb
Attended by the glory meant for you.
I die that absolute power in Rome may die;
But if you'd wished it, I'd have lived for you.'

CINNA

You want it: then you must be satisfied:
1050   I must avenge your father and free Rome;
I must mete out a tyrant's just desert.
But you're a more cruel tyrant than Augustus:
He robs us of our lives, our goods, our wives,
But never does he commandeer our souls;

The ruthless sovereignty your beauty wields
Controls the spirit and subdues the will.
You make me prize that which dishonours me;
You make me hate that which my soul reveres;
You make me shed that blood for which I should
Shed all of mine a thousand times and more.   1060
You wish it, I obey, you have my word:
But my own hand at once will turn on me
In sacrifice to that great ruler's shade,
And link my punishment with my forced crime;
So by confounding those two deeds I shall
Straightway retrieve my forfeited good name.
Farewell.

    Exit CINNA.   [III.v]

FULVIA

       You've plunged his soul into despair.

EMILIA

To love me means to do what must be done.

FULVIA

In doing what you ask of him he'll die.
You're weeping!

EMILIA

       Ah, Fulvia, seek him out and, if   1070
You care for me enough to succour me,
Tear from his heart his plan to end his life:
Say—

FULVIA

    That to save him you will spare Augustus?

EMILIA

Ah! That would wrong the hatred in my heart.

FULVIA

What then?

EMILIA

     He must go on and keep his oath;
When that is done, he must choose me or death.

ACT IV

Augustus' apartment

AUGUSTUS, EUPHORBUS,

[IV.i]   POLYCLETUS, GUARDS

AUGUSTUS

Euphorbus, this is quite beyond belief.

EUPHORBUS

My lord, the telling of it chills the blood:
It's frightening to conceive such furious rage;
1080   The thought of it strikes terror to the heart.

AUGUSTUS

What? Cinna? Maximus? My dearest friends!
The two I honoured with such high regard,
Opened my heart to, and selected for
Positions of the greatest weight and honour!
I place my sovereign power in their hands,
And they conspire to tear my life from me!
Maximus has repented and forewarns me:
He shows a heart moved justly by remorse.
But Cinna!

EUPHORBUS

           Cinna alone still rages, made
1090   The more rebellious by your favours to him;
Alone he fights against the wholesome impact
Of Maximus' remorse upon the plotters.
He tries to quash their fear and their contrition
And fire their shaken souls with fresh resolve.

AUGUSTUS

Only he spurs them, only he corrupts them!
The vilest traitor that the world has known!
Perfidy nurtured in a Fury's breast!*
Too cruel a blow from such a cherished hand!
Betrayed by Cinna! Polycletus, hear me.
(*He whispers to him.*)

POLYCLETUS

1100   My lord, all your commands will be obeyed.

AUGUSTUS

Erastus meanwhile can bring Maximus
Here to receive a pardon for his crime.
        Exit POLYCLETUS.

EUPHORBUS

He has condemned himself for it already:
He'd scarcely come home from the palace when,
With wild gaze and unseeing eyes, his heart
Bursting with sighs, his mouth convulsed with sobs,
He cursed his life and the ill-fated plot,
Explained it all to me as I have told you,
Ordered me to alert you to the danger,
And added: 'Tell him I am passing sentence   1110
On myself and know my just deserts.'
Then he abruptly plunged into the Tiber;
The swift, swollen waters and the murky night
Concealed from me his tragic story's ending.

AUGUSTUS

By yielding too meekly to his fierce remorse
He has deprived himself of my forgiveness;
There is no wrong to me repentance will
Not wipe away. But since he's chosen to
Reject my pardon— Guards! Go and arrest
The others, and hold this faithful witness fast.   1120
        Exeunt GUARDS *with* EUPHORBUS.   [IV.ii]

AUGUSTUS (*alone*)

O Heaven! After this to whom would you
Have me entrust my life and secret thoughts?
Take back the mighty power you've lent me, if
The gift of subjects means the loss of friends,
If it must be the lot of sovereigns to
Be hated for the blessings we bestow,
And cruelly condemned by you to love
Those you incite to bring about our death.
We're never safe: omnipotence is fear.

        Augustus, face the truth: you were Octavius.   1130
You spared none then, so why should you be spared?
Your arm has bathed in rivers of blood! Remember

The streams of it that reddened Philippi,
That flowed at Antony's defeat, that flowed
When Sextus fell; see, drowning in her blood,
The city of Perugia and her people.*
After that carnage, reflect upon the blood
That your proscriptions shed, where you yourself,
The executioner of your own friends,
Buried the knife in your own tutor's breast:
Then dare accuse Fate of injustice, when
You see your friends prepared to murder you,
When, spurred to kill you by your own example,
They break the laws that you have not observed!
Their perfidy is just; Heaven sanctions it:
Lose your dominion as you came by it;
Yield your unfaithful blood to faithlessness;
Suffer ungrateful treachery in your turn.
      But where's my judgement when I need it most?
What madness, Cinna, damns me and not you?
You hypocritically make me keep
The power you plan to kill me for possessing,
Condemn me for the crime that you provoked,
Raise an illicit throne to shatter it,
Sugar your murder with patriotic zeal,
And to destroy me jeopardize the State!
And I'm to make myself forget all that!
Leave you in peace when you've filled me with fear!
No, no, I betray myself to think of it!
Who pardons lightly begs to be abused:
Punish the leader, proscribe the accomplices.
      What then? An endless round of blood and slaughter?
My cruel hand grows tired but cannot rest;
I try to be feared and only stir rebellion;
Rome is a hydra eager to destroy me:
One head cut off gives rise to hundreds more;*
The more I spill the blood of scheming traitors,
The more my life's not more secure but cursed.
Octavius, do not wait for some new Brutus:
Die: rob him of the glory of your fall;

1140

1150

1160

1170

Die: straining to survive is vain and base
If brave men in such numbers want your death,
If all the finest flower of Rome's youth
Is bent in turn on cutting short your days;
Die, since there is no cure for this disease;
Die, since you must destroy or be destroyed.
Life is but paltry, and what remains to you
Is not worth buying at so grim a price.
Die; but at least depart this life in splendour:
Quench your brief candle in the traitor's blood.   1180
As you expire, let him be sacrificed;
Grant him his wish while punishing his crime;
Let your death torture him by letting him
Observe it with no joy; let you instead
In dying rejoice to watch him die. If Rome
Must hate me, let me glory in her hate.

   O Romans, O revenge, O supreme power,
O desperate struggle of a wavering heart
That flees from resolutions as they form,
Order the fate of this beleaguered sovereign: 1190
Which path should I pursue and which renounce?
Let me be emperor still, or let me die.

   Enter LIVIA.   [IV.iii]

AUGUSTUS (*continues*)

Livia, I've been betrayed; and the hand poised*
To murder me has crushed my will with sorrow.
Cinna's the traitor, Cinna—

LIVIA

                  Euphorbus told me;
I blenched with horror when I heard his story.
But will you listen to a woman's counsel?

AUGUSTUS

Ah! Is there any counsel I can follow?

LIVIA

My lord, to date your harsh severity
Has thundered noisily to no avail.   1200
To see another put to death scares no one:
Lepidus rose by Salvidienus' fall;

Murena followed, then came Cepio;
The death by torture of them both struck no
Restraining fear into Egnatius' fury;*
And Cinna now dares follow in his wake.
Even the lowest of the low have sought
To rise by such a lofty undertaking.
In vain you've punished their temerity:
1210   With Cinna see what mercy can achieve;
Let him be tortured only by his shame.
This time seek out the most expedient way:
His execution may provoke the people;
His pardon may embellish your renown:
Those whom your harshness drives to savage rage
May well be moved by your benevolence.

AUGUSTUS

I'll win their hearts outright by giving up
The hated power that makes them plot my death.
I'm tired of pondering over your advice;
1220   No more of it: I've done with pondering.
    Rome, sigh no more for your lost liberty:
If I enslaved you, I shall set you free;
I'll give you back the empire that I conquered,
Greater, more peaceful than before my rule.
If you must hate me, hate me openly;
If you can love me, love me without fear:
Weary, as Sulla was, of power and rank,
My own contentment now is all I seek.

LIVIA

Sulla's good fortune has too long beguiled you;
1230   Beware: your fate may take a different course;
The famed good luck that saved his life would not
Be deemed good luck if it were always so.

AUGUSTUS

Well, if it is too much for me to ask,
I'll give my blood to those who thirst for it.
After a lengthy storm one needs a harbour;
The only two I see are rest and death.

LIVIA

Would you renounce the fruit of so much toil?

AUGUSTUS

Would you retain the cause of so much hate?

LIVIA

My lord, to adopt a measure so extreme
Looks like despair, not magnanimity.   1240

AUGUSTUS

To rule and pardon such foul treachery
Would not show strength but weakness.

LIVIA

                                    It would show
That you can rule yourself with noble strength
And make the choice that most befits a king.

AUGUSTUS

It was a woman's counsel that you promised:
You've kept your word and given it, my lady.
After so many enemies laid low
And twenty years of rule, I know the kind*
Of strength required, the due priorities,
My duty when I meet with mutiny.   1250
To plot the sovereign's death wounds all his subjects;
The thought alone is a crime against the State,
An outrage to his whole dominion, which
Either he must avenge, or cease to rule.

LIVIA

Don't be so influenced by your emotions.

AUGUSTUS

Don't be so weak, or fond of your own rank.

LIVIA

You should not treat wise counsel with such scorn.

AUGUSTUS

Heaven will make clear to me what I should do.
Farewell; we're wasting time.

LIVIA

                          I will not leave you
Until you let my love prevail in this.   1260

AUGUSTUS
  You love being empress: that's why you persist.
LIVIA
  It's you I love, not Fortune's gifts to you.
      Exit AUGUSTUS.
LIVIA (*alone*)
  He's fleeing from me, but I'll make him see
  That by forgiveness he will reinforce
  His power, that the true monarch stamps himself
  Most nobly on the world by clemency.
      Exit LIVIA.*

Emilia's apartment

[IV.iv]   EMILIA, FULVIA

EMILIA
  Why am I so content? Against all reason
  My mind is utterly at peace! Augustus
  Has sent for Cinna and I feel no fear!
1270 My heart gives forth no sighs, my eyes no tears,
  As if some inner knowledge told me that
  All things will be resolved as I desire!
  Fulvia, have I rightly understood you?
FULVIA
  I had persuaded Cinna not to end his life,
  And calmly he was coming back with me
  To try a second time to soothe your anger;
  I had done well. Just then came Polycletus,
  The usual agent of Augustus' will.
  At his behest at once, discreetly, with
1280 No guard, he escorted Cinna to the palace.
  Augustus is disturbed; it's not known why.
  Conflicting speculations are put forward:
  Everyone thinks that some deep trouble grieves him,
  And that he's summoned Cinna to give counsel;
  But I'm confused by what I've just been told:
  Evander, Cinna's freedman, has been seized,
  Euphorbus arrested with no reason given,
  And rumours are spread abroad about his master,

Maximus: that he's a victim of despair:
The depths, they hint, the Tiber; nothing more.   1290

EMILIA

So many reasons to abandon hope,
Yet my sad heart refuses to be troubled!
In every case Heaven wills it to respond
With feelings contrary to what seems due:
Before, I was assailed by needless fear;
Now fear is justified, and I'm composed.
Great gods, I understand you! By your grace,
Which I revere, you keep my honour safe:
By not permitting me to groan and weep
You keep me steadfast in calamity.   1300
You wish to see me die as great of heart
As when I first embraced the glorious task;
And my wish is to die as you ordain,
With that same constancy you breed in me.
Freedom for Rome! O shade of my father, hear me!
I have done everything within my power:
I've spurred his friends to slay your murderer,
And ventured more for you than was my right.
If I have failed, my honour is intact;
If I cannot avenge you, I shall join you,   1310
But blazing still with fury of such splendour,
And by a noble death so worthy of you,
That you will recognize the blood of those
Great heroes whom you made my ancestors.

    Enter MAXIMUS.   [IV.v]

EMILIA (*continues*)

Maximus! It was rumoured you were dead!

MAXIMUS

Euphorbus led Augustus to believe so.
The plot discovered, they arrested him;
To save my life, he said I'd killed myself.

EMILIA

And Cinna?

MAXIMUS

        What grieves him most is that Augustus

1320 Knows of your part in the conspiracy;
He cannot shield you: his man, Evander, had
In his defence revealed that you incited
Cinna. The order for your arrest is given.

EMILIA
Whoever received it shows no haste: I'm quite
Prepared and weary of the wait.

MAXIMUS
                                      He expects
You at my house.

EMILIA
                              At your house!

MAXIMUS
                                            You're surprised:
But see the care that Heaven takes of you:
The messenger is one of us, and he
Will flee with us. Let's go before we're followed:
1330 We have a ship prepared to leave at once.

EMILIA
Maximus, do you know me, and who I am?

MAXIMUS
For Cinna's sake I'm doing all I can:
From this disaster I'm trying to rescue you,
The finest part of him that still remains.
Let us escape, Emilia, and live;
In time we'll come back and avenge his death.

EMILIA
When men like Cinna fall, they're to be followed,
Not avenged; they're not to be outlived.
He who would save himself when Cinna's lost
1340 Does not deserve the life to which he clings.

MAXIMUS
What's this? The madness of your blind despair?
O gods! What weakness in a soul so strong!
A noble heart that will not fight, that is
Laid low by one defeat at Fortune's hand!
Call back the sublime courage that was yours;
Open your eyes and see me as I am:

In me you look upon a second Cinna;
In me Heaven gives you back the love you've lost:
Since friendship made one soul of him and me,
Bestow your love for him upon his friend,   1350
And I will cherish you as tenderly—

EMILIA

You dare to love me and you dare not die!
You are presumptuous: if you must presume,
At least deserve what you are asking for.
Don't like a coward flee from glorious death,
Or offer me a heart you show so base.
Arouse my envy of your strength and courage;
If I can't love you, make me mourn your loss;
Show a true Roman's utmost fortitude
And earn my tears, since you're denied my heart.   1360
If friendship for Cinna be your motive, is
It fitting to beguile me, whom he loves?
Learn, learn from me what duty is owed to friendship,
And either show it, or be shown by me.

MAXIMUS

Your natural grief makes you too quick to judge.

EMILIA

And yours makes you too quick to serve yourself.
You speak already of return and vengeance,
And in your sorrow you can think of love!

MAXIMUS

Newborn my love may be, but it is strong:
In you I love my friend, the man who loved you,   1370
And with the selfsame ardour that inflamed him—

EMILIA

A wise man, Maximus, would curb his tongue.
This news has shocked me, but not blurred my mind;
Despair in me is noble, but not blind.
No rash emotion clouds my constancy,
And I see more than I would wish to see.

MAXIMUS

You don't suspect me of some base deception?

EMILIA
    Since you would have me say so, yes, I do.
    The plan for our escape is much too neat
1380   Not to cast doubt on your integrity:
    If you had not contrived our flight, the gods
    Would need to have rained miracles to save us.
    Flee without me: your love is wasted here.

MAXIMUS
    Ah! You have said enough.

EMILIA
                     I could say more;
    Yet you need fear no angry words from me.
    But do not hope to dazzle me with lies.
    If I am wronging you by my mistrust,
    Your vindication is to die with me.

MAXIMUS
    Emilia, live, and let my love for you—

EMILIA
1390   I'll hear you in the presence of Augustus.
    Come, Fulvia.

[IV.vi]   *Exit* EMILIA *with* FULVIA.

MAXIMUS (*alone*)
               Crushed, despairing, meriting,
    If possible, a crueller rejection,
    What's left now, Maximus? What penance will
    Atone for your cheap stratagem?
    No more delusions: as she dies, Emilia
    Will blazon forth the truth to all the world;
    On that same scaffold where she ends her days
    Will be displayed her glory and your shame:
    Her death will pass on to posterity
1400   The record of your villainous betrayal.
    By vile deception in one day you've failed
    Your sovereign, your friend, and the woman that you love.
    And from so many sacred ties defiled,
    From sacrificing two lovers to the tyrant,
    All you have garnered is the burning shame
    Set raging in your heart by vain remorse.

Euphorbus, your base counsel is the cause.
But what can be expected of your kind?
Freedmen are never more than scurvy slaves;
Their state may change, their soul remains the same.   1410
Yours is still servile: freedom has not brought you
The slightest tincture of nobility.
You've made me reinstate an unjust power;
You've made me stain the honour of my name.
My heart resisted you, but you fought on
Till your duplicity had tainted it.
For that I forfeit life and reputation,
And I deserve it all for trusting you.
But, please the gods, before the lovers' eyes
I'll sacrifice you in my bitter rage,   1420
And trust that my blood will be pure enough
To expiate the wrong I've done to them,
If in your blood, as vengeance justly due,
I cleanse the crime of hearkening to you.

ACT V

Augustus' apartment
AUGUSTUS, CINNA   [V.i]

AUGUSTUS
Cinna, sit down. Yes, sit; and see that you
Meticulously follow this instruction:
Listen in silence to what I'm going to say.
Don't interrupt me with a word, a sound;
Master your tongue; if to be quiet so long
Puts an unnatural pressure on your feelings,   1430
You shall reply at length when I have done.
On this point only let me have my way.
CINNA
My lord, I shall obey you.
AUGUSTUS
                        Don't forget
To keep your word, and I'll be true to mine.

You're living, Cinna, yet you spring from those
Who were my father's enemies and mine.*
In their camp you first saw the light of day,
And, when they died and I became your master,
Their hatred was so rooted in your breast
1440   That already you had raised your sword against me.
Before you were born you were my enemy,
And, when you came to know me, you remained so:
Your natural inclination ratified
The blood that ranked you with my enemies.
What you could do to harm me, that you did.
And what was my revenge? To let you live.
I held you captive to shower blessings on you;
My Court was your prison, my favour was your shackle.
First I restored to you your patrimony;
1450   Antony's spoils I then enriched you with;
And you know well enough how since, at every turn,
I've waxed profuse in pouring gifts on you.
The dignities and honours you've requested*
I've granted you at once without demur.
I've even favoured you before the sons
Of former allies of the highest rank,
Those who bought me my empire with their blood,
Those who preserved for me the air I breathe.
The way I've treated you has made the victors
1460   Envy the happy fortune of the vanquished.
When Heaven, after so long indulging me,
Hardened its heart and snatched Maecenas from me
By untimely death, I gave his place to you,*
Made you, like him, my closest confidant.
This very day, when my divided soul
Urged me to abdicate, it was from you
And Maximus alone I sought advice.
His I rejected, and chose to follow yours.
Today again I even offered you
1470   Emilia, deservedly adored by all
And raised so high by my devoted care
That you'd have less if I had crowned you king.

You've not forgotten, Cinna; you could not
So soon forget so many favours, blessings;
But, Cinna, what's beyond belief is true:
You've not forgotten, and you mean to kill me.

CINNA

I, my lord! Guilty of such treachery!
If such a vile intention—

AUGUSTUS

                      Keep your promise.
Sit down. I've not said all I want to say.
Then, if you can, you shall defend yourself.   1480
Listen, and take more care to keep your word.
   You plan to kill me in the Capitol
At the sacrifice tomorrow: as the signal
Your hand will give me, not incense, but death.
Half of your men will stay to guard the door,
The rest will follow you as reinforcement.
Am I well briefed, or full of false suspicions?
Shall I rehearse for you the murderers' names?
Proculus, Glabrion, Rutilus, Plautus, Lenas,
Marcellus, Pomponus, Albinus, Icilius, Virginius,   1490
Maximus – whom next to you I loved the most;
The rest do not deserve the honour of
Being named: a paltry crew of desperate men
Undone by debt and crime, who know that soon
The rigour of my laws will strike them, that
Without a revolution they are doomed.
   You've nothing now to say; your tongue is tied,
By shame more than obedience to my will.
What was your plan? What did you hope to gain
When in the temple you had hacked me down?   1500
To free your country from a tyrant's rule?
You told me earlier today, I think,
That Rome's security depended on
A sovereign's absolute and sole command.
If your objective was Rome's freedom, you
Would not have stopped me from restoring it;
In her name you'd have accepted it from me,

Not planned to seize it by assassination.
What was your goal, then? To occupy my throne?
1510 Rome's destiny is curiously sick
Indeed, if I'm the only obstacle
To your accession as her sovereign lord;
If so pathetic are her fortunes that
You are her greatest asset after me,
That my demise will leave the mighty empire
Entrusted to no better hands than yours.
Look deep into yourself; learn what you are:
In Rome you're honoured, you're sought after, loved;
Everyone fears you, everyone's your slave;
1520 Your state is lofty, you can do your will.
But even your enemies would pity you,
If I let you depend on your own feeble
Merit. Try to disprove me; tell me what
You're worth, tell me your strengths, your glorious deeds,
Your special gifts that must have so impressed me,
That raise you up above the common herd.
My favour makes you great and gives you power;
That alone raises you and underpins you;
That is what people worship, and not you.
1530 Apart from that you have no rank or credit,
And all I have to do to make you fall
Is to withdraw the hand that props you up.
But I prefer to give you what you want:
Rule, if you can, by cutting short my life.
But do you think that the Servilii,
The Cossi, the Pauli, the Metelli, the Fabii,*
And all the others whose great hearts reflect
Their mighty ancestors will lay aside
Their pride in noble lineage so far
1540 As to endure that you reign over them?
Speak. Speak: the time has come.

CINNA

                                        I'm stupefied.
No, I'm not frightened by your anger or
By death. I see that I'm betrayed; that gives

Me pause: I cannot think who'd be the traitor.
But that must not preoccupy me now.
   My lord, I'm Roman, and of Pompey's blood;
The slaughter of him and his two sons was not*
Avenged in full by Caesar's death. That vengeance
Was the sole glorious goal of our design.
Betrayed, I must endure your cruelty,   1550
But don't expect from me snivelling repentance,
Futile regrets or shameful pleas for mercy.
Fate is your friend and equally my foe;
I know what I have done, and what you must do:
You owe posterity a stern example:
Your own security demands my death.

AUGUSTUS

So you defy me, Cinna, you play the hero;
Quite unremorseful, you compound your crime.
We'll see if you are resolute to the last.
You see that I know all; you know your due: 1560
Sentence yourself; pronounce your punishment.

   Enter LIVIA *and* EMILIA *with* FULVIA.   [V.ii]

LIVIA

Who all the plotters are you don't yet know:
Your Emilia here, my lord, is one of them.

CINNA

O gods, Emilia here!

AUGUSTUS

             You too, my child!*

EMILIA

Yes: everything he did, he did for me.
I was the cause, my lord, and the reward.

AUGUSTUS

The love I planted in your heart today
Is driving you to die for him already?
You've wasted little time in learning to
Adore the husband that I offered you.   1570

EMILIA

The love you seem to hold against me was
Not born in swift response to your command;

It filled our hearts without your bidding, and
Has been our treasured secret for four years.
But though our mutual feelings are so strong,
A stronger hatred has ruled both our lives:
I offered him no hope of winning me
Until he had avenged my father's death.
I made him swear it; he found accomplices.
1580   Heaven robs me of the outcome I desired,
And as your victim I am here, my lord,
Confessing guilt, but not to save his life:
Death justly follows what he planned to do;
A crime against the State brooks no defence.
To die with him and join my father, that
Is all I hope for and what brings me here.

AUGUSTUS

How long, O Heaven, and why must I be pierced
With arrows shot by my own family?
I had to banish Julia in disgrace,*
1590   And in her place Emilia had my love;
Now she too proves unfit to be my daughter.
One shamed me, and the other wants my blood.
Both yielded to base passion: one embraced
Immodesty, the other parricide.
My child, is this how you repay my kindness?

EMILIA

It's how you paid my father back for his.

AUGUSTUS

Think of the loving care with which I raised you.

EMILIA

He brought you up with equal tenderness;
He was your tutor and you slaughtered him;
1600   You taught me how to tread the path of crime.
The difference between us is just this:
You sacrificed my father to your ambition,
While I, ablaze with my just anger, tried
To sacrifice you to his innocence.

LIVIA

Not so, Emilia; pause; reflect that he

Has amply paid you for your father's kindness.
His death, which so enrages you, was caused,
Not by Augustus Caesar, but Octavius.
Those crimes committed to obtain the crown
Heaven pardons when it grants us sovereignty.   1610
In crowning him, Heaven justified his past,
And made his future rule legitimate.
He who can gain the throne can bear no guilt:
Whatever he has done, or does, he is
Inviolate, our goods and lives are his.
The sovereign's life is never ours to take.

EMILIA

Just so. My aim in speaking as I did
Was to provoke him, not to protect myself.
    So punish me, my lord, the vile seductress
Who turns your favourites into thankless heroes.   1620
Cut short my deadly life to shield your own.
Cinna is not the last I shall corrupt!
I'll be more dangerous if I have both
My father and my lover to avenge.

CINNA

I was corrupted by you? And I am now
To let you, whom I love, dishonour me?
    My lord, the truth must now be plainly spoken:
I'd planned this enterprise before I loved her.
Finding her cold to my most chaste desires,
I sought new means to waken a response: 1630
I spoke of her father and your ruthlessness;
And with my heart I offered her revenge.
How sweet to women is the thought of vengeance!
With that pledge I besieged and conquered her.
My undeserving self she scorned; she could
Not scorn the man who would avenge her father.
I tempted her; because of me she fell;
She's an accomplice, I the source and spur.

EMILIA

Cinna, how can you say so? Is it love
To snatch my honour from me as I die?   1640

CINNA
>Die; but in dying do not soil my name.

EMILIA
>Mine withers, if Augustus trusts your word.

CINNA
>Mine perishes, if you seize all the glory
>That flows from deeds so noble as our goal.

EMILIA
>Well, have your share in it, and leave me mine.
>It would diminish if I lessened yours.
>To those who truly love, renown and joy,
>Torment and shame are shared in equal measure.
>   Our two souls are, my lord, two Roman souls;
>Joining in love, we're joined in hatred too;
>The bitter loss of kin for which we grieved
>Taught us our duty, both of us together.
>In that great enterprise our hearts concurred;
>Together our exalted minds devised it;
>Together we desire a noble death.
>You wished to unite us; do not divide us now.

AUGUSTUS
>Yes, I'll unite you, you treacherous, thankless pair,
>Who hate me more than did Mark Antony
>Or Lepidus; yes, I'll unite you, since
>You wish it: your desire shall be appeased.
>And the whole world, discovering what incites me,
>Shall marvel at both crime and punishment.

[V.iii]   *Enter* MAXIMUS.

AUGUSTUS (*continues*)
>Maximus! So Heaven smiles on me and has
>Reclaimed you from the raging river's depths.
>Come here to me, my only faithful friend.

MAXIMUS
>A criminal, my lord, deserves less honour.

AUGUSTUS
>Don't talk of crime when you have shown remorse,
>When you have rescued me from mortal danger:
>To you I owe my life and sovereignty.

1650 (line marker)
1660 (line marker)

MAXIMUS

    Of all your enemies I am the worst: 1670
    If you still reign, my lord, if you still live,
    It is my jealous fury you must thank.
    No virtuous remorse took hold of me:
    To kill my rival I betrayed his plot.
    Euphorbus made you think I'd drowned myself
    So that you would not send in search of me:
    I planned to deceive Emilia, to frighten her
    So that she'd flee from Italy with me,
    Persuading her by holding out the hope
    That we'd return to avenge her lover's death.   1680
    She was not tempted by my sordid bait;
    Her virtue under siege acquired new strength:
    She saw into my heart. You know the rest;
    There is no need for me to tell you more:
    You see the outcome of my squalid trick.
    But if my warning merits some reward,
    Then let Euphorbus die in torment, and
    Let me die in the sight of these two lovers.
    That villain caused me to betray my friend,
    My love, my sovereign, and my country,   1690
    Yet I shall rest contented if I die
    Knowing he's suffered all that he deserves.

AUGUSTUS

    Heaven, is this all? Or has my cruel fate
    Corrupted more of those most dear to me?
    Though it be aided by the powers of hell,
    This ruler of the world shall rule himself.
    I must; I will. Posterity, for ever
    Preserve the record of this victory.
    Today I master the most righteous anger
    Of which the memory will descend to you.   1700
      Cinna, let us be friends: here is my hand.
    I spared your life as my born enemy;
    And now, despite your rabid, vile intent,
    Again I spare it as my murderer.
    Let's see which of us acts with better grace,

The donor or recipient of your life.
You spurn my favours, I'll redouble them;
I've showered them on you, now I'll crush you with them:
Take, with this bride that I had promised you,
1710   The rank of consul for the coming year.
        My child, love Cinna in that glorious role;
Prefer its crimson to my crimson blood.*
Like me subdue your anger: in a husband
More than a father I restore to you.

EMILIA

And I'm restored to you by these resplendent
Blessings which reform my ailing sight.
What I thought just, I now perceive as evil;
The fear of death did not arouse what now
Is raging in my soul: a fierce remorse
1720   To which my heart surrenders silently.*
Heaven smiles upon your sovereignty, my lord;
Of that I'm proud to be the proof: by changing
My heart's desire, Heaven signifies its wish
That Rome should change her form of government.
My hatred, which I thought immortal, now
Must die; it's dead; my heart is true to you.
That hatred I abhor from this time forth;
Its rage gives way to burning loyalty.

CINNA

My lord, what can I say when our transgressions
1730   Meet with rewards instead of punishments?
O matchless worth! O clemency which makes
Your power more just and more corrupt my crime!

AUGUSTUS

No more: in sweet oblivion let it rest.
Now join me both in pardoning Maximus.
All of us he betrayed: but so he kept
You guiltless and restored my friends to me.
Maximus, take your place again beside me;
Enjoy once more your credit and renown.
Forgive Euphorbus too, all three of you.

Tomorrow shall Cinna marry Emilia: that's   1740
Your penance, Maximus, if you still love her.

MAXIMUS

It is too just for me to make complaint;
I'm more shamed by your kindnesses, my lord,
Than envious of the joy that I'm denied.

CINNA

Let my restored integrity, my lord,
Devote to you that faith so basely broken,
But which is now so strong and firmly rooted
It could withstand the downfall of the skies.
May the first mover of great destinies
By cutting short our lives prolong your days,   1750
And I be privileged to lose for you
A hundredfold what you've bestowed on me.

LIVIA

That is not all, my lord: my soul is fired
By a prophetic ray of holy light.
Pay heed to what the gods impart through me:
The edict of your blessed destiny.
    This day's event makes you inviolate:
Your yoke will now be borne without complaint;
The most rebellious heart will now be true,
And find it glorious to die for you.   1760
No treacherous design, no envious gaze
Will cloud the course of your triumphant days,
No faithless friend, no base conspiracy:
You've found the art of breeding loyalty.
Rome, with a sense of deepest joy unfurled,
Entrusts to you dominion of the world.
Your virtues will protect your sovereignty
And safeguard her long-lived prosperity.
Beguiled no more by freedom's spurious dream,
Always she'll grant one ruler power supreme.   1770
You shall have hallowed temples here on earth;
In Heaven a seat to honour your true worth.
Your star for future nations in this world's dark night,

    Guiding all mighty monarchs, ever shall shine bright.

AUGUSTUS

    This augury I trust: may it come to pass;
    And ever may the gods inspire you so!
      Tomorrow let redoubled sacrifices
    Be offered them with happier auspices,*
    While your conspirators throughout Rome hear it said:
1780   Augustus all has learnt and learnt all to forget.*

CRITIQUE OF *CINNA*

(1660)

This tragedy has been given pride of place in my works by so many illustrious voices that I should make too many prestigious enemies if I spoke ill of it; I am not so inimical to myself as to seek out shortcomings where they have been pleased to discern none, and question the judgement they have passed on it, thus to tarnish the splendour of the accolade they have thought fit to grant me on its account. Such weighty and widespread approbation springs no doubt from the fact that verisimilitude is so judiciously maintained in the play in areas where it lacks veracity that no appeal to the strictures of theatrical convention is required in extenuation. Nothing in the work is at variance with the historical facts, although many things have been added to them; they are in no way violated by the necessities of dramatic representation, nor by the unity of time, nor by that of place.

It is true that the setting contains two specific areas. Half of the play takes place in Emilia's apartment, and the other half in that of Augustus. It would have been ridiculous of me to give the impression that the Emperor would have asked Maximus and Cinna for advice concerning his mooted abdication in the very same location where Cinna had delivered his report to Emilia concerning the conspiracy he was mounting against him. For the same reason I broke with the scene-linking convention in the fourth act, being unwilling to have Maximus deliver his warning to Emilia, that the conspiracy had been discovered, in the very same place where he himself had ordered that Augustus be informed about it, and from which the Emperor had just departed in such an extreme state of anxiety and vacillation. It would have been exceptionally imprudent and totally lacking in verisimilitude for Maximus to appear in the apartment of the Emperor a moment after he had caused him to be told about the conspiracy of which he was one of the leaders and to be falsely informed that he, Maximus, was dead. Far from being able to stupefy Emilia with the fear of finding herself arrested, he would have been inviting his own arrest and creating an insurmountable obstacle to the plan he wanted to implement. I therefore ensure that Emilia never speaks in the same location as Augustus, with the exception of the fifth act; but that does not preclude the play, taken in its entirety, from observing the unity of place, since all the action occurs not only in Rome, and in the same quarter of the city, but even within Augustus' palace, provided you allow that Emilia has an apartment there which is at some distance from his.

The account which Cinna gives of his conspiracy is consistent with what I have said elsewhere: that an embellished narration is endurable only when both speaker and listener are sufficiently at ease and sufficiently pleased by it to vouchsafe it all the patience it demands. Emilia is delighted to learn from her suitor's lips how eagerly he has fulfilled her wishes; and Cinna is no less delighted to be able to afford her such high hopes of achieving her desired objective; that is why, however lengthy the narration, with no interruption whatsoever, she does not find it in the least tedious. The rhetorical decoration with which I have endeavoured to enrich the account does not cause her to deem it too contrived and unnatural, and the varied literary devices it contains ensure that the time I accord it is in no way begrudged; but if I had deferred it until after Evander had unsettled the couple by the news he brings them, Cinna would have been compelled either to abstain from delivering it, or to convey the substance in a few words, for Emilia would have been unable to tolerate any more.

Just as the verse in *Horace* is somewhat more direct and less stilted than that of *Le Cid*, one might say that in this play it is more refined than in *Horace*, and that one of the reasons for the high praise it has received is doubtless the easy flow of the action, neither overburdened with incident not cluttered with narrations of what occurred before the play begins. The audience likes to devote its attention entirely to what is happening on the stage at the moment, and not, in order to comprehend what it is seeing, to have to recall what it has already seen and to cast its mind back to the first acts while the final ones are unrolling before it. That is the disadvantage of involved plays such as *Rodogune* and *Héraclius*, which are described in literary jargon as 'implex', a word derived from Latin. This drawback is not found in simple plays; but while the complicated ones surely require greater intellectual capacity to conceive them and finer artistry to execute them, the simple ones, lacking the support of complex action, can be sustained only by greater strength in the verse, the arguments and the sentiments.

MOLIÈRE

THE MISANTHROPE

A Comedy

LE MISANTHROPE

Comédie

*First performed on 4 June 1666 at the
Théâtre du Palais Royal in Paris*

CHARACTERS

ALCESTE, suitor to Célimène
PHILINTE, friend of Alceste
ORONTE, suitor to Célimène
CÉLIMÈNE, a young widow courted by Alceste
ÉLIANTE, cousin of Célimène
ARSINOÉ, friend of Célimène
ACASTE ⎫
CLITANDRE ⎭ young marquesses
BASQUE, servant of Célimène
OFFICER of the Marshals of France
DU BOIS, servant of Alceste

The action takes place in Paris, in the drawing-room of
Célimène's house, which is also the home of Éliante

ACT I

PHILINTE, ALCESTE

PHILINTE

What is it? What's upset you?

ALCESTE

Leave me, please.

PHILINTE

No, tell me: why this strange behaviour, what's—

ALCESTE

Leave me, I say; get out; just go away.

PHILINTE

You might at least hear me speak without exploding.

ALCESTE

I will explode and I won't hear you speak.

PHILINTE

I'm baffled by these moody fits of yours.

Friends though we are, I seem to be the first—

ALCESTE

Friends? You and I? Forget it: that's all over.

Until today I have called you my friend,

But after seeing in you what I've just seen,   10

I tell you plainly you're no friend of mine.

I want no share in a corrupted heart.

PHILINTE

So you think I've done something bad, Alceste?

ALCESTE

Philinte! You ought to die of shame; what you've

Just done is unforgivable; it would disgust

And outrage any man of honour.

I see you crush a man with fervent hugs

And show him every sign of fond affection;

You reinforce your frenzied, wild embraces

With vows of friendship, oaths and protestations;   20

Then, afterwards, when I say, 'Who was that?'

You're scarcely able to recall his name!
He moves away, your warmth evaporates
And you confess that he means nothing to you!
For God's sake! It's unworthy, squalid, vile
To be so faithless to your own true self.
If by mischance I'd sunk so low, at once,
In sheer remorse, I'd go and hang myself.

PHILINTE

It doesn't seem to me a hanging matter,
30   And I entreat you kindly to permit me
To mitigate the harshness of your sentence,
And not, please sir, to hang myself for that.

ALCESTE

Facetiousness betrays a vulgar mind.

PHILINTE

Well, seriously, what's one supposed to do?

ALCESTE

Just be sincere, and as a man of honour
Say nothing that does not come from the heart.

PHILINTE

When a man joyfully embraces us,
We have to pay him back in the same coin,
Respond as best we can to his effusions
40   And match his oaths and pledges with our own.

ALCESTE

No, I can't stomach the slavish rituals
Your people of fashion almost all affect.
There's nothing I hate so much as the wild antics
Of those prolific protestation-mongers,
Those genial lavishers of hugs and kisses,
Those sycophantic spouters of empty words
Who make a contest out of social graces
And treat alike sound, cultured men and fools.
What do you gain when someone shows affection,
50   Swears friendship, truth, esteem, devotion, love,
And makes you an elaborate panegyric,
If every idiot hears the same from him?
No, no: a man with any self-respect

Disdains esteem that's been so prostituted.
The greatest praise means nothing when you see
The whole world rated just as high as you.
Esteem is based on preference: to esteem
Everyone is not to esteem at all.
Since you adopt these vices of the age,
Good God! you're not the kind of man for me;   60
I spurn the universal, cheap affection
That treats degrees of merit equally.
I wish to be selected; to be blunt:
The friend of all men is no friend of mine.

PHILINTE

But in society we must observe
The normal customs of polite behaviour.

ALCESTE

No, no: that shameful traffic in false shows
Of friendship we should mercilessly scourge.
I want us to be true: when we converse,
I want our hearts to speak without disguise;   70
I want our hearts exposed, so that our feelings
Are never masked by empty compliments.

PHILINTE

In many situations perfect candour
Would be absurd and unacceptable.
With due respect to your stern sense of honour,
It's sometimes right to hide what's in one's heart.
Would it be fitting and correct to say
To all and sundry what we thought of them?
When we detest or disapprove of someone,
Are we supposed to make our feelings plain?   80

ALCESTE

Yes.

PHILINTE

What! You'd go and tell old Émilie
That she should give up trying to be a beauty,
And that her clownish make-up is a joke?

ALCESTE

Of course.

PHILINTE
    And Dorilas that he's a bore,
That everyone at Court is sick of hearing
About his derring-do and grand relations?

ALCESTE
Why not?

PHILINTE
     You can't be serious.

ALCESTE
          Yes, I am;
And in this matter I'll spare nobody.
I'm pained by what I see; in Court and town
90 There's nothing that does not stoke up my bile;
A black mood overcomes me, deep despair,
To see how human beings treat each other.
Everywhere I find crawling flattery,
Injustice, self-interest, perfidy, deceit:
I've had enough! I'm seething; I've decided
To go to war with all the human race.

PHILINTE
Your philosophic spleen is so barbaric!
I find these gloomy fits of yours quite funny:
The two of us, who were brought up together,
100 Are like those brothers in *The School for Husbands*,*
Who—

ALCESTE
   Lord! Spare me your inept comparisons.

PHILINTE
Well, really, spare me these expostulations.
Your efforts are not going to change the world;
And, since you find plain-speaking so attractive,
I tell you candidly that your bad temper
Provides amusement everywhere you go.
Such fury at the manners of the age
To many people seems ridiculous.

ALCESTE
That's fine, by Heaven! That's fine! That's what I want.
110 That's a good sign; I'm overjoyed to hear it.

I find all humans so detestable
That I'd be sorry if they thought me wise.

PHILINTE
You bear extreme ill-will towards mankind.

ALCESTE
Yes: I've conceived a monstrous hatred for it.

PHILINTE
Are all poor mortals, without one sole exception,
To be enveloped in this great aversion?
In our age there are still some to be found—

ALCESTE
No, I hate all of them, all human beings:
Some because they're malicious evil-doers,
The rest because they wink at the evil-doers   120
And don't regard them with that fierce abhorrence
That vice should kindle in all virtuous souls.
You see with what injustice they indulge
That downright scoundrel I'm fighting in the courts.
Behind his mask it's clear that he's a crook;
Everyone knows exactly what he is;
His rolling eyes and oily tongue don't take
In anyone who's not a stranger here.
The little tyke wants crushing; it's well known
He rose up in the world by sordid frauds;   130
The glittering success they bought for him
Offends true worth and makes true virtue blush.
For all the public honours he receives
No one defends his shameful reputation:
Call him a rogue, a cur, an odious blackguard,
Everyone nods and nobody dissents.
Yet everywhere the humbug gets a welcome,
A smile, a hug; he creeps through every door;
And any post that lobbying can win
He'll get, before the worthiest gentleman.   140
Good grief! It's like a knife plunged through my heart
To see vice cosseted and pampered so.
At times I have a sudden urge to flee
To some desert far away from human beings.

PHILINTE

    Heavens! Just accept the manners of the time
    And make allowances for human nature;
    Don't judge it by the most exacting standards;
    Indulge its failings. In society
    We need a flexible morality;
150   To be too virtuous can be a fault.
    Good sense avoids extremes, and calls on us
    To couple righteousness with temperance.
    The stern austerity of ancient days
    Jars with our age and its accustomed ways;
    It asks too much perfection of poor mortals.
    One must bend with the times, not be too rigid.
    To take it on oneself to mend the world
    Is, let me tell you, sheer unrivalled folly.
    Like you, I'm constantly aware of things
160   Which, handled differently, could be improved;
    But, unlike you, no matter what I see,
    I never let myself become enraged.
    I calmly take my fellows as they are;
    I train myself to suffer what they do;
    And I think that in Court and town my phlegm
    Is no less philosophic than your bile.*

ALCESTE

    But can this reasonable phlegm of yours
    Never be whipped up, sir, by anything?
    Suppose you found a friend had double-crossed you,
170   Or someone schemed to steal your property,
    Or tried to smear you with malicious rumours,
    You'd see all that and not become enraged?

PHILINTE

    Yes: those faults you complain about I view
    As vices integral to human nature;
    And so I'm no more horrified to see
    My fellows selfish, wily and unjust
    Than to see vultures crave for carrion flesh,
    Monkeys make mischief, or rabid wolves rampage.

ALCESTE

So I'm to be cheated, ripped apart and robbed
Without— Good grief! I've nothing more to say,   180
Your reasoning is so devoid of sense.

PHILINTE

I tell you, your best course is to say nothing.
Spend less time railing at your adversary
And give the lawsuit more of your attention.

ALCESTE

I'll give it none, that's categorical.

PHILINTE

But then what canvassers will speak for you?*

ALCESTE

Canvassers? Reason, my rights, and equity.

PHILINTE

But won't you visit any of the judges?

ALCESTE

No. Is my cause unjust or dubious?

PHILINTE

Agreed. But backstairs intrigues can be harmful.   190
And if—

ALCESTE

       No; I'm determined not to stir.
Either I'm right or wrong.

PHILINTE

                Don't trust to that.

ALCESTE

I will not budge.

PHILINTE

          Your opponent's powerful;
His friends might influence the—

ALCESTE

                   Never mind.

PHILINTE

It's foolish.

ALCESTE

       So. I want to see what happens.

PHILINTE
  But you—
ALCESTE
            To lose my case will give me pleasure.
PHILINTE
  Alceste! You—
ALCESTE
               In this trial I'll find out
  If human beings are insolent enough,
  Malicious and depraved enough, to let
200 The whole world see them treat me with injustice.
PHILINTE
  What a man!
ALCESTE
          I should like, cost what it may,
  For the sheer beauty of it, to lose my case.
PHILINTE
  If people heard you speak like that, Alceste,
  You really would become a laughing-stock.
ALCESTE
  How sad for those who laughed.
PHILINTE
                 But in this house
  Do you find the rectitude that you demand,
  The perfect probity that you insist on:
  Do you find it in the lady that you love?
  I marvel that, despite declaring war
210 On all your fellow-creatures, sickened though
  You are with all the human race, you find
  One member of it irresistible.
  And what astonishes me even more
  Is the strange choice your heart has fixed upon.
  The sincere Éliante is fond of you;
  The modest Arsinoé likes you well;
  Yet their affection leaves you quite unmoved,
  And you're beguiled instead by Célimène,
  Whose backbiting and coquetry would seem
220 To epitomize the manners of the age.
  How is it that you tolerate in her

The very faults you loathe in other people?
Are they redeemed by her attractiveness?
Do you not see them, or do you forgive them?

ALCESTE

Oh, no, my love for the young widow does
Not blind me to the blemishes she has;
For all the passion she awakes in me
I'm still the first to see and to condemn them.
But, even so, I'm helpless; I confess
My weakness: she knows how to captivate me.   230
I see her faults; I chide her for them; yet
Despite them, she bewitches me. Her charm
Is invincible; and I've no doubt my love
Will purge her of the vices of the age.

PHILINTE

No small achievement that would be. And so
You're quite convinced that she loves you?

ALCESTE

                                        Lord, yes!
Unless I thought so, I should not love her.

PHILINTE

But if it's clear that you're the one she cares for,
Why do her other suitors trouble you?

ALCESTE

Because a man in love claims full possession.   240
And so I've come here now prepared to tell her
Exactly what my love for her demands.

PHILINTE

I tell you, if I could freely make my choice,
Her cousin Éliante's the one I'd pick.
Her heart's sincere and true, she's fond of you,
And with her you'd be so much better suited.

ALCESTE

Yes, so my reason tells me constantly;
But reason has no power over love.

PHILINTE

I fear for this love of yours: the hopes you cherish
May be—   250

    Enter ORONTE.   [I.ii]

ORONTE

   I learnt downstairs that Célimène
Has gone with Éliante to do some shopping;
But when they told me you were in the house,
I came straight up to tell you, hand on heart,
That you have won my wildest admiration;
My high regard has long made me desire
Most ardently to count myself your friend.
Yes, my heart loves to recognize true worth;
I long for friendship's knot to bind us close.
I cannot think a warm friend, of my rank,
260 Could ever be the kind to be rejected.
I'm speaking, if you please, to you, Alceste.
  (*During this speech* ALCESTE *seems to be daydreaming
  and unaware that he is being addressed by* ORONTE.)

ALCESTE

To me, sir?

ORONTE

   Yes, to you. Do I offend you?

ALCESTE

No, but this comes as a great surprise to me;
This is an honour I was not expecting.

ORONTE

My high regard for you should not surprise you:
You have the right to claim it from the world.

ALCESTE

Sir—

ORONTE

   In the land there's nothing to exceed
The dazzling merit that is seen in you.

ALCESTE

Sir—

ORONTE

   Yes, my judgement rates you far above
270 The most distinguished of our countrymen.

ALCESTE

Sir—

ORONTE

      May Heaven strike me down if I should lie!
And here and now, to show you how I feel,
Permit me, sir, to embrace you heartily,
And crave that I may rank among your friends.
Your hand, I beg; you promise it to me,
Your friendship?

ALCESTE

                Sir, I—

ORONTE

                        What, are you reluctant?

ALCESTE

Sir, I am honoured by what you propose;
But friendship calls for rather more discretion.
Assuredly we do profane its name
To have it on our lips at every turn.   280
The bond should spring from wise discrimination;
To be friends we should know each other better.
It may be that our temperaments are such
That we should both repent of the transaction.

ORONTE

Upon my life, there's wisdom in your words:
My high regard for you soars higher still;
Let time, then, forge that tender link between us.
But meanwhile I shall be entirely yours:
If you've some business to be raised at Court,
It's known His Majesty thinks well of me: 290
He values my advice; in every way,
By Heaven, he treats me very civilly.
Remember, I'm completely at your service.
Now, since you have so fine an intellect,
To inaugurate the noble bond between us
I've brought a sonnet that I've just composed
To ask if I ought to publish it.

ALCESTE

Sir, I am ill-equipped to judge your work:
I beg to be excused.

ORONTE
                              Why?

ALCESTE
                                    In such matters
300   I err in being rather too sincere.

ORONTE
       That's what I want: I should be most aggrieved
       If, when I'd asked you to speak candidly,
       You failed me and disguised your true opinion.

ALCESTE
       Since that is what you wish, sir, I consent.

ORONTE
       A Sonnet— It's a sonnet. *Hope may*— A lady
       Had fed with hope my admiration for her.
       Hope may— It's not one of those great solemn poems,
       Just a few tender, wistful little verses.
           (*He looks at* ALCESTE *each time he interrupts himself.*)

ALCESTE
       We'll see.

ORONTE
                      Hope may— I don't know if you'll think
310   The style sufficiently direct and simple,
       Or if you will approve my choice of words.

ALCESTE
       That we'll discover, sir.

ORONTE
                              You understand,
       I spent no more than fifteen minutes on it.

ALCESTE
       Come, sir: the time it took is not what matters.

ORONTE

       Hope may, it is true, give us ease,
       And lull for a time our heart's ache;
       But, Phyllis, how wretched that peace,
       When nothing arrives in its wake.

PHILINTE
       That's a nice opening; I'm quite charmed already.

ALCESTE (*sotto voce*)
  What! Have you got the nerve to say that's good?   320
ORONTE

  Kindness you did dispense:
  'Twere kinder to let me mope
  And spare yourself expense
  Than give me only – hope.

PHILINTE
  Ah! Very stylishly put! Well done, well done!
ALCESTE (*sotto voce*)
  God! You vile flatterer, how can you praise such twaddle?
ORONTE

  If an eternal wait
  Must be my passion's fate,
  To death I shall repair.
  You cannot change my course: 330
  Unending hope perforce,
  Fair Phyllis, breeds despair.

PHILINTE
  A sweet, romantic dying fall – quite splendid.
ALCESTE (*sotto voce*)
  To hell with the dying fall: I wish you'd fall
  And break your nose, you poisonous little toady!
PHILINTE
  I've never heard such polished lines of verse.
ALCESTE
  My God!
ORONTE
              You flatter me, and think perhaps—
PHILINTE
  No, I don't flatter.
ALCESTE (*sotto voce*)
                    Don't you now, you humbug?
ORONTE
  Alceste, we've an agreement, you and I.
  Please be sincere and tell me what you think.   340

ALCESTE

   Sir, this is always delicate terrain:
   We all like to be told that we have talent.
   But once, to someone that I shall not name,
   Seeing the sort of poetry he wrote,
   I said a gentleman should always keep
   A firm rein on the urge one has to write;
   That he should hold in check his keen compulsion
   To show his scribblings to the world; that by
   Displaying them he took the risk of cutting
350   A feeble figure in society.

ORONTE

   By that do you mean to make me understand
   That I am wrong to want—

ALCESTE

                        I'm not saying that.
   But I did tell him that lame verse is fatal;
   That such a weakness in a man can wreck him:
   He may have many splendid qualities,
   But it's always by one's defects that one's judged.

ORONTE

   Do you find something lacking in my sonnet?

ALCESTE

   I'm not saying that. But, to discourage him
   From writing, I made him see how in our time
360   That foible has destroyed some splendid men.

ORONTE

   Do I write badly? Would I be like them?

ALCESTE

   I'm not saying that. But then I said to him:
   What pressing need have you to versify?
   And why the devil do you print the stuff?
   Those who unleash bad books we don't forgive,
   Unless they're sorry hacks who write to live.
   Take my advice and conquer your temptation;
   Conceal these dabblings from the public gaze;
   Don't sacrifice, however hard you're pressed,
370   The high esteem in which you're held at Court

To let some greedy printer foist on you
A wretched writer's ludicrous repute.
That's what I tried my best to make him see.

ORONTE

That's clear enough: I think I understand you.
But won't you tell me where my sonnet fails—

ALCESTE

Frankly, you should consign it to your closet.
You've taken bad examples as your model
And your expressions are not natural.
What do you mean by *lull for a time our heart's ache*?
And *nothing arrives in its wake*?   380
And *spare yourself expense*
Than give me only hope?
And *unending hope, perforce,*
Fair Phyllis, breeds despair?
This figurative style that's thought so clever
Forsakes all notion of reality;
It's only playing with words, pure affectation;
It doesn't sound a bit like natural speech.
In this the bad taste of the age appals me;
Crude though our fathers were, they knew much better.   390
I think what's praised today is not a patch
On this old song I shall recite to you:

> *If the King to me should give*
> *His dearest town, fair Paris,*
> *So that my darling I should leave,*
> *And lose her love, I wis,*
> *To King Harry I would say,*
> *Keep your Paris, I thee pray,*
> *For to my true love I will cleave*
> *And with my darling stay.*   400

The rhymes are weak, the style is out of date;
But don't you see that that is worth much more
Than those frills which insult one's common sense,
That these words come directly from the heart?

If the King to me should give
His dearest town, fair Paris,
So that my darling I should leave,
And lose her love, I wis,
To King Harry I would say,
410 *Keep your Paris, I thee pray,*
For to my true love I will cleave
And with my darling stay.

A man truly in love would speak like that.
(*to* PHILINTE)
Sir, you may laugh: for all your clever critics,
I prize that more than the false, flowery verses,
The gaudy trash that's all the rage these days.

ORONTE
And I maintain my poetry is good.

ALCESTE
You have your reasons for supposing so,
But you'll permit me to hold different views
420 Which, by your leave, will not give way to yours.

ORONTE
For me the praise of others is enough.

ALCESTE
They have the art of feigning; I can't bluff.

ORONTE
I wonder why you think you're such a genius?

ALCESTE
To praise your poem I'd have to be *in*genious.

ORONTE
I can well do without your approbation.

ALCESTE
You've no choice but to bear the deprivation.

ORONTE
I'd like to know how, just to see, of course,
You'd write a poem describing *your* amours.

ALCESTE
I could write sonnets just as bad as yours,
430 But I'd make sure they never left locked drawers.

ORONTE
  You use strong words; your arrogance, I swear—
ALCESTE
  For flattery you'd better go elsewhere.
ORONTE
  Now, little man, just mind what tone you use.
ALCESTE
  By Heaven, great sir, I'll take what tone I choose.
PHILINTE (*placing himself between them*)
  Stop, gentlemen; you go too far: enough!
ORONTE
  Ah, yes! I'm in the wrong; I quit the field.
  My duty to you, sir, with all my heart.
ALCESTE
  And I am, sir, your very humble servant.
    Exit ORONTE.   [I.iii]
PHILINTE
  Well there, you see: for being too sincere
  You're landed with an awkward situation.   440
  I saw that, if you'd praised him, Oronte would—
ALCESTE
  Don't speak to me.
PHILINTE
                    But you—
ALCESTE
                              Leave me alone.
PHILINTE
  But you—
ALCESTE
          Leave me, I say.
PHILINTE
                          If I—
ALCESTE
                                Enough.
PHILINTE
  What—
ALCESTE
        I'm not listening.

PHILINTE

But—

ALCESTE

Still there?

PHILINTE

Insulting—

ALCESTE

By Heaven, it's too much! Will you let me be?

PHILINTE

Don't be absurd: you won't get rid of me.

ACT II

[II.i]   ALCESTE, CÉLIMÈNE

ALCESTE

Madam, will you permit me to be blunt?
I'm far from satisfied with your behaviour;
It stirs my bile, it puts me in a rage;
450   We'll have to part company, I feel it coming.
Yes, not to tell you so would be deceitful:
Indubitably, there'll be a breach between us;
Even if I promised you the contrary
A thousand times, I'd have to break my word.

CÉLIMÈNE

I see: so it was just to quarrel with me,
Was it, that you were so keen to see me home?

ALCESTE

No, I'm not quarrelling; but you admit
All comers to an intimate acquaintance.
You have too many admirers flocking round you;
460   My feelings for you put that out of court.

CÉLIMÈNE

Am I to blame if I attract admirers?
Can I prevent men finding me alluring?
When they come sweetly crowding in to see me,
Am I to take a stick and drive them out?

ALCESTE
   No, madam, it's not a stick you need, but just
   A heart less open, less accessible.
   I know that your attractions draw men to you,
   But then you welcome them and so they stay.
   Your beauty lures them to you, yes, but it's
   The warmth of your response that binds them fast;   470
   The promise you hold out too readily
   Keeps them assiduously at your side.
   A little less encouragement from you
   Would soon disperse your army of admirers.
   At least, I beg you, do explain to me
   Just why Clitandre enjoys your special favour.
   What shining talents, what sublime distinction
   Does he possess to warrant your approval?
   Is it the long nail on his little finger
   That qualifies him for your high regard?   480
   Have you succumbed, like all the world of fashion,
   To the resplendence of his golden wig?
   Do you love him for the great frills round his knees
   Or his display of ribbons? Were you conquered
   By his great German breeches while he posed
   As your adoring slave? Or could it be
   The way he giggles and his shrill falsetto
   That found the secret passage to your heart?
CÉLIMÈNE
   It's so unfair of you to pick on him!
   Don't you know well enough why I indulge him?   490
   Because of my lawsuit: so that, as he's promised,
   He'll influence all his friends on my behalf.
ALCESTE
   Then, madam, be prepared to lose your lawsuit,
   But don't indulge a man I find offensive.
CÉLIMÈNE
   But not a man escapes your jealousy.
ALCESTE
   Because there's not a man you don't encourage.

CÉLIMÈNE

That's where your fearful heart should find its comfort:
My bounty's shared out universally.
You'd have much greater cause to be offended
500   If I bestowed it all on one alone.

ALCESTE

You chide me for my jealousy: pray tell me,
What more do I have, madam, than the rest?

CÉLIMÈNE

The happiness of knowing you are loved.

ALCESTE

What reason has my aching heart to think so?

CÉLIMÈNE

Surely, since I've been bold enough to say so,
Such a confession should allay your doubts.

ALCESTE

But how can I be sure that every day
You don't say just the same to all the rest?

CÉLIMÈNE

Well, that's a pretty lover's compliment!
510   I see you have a high opinion of me.
All right, to ease your mind of any doubt,
I take back everything I've ever said.
Now nothing can deceive you but yourself,
So be content.

ALCESTE

                        Gods! Why do I have to love you?
Oh, if I get my heart back from your clutches,
I'll bless Heaven for a gift beyond all price.
I make no secret of it: I do my best
To break the fearsome bond that makes it yours;
But so far all my struggling has been futile:
520   It must be for my sins I love you so.

CÉLIMÈNE

Never have I seen love like yours, it's true.

ALCESTE

Yes, there I challenge all the world to match me.
Madam, my love is unimaginable:

Never has anybody loved like me.

CÉLIMÈNE

You have a new approach to it, indeed:
Loving for you means constant quarrelling;
Your passion breaks out only in resentment.
Never was love so critical and cross.

ALCESTE

But you have power to banish my ill-humour.
Let's end our differences, for pity's sake,   530
Speak to each other honestly, and stop—
   Enter BASQUE.   [II.ii]

CÉLIMÈNE

What now?

BASQUE

      Acaste's downstairs.

CÉLIMÈNE

            Well, show him up.
   Exit BASQUE.   [II.iii]

ALCESTE

What, can one never speak to you alone?
Are your doors always open to the world?
Can you not just for once be resolute
And send to say that you are not at home?

CÉLIMÈNE

Do you want me to give him cause to take offence?

ALCESTE

That it matters to you is an offence to me.

CÉLIMÈNE

I'd never be forgiven by that man
If he suspected I'd refused to see him.   540

ALCESTE

And so? Why should you incommode yourself?

CÉLIMÈNE

Heavens! Such people's good will is important:
That kind of person somehow has acquired
The right to speak out openly at Court;
They have their say in every conversation.
They can't be helpful, but they can do harm.

No matter what support one has elsewhere,
Those loudmouths must not be antagonized.
ALCESTE
So, for whatever reasons you concoct,
550   You justify admitting all and sundry,
And in your judgement what's important is—
[II.iv]   *Enter* BASQUE.
BASQUE
Madam, Clitandre is here as well.
ALCESTE

                       Exactly.

   (*He makes to leave.*)
CÉLIMÈNE (*to* ALCESTE)
Where are you going?
ALCESTE

             I'm off.

CÉLIMÈNE

                 No, stay.

ALCESTE

                     For what?

CÉLIMÈNE
Do stay.
ALCESTE

      I can't.

CÉLIMÈNE

          I want you to.

ALCESTE

               It's pointless.
That kind of chit-chat wearies me to death.
You really shouldn't ask me to endure it.
CÉLIMÈNE
I want you to. I want you to.
ALCESTE

            I can't.

CÉLIMÈNE
Oh, well, then, please yourself: you'd better go.
[II.v]   *Enter* ÉLIANTE *and* PHILINTE.

ÉLIANTE
The pair of marquesses are coming up.
Had you been told?
CÉLIMÈNE
Yes.
(*to* BASQUE)
Chairs for everyone! 560
(*After distributing chairs* BASQUE *exits.*)
CÉLIMÈNE (*continues, to* ALCESTE)
You haven't gone yet?
ALCESTE
No: I want you, madam,
To clarify your preference: them or me.
CÉLIMÈNE
Be quiet!
ALCESTE
You must make your choice at once.
CÉLIMÈNE
You're mad.
ALCESTE
Oh, no: you must decide between us.
CÉLIMÈNE
Really!
ALCESTE
Make up your mind.
CÉLIMÈNE
You can't be serious.
ALCESTE
You have to choose; my patience is exhausted.
Enter CLITANDRE *and* ACASTE.
CLITANDRE
Madam, I've just come from the palace – Lord!
At the levée Cléonte was a perfect clown!*
Has he no charitable friend to pull
Him up about his ludicrous behaviour? 570
CÉLIMÈNE
True, he's committing social suicide;

He makes himself a sideshow everywhere;
And, when you haven't seen him for a while,
You find him even weirder than before.

ACASTE

Lord! Talking of weirdies, madam, I've just been tortured
By the most tiresome bore: that Damon, you know,
The argufier; he kept me from my sedan
A whole hour – just imagine! – in the sun.

CÉLIMÈNE

He does go on, he's master of the art
580   Of making speeches full of emptiness.
His babble never deviates into sense:
It's just a noise you hear, a stream of sound.

ÉLIANTE (*to* PHILINTE)

That's not a bad beginning: the dissection
Of friends and neighbours is gathering momentum.

CLITANDRE

Then Timante, madam, is a curious creature.

CÉLIMÈNE

From top to toe a man of mystery!
He throws you a glazed look as he runs by –
A busy bee who has, in fact, no business.
He hints at things by pulling knowing faces,
590   And makes one's head spin with his strange grimaces.
He's always butting in to tell you, slyly,
Some shattering secret that's not worth repeating.
Each word he speaks is said in confidence:
He whispers in your ear to say hello.

ACASTE

And Géralde, madam?

CÉLIMÈNE

                                        Oh, the tedious snob!
Great lords are all he ever thinks about;
He floats in an eternal royal round,
Enamoured of princesses, princes, dukes.
Titles enrapture him: he talks of nothing
600   But carriages and horses, hunts and hounds;
He calls the grandest folk by their first names

And never soils his lips with plain *Monsieur*.

CLITANDRE

He and Bélise, I hear, are very close.

CÉLIMÈNE

Dull woman quite incapable of speech!
I suffer martyrdom each time she calls;
One sweats to think of things to say to her.
Then she's so bad at putting words together
The conversation keeps on fizzling out.
To try to breach her wall of stupid silence
One summons every platitude – in vain.   610
Fine weather, rain, how hot it is, how cold:
They're springs of thought that soon run dry with her.
Yet, painful though her visit is, she drags
It out to an excruciating length.
One asks the time, one yawns, one yawns again,
And still she sits there like a block of wood.

ACASTE

And what about Adraste?

CÉLIMÈNE

                          Oh, such conceit!
There's a man blown up with his own importance.
The Court, he thinks, does not appreciate him,
And so his daily task is to revile it.   620
Each post or charge assigned to someone else
Insults his bloated vision of himself.

CLITANDRE

But tell us what you think about young Cléon,
Whom everyone is visiting these days.

CÉLIMÈNE

I think he's trading on his clever chef,
And it's his table that they're visiting.

ÉLIANTE

The food he serves is really quite delicious.

CÉLIMÈNE

Yes, if he didn't also serve himself.
His silliness is an insipid dish
That ruins every meal he offers one.   630

PHILINTE

    Damis his uncle is very much admired:
    What do you think of him?

CÉLIMÈNE

                     He is my friend.

PHILINTE

    I'd say a true gentleman and sound enough.

CÉLIMÈNE

    Yes, but he always has to be so clever!
    It drives me mad: you see him straining
    To make his every word a pearl of wit.
    Now that he poses as an intellectual,
    Nothing can rise to his exalted taste;
    In every writer's work he looks for faults.
640   He thinks praise is beneath a cultured mind,
    That being a scholar means to carp and quibble,
    That only imbeciles admire or laugh,
    And that by damning every modern work
    He hoists himself above the hoi polloi.
    He even criticizes conversations:
    Their trivial topics are too vulgar for him,
    And from his dizzy heights, with folded arms,
    He lends a pitying ear to what one says.

ACASTE

    God damn me! That's his portrait to the life!

CLITANDRE

650   You're marvellous at hitting people off!

ALCESTE

    Go to it, press on, back-stabbing hypocrites!
    No one's left off the hook, to each his turn.
    But there's not one of them you wouldn't rush
    To greet, clasp hands with, hug close to your bosom,
    And with a Judas kiss renew your vows
    Of friendship, loyalty and admiration.

CLITANDRE

    Why blame us? If you don't like what you hear,
    Your hostess is the one you should reproach.

ALCESTE

Oh, no, by Heaven, it's you: your toadying laughter
Draws from her these malicious shafts of wit.   660
Her mocking humour's nurtured constantly
By the foul poison of your flattery;
If scoffing and sneering earned her no applause,
She'd find it less rewarding to poke fun.
It's always flatterers who are to blame
When human beings are tempted into vice.

PHILINTE

But why do you defend her victims, you,
Who would yourself condemn the faults she mocks?

CÉLIMÈNE

Doesn't Sir always have to be contrary?
Is he to stoop to thinking like the rest   670
And not to blazon everywhere the spirit
Of contradiction he received from Heaven?
The views of others he can't bear to share;
He always has to mount an opposition.
He thinks he would appear a common fellow,
If he were heard to say, 'I quite agree.'
To contradict he finds so glorious
That often he takes arms against himself,
And eagerly refutes his own opinions
The moment someone else expresses them.   680

ALCESTE

Madam, the mockers are clearly on your side:
You're free to aim your ridicule at me.

PHILINTE

It's true, though, that your temperament compels you
To fight against your fellow-creatures' views:
No matter if they utter praise or blame,
Your self-confessed ill-humour contradicts them.

ALCESTE

Because, God dammit, they always get it wrong!
In every case it's right to shoot them down:
All I hear given out on every side

690   Is undue praise or ill-considered blame.

CÉLIMÈNE

But—

ALCESTE

      No, no, madam, if I die for it,
    The pleasures you delight in I can't bear;
    And it's not right to nourish in you here
    The very faults you're censured for elsewhere.

CLITANDRE

    Well, I don't know, but for my part I swear
    That I have always found the lady faultless.

ACASTE

    I see that she's endowed with charm and grace,
    But any faults she has escape my eyes.

ALCESTE

    Not mine. My eyes aren't closed to them, she knows:
700 I take good care to remonstrate with her.
    The more we love, the less we ought to flatter:
    Pure love forgives no faults. If I were in
    Her place, I'd show the door to those pathetic
    Admirers who tamely echoed all my views
    And with their sycophantic sniggering
    Pandered to my unseemly foolishness.

CÉLIMÈNE

    So, if all lovers followed your advice,
    They'd make sure they said nothing sweet or kind,
    And, as the strongest proof of perfect love,
710 They'd roundly abuse the person they adored.

ÉLIANTE

    That's not the usual way love shows itself:
    Lovers are prone to boast about their choice.
    Their passion blinds them to all faults: to them
    The loved one's weaknesses are lovable.
    Failings are seen as items of perfection
    And given names that make them sound attractive.
    A pale girl is described as 'jasmine-white';
    A scary dark one? She's 'a dear brunette';
    If she's a skinny thing, she's 'slim and graceful';

She's fat? She has 'a majesty of gait';   720
And, if she's charmless, sluttish and unkempt,
She's said to have 'a simple, unspoiled beauty'.
The giantess becomes 'a glorious goddess';
The midget? 'A miracle in miniature'.
Obnoxious pride is 'regal dignity'.
She's wily? No, she's 'clever'. A fool? She's 'artless'.
She prattles? She has 'such a genial nature';
She never speaks? She's 'modest and demure'.
So does a truly passionate admirer
Adore the very faults of her he loves.*   730

ALCESTE
I don't agree, my view—

CÉLIMÈNE
                   Let's leave it there,
And walk a little in the gallery.
What, you aren't leaving us, you two?

CLITANDRE *and* ACASTE
                           Oh, no.

ALCESTE
You seem to be afraid that they might leave.
Go when it suits you, gentlemen; I warn you,
I shall remain till after you have gone.

ACASTE
Unless I should impose upon our hostess,
I'm free to stay until the close of day.

CLITANDRE
As long as I attend the King's retiring,
I have no business calling me away.   740

CÉLIMÈNE
You're joking, I presume?

ALCESTE
                Oh, no, I'm not.
We'll see if I'm the one you wish to go.
    Enter BASQUE.   [II.vi]

BASQUE (*to* ALCESTE)
Sir, there's a man who wants to talk to you;
He says the matter must be dealt with now.

ALCESTE

  Tell him from me I've no such urgent business.

BASQUE

  He's wearing a long coat with pleated skirts
  And gold on it.

CÉLIMÈNE (*to* ALCESTE)

                 Go and see what he wants,
  Or bring him in.

[II.vii]   *An* OFFICER *of the Marshals of France appears.*
     Exit BASQUE.

ALCESTE

               So what do you want with me?
  Come in, sir.

OFFICER

          Sir, there's something I have to tell you.

ALCESTE

750 Sir, you can tell me without whispering.

OFFICER

  The Court of Marshals summons you, by me,
  To place yourself before it instantly,
  Sir.

ALCESTE

  Whom, sir? Me?

OFFICER

          The very same.

ALCESTE

                 What for?

PHILINTE

  It's about that silly quarrel with Oronte.

CÉLIMÈNE

  What's this?

PHILINTE

        Oronte and he clashed earlier today
  About a sonnet he disliked. The Marshals
  Want them to patch it up and avoid a duel.*

ALCESTE

  They'll get no feeble backing-down from me.

PHILINTE

  You must obey the summons. Come, let's go—

ALCESTE

   And how do they think they're going to reconcile us?   760
   Can they compel me to consider good
   The sonnet over which we disagreed?
   I take back nothing that I said before:
   I think it's dreadful.

PHILINTE

                  Don't be so aggressive—

ALCESTE

   I shan't retract: the sonnet's execrable.

PHILINTE

   Your attitude must be more flexible.
   Come on.

ALCESTE

        I'll go, but nothing will compel
   Me to retract.

PHILINTE

          Come and present yourself.

ALCESTE

   Unless the King sends his express command
   That I approve the sonnet in dispute,   770
   I shall maintain, by Heaven, that it is bad
   And that the writer of it should be hanged.
      (*to* CLITANDRE *and* ACASTE, *who are laughing*)
   By jingo, gentlemen, I did not know
   That I was so amusing.

CÉLIMÈNE

              Run along:
   Go where you're summoned.

ALCESTE

                 Madam, I shall walk,
   And come back shortly to conclude our talk.

ACT III

CLITANDRE, ACASTE

CLITANDRE

You seem, dear marquess, mightily contented:
All things delight you, nothing casts you down.
Can you say frankly, with no self-deception,
780   That you have cause to be so full of joy?

ACASTE

Lord! When I scrutinize myself, I see
No reason why I should be miserable.
I'm rich, I'm young, and from a family
That has some right to claim nobility;
I think that, with the rank bestowed on me
By birth, there are few posts beyond my reach.
Courage we all rate highly, and I make
No boast in saying I'm known to have my share:
Pistols or sword, when called upon, I've used
790   With no small vigour and with some panache.
I've taste, of course, and brains: I can at once
Pronounce on any subject; I've no need
To think about a thing to give my view.
At first nights, which I love, I play the critic:
Up on the stage I lead the claps and boos*
And at the best bits stamp and scream Bravo!
I'm deft, I move with grace, I have charisma,
I've a slim waist, my teeth are much admired;
And as for dress-sense, in all modesty,
800   I think he'd be a fool who challenged me.
I'm as well thought of as a man could wish,
Adored by the ladies, and favoured by the King.
With that I think, dear marquess, I do think
A man has every cause to be content.

CLITANDRE

But if elsewhere you make such easy conquests,
Why do you come here where you've no success?

ACASTE

Lord! I'm not of the breed or humour to

Endure a lady's cold discouragement.
It's for the gawky fellows, the dreary ones,
To burn devotedly for frigid beauties,   810
To languish at their feet, endure their torments,
Resort to sighs and tears to plead their cause,
And try, by persevering endlessly,
To win what is denied their paltry worth.
But men of my stamp, marquess, are not made
To love on credit and do all the paying.
However fine and fair the ladies are,
I think, thank God, one also has one's price;
It can't be right that they should grace themselves
With such a heart as mine at no expense;   820
At least, to keep the scales weighed evenly,
Advances must be made at equal cost.

CLITANDRE
You think then, marquess, that you're well in here?

ACASTE
I have my reasons, marquess, for thinking so.

CLITANDRE
Do free yourself from that grave misconception:
Believe me, friend, you're blind and self-deluded.

ACASTE
Of course, I must be: blind and self-deluded.

CLITANDRE
But what makes you imagine that you're favoured?

ACASTE
I'm blind.

CLITANDRE
            What grounds d'you have for thinking so?

ACASTE
I'm self-deluded.

CLITANDRE
                    Have you certain proof?   830

ACASTE
I'm dreaming, don't you know.

CLITANDRE
                              Has Célimène
Confessed to you in secret that she loves you?

ACASTE
  No; I'm ill-treated.

CLITANDRE
                 Answer me, I beg you.

ACASTE
  I only get rebuffs.

CLITANDRE
             Oh, do stop fooling!
  Tell me what cause for hope she's given you.

ACASTE
  I'm the poor reject, you're the chosen one;
  For me she has a hearty detestation.
  One of these days I'll have to hang myself.

CLITANDRE
  Idiot! Look here now, marquess, what d'you say
840 We work together on this courtship business?
  As soon as one of us can show clear proof
  That Célimène is more inclined to him,
  The other will at once withdraw, and so
  Remove a strong contender from the field?

ACASTE
  Ah, dammit, man! Yes, now you're making sense:
  I'll put my hand to that with all my heart—
  But ssh!

[III.ii]   *Enter* CÉLIMÈNE.

CÉLIMÈNE
        Still here?

CLITANDRE
             Love roots us to the spot.

CÉLIMÈNE
  I heard a carriage down below. Who is it,
  Do you know?

CLITANDRE
      No.

[III.iii]   *Enter* BASQUE.

BASQUE
          Madam, Arsinoé is here
  To see you.

CÉLIMÈNE
                    What does that woman want with me?   850
BASQUE
   Éliante is down there having a chat with her.
      Exit BASQUE.
CÉLIMÈNE
   What is she up to now? What brings her here?
ACASTE
   She's known to be a paragon of virtue:
   Her fervent piety—
CÉLIMÈNE
                    Yes, fervent humbug:
   She lives for this world, not the world to come.
   She's out to hook a husband; since she can't,
   Of course she's jealous of the fond admirers
   That flock incessantly round someone else.
   Left pining on the shelf, she's always whining
   That in our age men have no taste in women.   860
   Her frightful loneliness she tries to hide
   Behind a veil of spurious piety:
   To mask the failure of her homely looks,
   She claims that it's a sin to be attractive.
   The truth is she'd be thrilled to have a suitor.
   She has her eye on poor Alceste, and feels
   Insulted by his interest in me:
   She'd have it that I'm stealing him from her,
   And in her envious unconcealed resentment
   She vents her spite in underhand attacks.   870
   Never have I seen anything so stupid;
   She has the most supreme impertinence,
   And—
      Enter ARSINOÉ.   [III.iv]
CÉLIMÈNE (*continues*)
            Ah! What happy chance has brought you here?
   Truthfully, madam, I've been pining for you.
ARSINOÉ
   My duty brings me to offer some advice.

CÉLIMÈNE

   Ah! Goodness me, how pleased I am to see you!
     Exeunt ACASTE *and* CLITANDRE.

ARSINOÉ

   Their leaving now could not be more propitious.

CÉLIMÈNE

   Shall we sit down?

ARSINOÉ

                  That won't be necessary.
   Madam, true friendship should show itself most plainly
880   In matters of the gravest import to us;
   And, as no question can be more important
   Than that of reputation and decorum,
   I've come to show you what a friend I am
   By warning you about your reputation.
     Yesterday I called on some very pious folk,
   And in the conversation you were mentioned.
   I fear your colourful behaviour, madam,
   Had the misfortune not to be admired.
   The droves of men whose visits you permit,
890   Your coquetry, and the gossip it provokes,
   Found more detractors than there should have been,
   Who spoke more harshly than I could have wished.
   You can imagine which side I supported;
   I did my best to come to your defence:
   I pleaded strongly that you meant no harm
   And pledged myself as surety for your virtue.
   But, as you know, there are certain things in life
   That, with the best will, cannot be excused;
   And so, reluctantly, I did concede
900   That you were somewhat sullied by your conduct,
   That it gave an unfortunate impression,
   That it called forth a stream of unkind stories,
   And that, if you so wished, your mode of life
   Might give less cause for general condemnation.
   Not that I think your honour has been soiled –
   May Heaven preserve me from suspecting it!
   But semblance can be seen as truth: to be

Pure for oneself alone is not enough.
  Madam, I know you're much too sensible
To take amiss this beneficial counsel,   910
Or fail to see that it is prompted by
Solicitude for your best interests.

CÉLIMÈNE

Madam, I really am most grateful to you.
Your counsel puts me in your debt. And now,
Far from resenting it, I shall repay you
With counsel that concerns *your* reputation;
And, as you've shown me what a friend you are
By telling me the gossip spread about me,
I'm going to follow your so kind example
By telling you what people say of you.   920
  Somewhere, the other day, while visiting,
I chanced to meet some very worthy folk,
Who, listing the attributes of saintly souls,
Mentioned you, madam, in the conversation.
Your prudishness and blatant piety
Were not judged as a pattern to be followed:
The air of grave decorum you affect,
Your endless talk of modesty and honour,
The way you tut-tut when you hear some word
That sounds rude, though it's said in innocence,   930
The high esteem in which you hold yourself,
The pitying looks you cast on everyone,
Your frequent sermons, your acerbic censure
Of conduct that is blameless, pure and chaste:
All that, if I may speak with candour, madam,
Was felt by everyone to be repugnant.
They said: 'What good is a demure demeanour
If it's belied by everything she does?
She says her prayers with scrupulous correctness,
But beats her servants and withholds their wages;   940
In churches she parades her piety,
But paints her face and strives to seem a beauty;
In pictures she conceals the naked flesh,
But in real life she's quite a taste for it.'

Against them I defended you, of course,
Insisting that it was malicious slander,
But I was overruled by everyone;
And they concluded that you would do well
To take less interest in the lives of others,
950 And regulate your own with greater care;
That one should take a close look at oneself
Before presuming to condemn one's neighbour;
That only those whose own lives are unblemished
Should set about correcting other people;
And, even then, it's better left, if needed,
To those whom Heaven has charged with such concerns.
    Madam, you're also much too sensible
To take amiss this beneficial counsel,
Or fail to see that it is prompted by
960 Solicitude for your best interests.

ARSINOÉ

To rebuke is to expose oneself, I know,
But I was not expecting this reprisal.
Madam, I gather from its bitter tone
That my sincere advice has wounded you.

CÉLIMÈNE

No, madam, not at all: if we were wise,
Such mutual advice would be the rule.
By speaking in good faith we should amend
The blindness that obscures us from ourselves.
Just say the word, and with the same devotion
970 We'll make a habit of this friendly service,
And candidly report, in confidence,
You what you hear of me, and I of you.

ARSINOÉ

Ah, madam, no one does speak ill of you;
I am the one who's always criticized.

CÉLIMÈNE

All conduct may be rightly praised or blamed
Depending on one's age or inclination.
There is a season for flirtatiousness,
And, in due course, a time for prudishness:

Discretion may persuade us to adopt it
When the bright bloom of youth has blown away;   980
It serves to mask humiliating failures.
One day perhaps I'll follow your example:
Time will bring with it what must be, but, madam,
Twenty is not the age to play the prude.

ARSINOÉ

Really, you flaunt a pitiable advantage
In trumpeting your youth so mightily:
The gap between our ages does not warrant
Your using such a patronizing tone.
Indeed, I cannot think what drives you, madam,
To attack me in this unexpected way.   990

CÉLIMÈNE

Nor can I think what drives you, madam, to blacken
My reputation everywhere you go.
Must you blame me for all your disappointments?
Is it my fault if no one cares for you?
If my looks make men fall in love with me,
If I'm plied daily with devotion which
You'd dearly like to see denied to me,
I can't prevent it, there's nothing I can do.
The field is open, I'm not stopping you
From having what it takes to attract admirers.   1000

ARSINOÉ

Oh dear! Do you think one's bothered by the horde
Of admirers that you boast so proudly of?
And that it isn't easy to assess
The current price for which they may be hired?
Are we to think, the world being what it is,
That it's your worthiness that draws the crowd?
That they're all fired with pure and honest love
And paying devoted homage to your virtue?
Transparent smokescreens don't blind anyone;
Society is not naïve: I see   1010
Women designed to kindle tender feelings
Who yet have no admirers at their door.
From that there are certain things we may deduce:

That men's hearts are not gained without concessions,
That no one courts us for our looks alone,
That flattering attentions must be bought.
So don't puff yourself up so pompously
Over the tawdry spoils of your mean triumphs;
And curb the conceit about your pretty face
1020   That leads you to think you're so superior.
If one looked enviously upon your conquests,
I'm sure that one could do as others do:
Abandon all restraint, and prove that, if
One wants admirers, they're not hard to get.

CÉLIMÈNE

Get some then, madam: show what you can do;
Employ your secret knowledge to attract them,
Without—

ARSINOÉ

                    Madam, let's cease this conversation
Or we shall both be driven much too far.
I should more properly have left already,
1030   If I'd not been obliged to await my carriage.

CÉLIMÈNE

Madam, remain as long as you desire;
You must not feel compelled to rush away.

          Enter ALCESTE.

CÉLIMÈNE (*continues*)

But my attentions shall not weary you:
I yield you up to better company.
This gentleman, arriving apropos,
Will entertain you more agreeably.
Alceste, I have a little note to write
Which it would be uncivil to delay.
Do stay with Arsinoé; she'll forgive
1040   My leaving with the best will in the world.

[III.v]   *Exit* CÉLIMÈNE.

ARSINOÉ

You see, she wishes me to entertain you
Until my carriage comes in just a moment;
And nothing she could do for me would equal
The pleasure of such company as yours.

Men of sublime worth, we all know, inspire
Respect and love in everyone; and you,
I must confess, have some mysterious power
That binds my heart to all your interests.
I only wish the Court would grace you with
Some proper recognition of your merit. 1050
You've a just grievance; it vexes me to see
Each passing day that nothing's done for you.

ALCESTE

I, madam? What claim have I to any favours?
What service to the State have I performed?
What glorious deeds give me the right to feel
Aggrieved if nothing's done for me at Court?

ARSINOÉ

Those whom the Court regards with special favour
Have not all done the State impressive service.
Ability needs opportunity,
And that great worth that you reveal to us 1060
Should really be—

ALCESTE

                    Good God! Forget my worth!
What do you expect the Court to do about it?
It would be busy, overworked indeed,
If it were meant to root out people's worth.

ARSINOÉ

Outstanding worth will root itself out: yours,
In many quarters, is esteemed most highly;
Yesterday you were praised, I'll have you know,
By powerful folk in two distinguished circles.

ALCESTE

Ah, madam, these days everyone is praised;
The present age makes no discrimination: 1070
Great worth is seen in everything alike;
To be praised nowadays is not an honour:
One's gorged with eulogies, one's pelted with them:
My valet gets his name in the *Gazette*.

ARSINOÉ

I wish that, to be seen to more advantage,
You could be tempted by a place at Court.

The merest nod to me that you'd accept it,
And strings could soon be pulled on your behalf.
I've those that I could set to work for you;
1080   They'd smooth your path to any goal you chose.

ALCESTE

And what should I do, madam, when I got there?
A temperament like mine had best avoid it.
Heaven did not deal to me, when I was born,
A soul in tune with the climate of the Court;
I do not have the qualities required
To carve my life and be successful there.
Being sincere and frank is my great strength;
I lack the art of speaking to deceive;
And he who cannot hide what he is thinking
1090   Does well to give that province a wide berth.
Outside the Court one must forgo, it's true,
The titles and support that are dispensed there;
But one forgoes as well, in compensation,
The tedious company of imbeciles;
One has no need to suffer harsh rebuffs,
To extol the verse of Monsieur So-and-So,
Rain compliments on Madame So-and-So,
Or stomach the witless whims of marquesses.

ARSINOÉ

Your dream is not a place at Court, I see!
1100   But where you have shown interest makes me grieve.
And on that theme, to share my thoughts with you,
I do so wish you'd made a better choice.
There's no doubt you deserve a kinder fate:
Your fair enchantress is unworthy of you.

ALCESTE

But, madam, in saying so have you forgotten,
Pray tell me, that she is a friend of yours?

ARSINOÉ

True, but it pricks my conscience, it really does,
To let you go on being so deceived.
Your false position gives me too much pain:
1110   Your love, I have to warn you, is betrayed.

ALCESTE

Madam, that shows some sympathetic feeling;
For such a warning a suitor must be grateful.

ARSINOÉ

Yes, friend of mine she may be, but I say
She is unworthy of a true man's heart:
The love she shows to you is all pretence.

ALCESTE

That may be, madam: hearts we cannot see;
But in your charity you might have paused
Before afflicting me with such a thought.

ARSINOÉ

If it's your wish not to be disabused,
That's very simple: I must hold my tongue.   1120

ALCESTE

No, but on such a matter to be plagued
By doubts is worse than facing any truth;
I should prefer for my part to be told
Only what could be clearly proved to me.

ARSINOÉ

All right; that's understood; upon this matter
You shall receive complete enlightenment.
Yes, you shall be convinced with your own eyes.
Simply escort me to my house, I pray;
There I shall show you faithful evidence
Of the unfaithful heart of your fair lady.   1130
And, if to another you could then be true,
Some consolation may be offered you.

ACT IV

ÉLIANTE, PHILINTE   [IV.i]

PHILINTE

No, never was there a man so hard to deal with,
Or such a painful reconciliation.
All their attempts to shift him were quite futile:
From his position he would not be budged.

Never can the Marshals have been called upon
To keep the peace in such an odd dispute.
'No, gentlemen,' he said, 'I won't retract.
1140   I'm at your service, save on this one point.
What's his complaint? With what does he reproach me?
Does writing badly reflect upon his honour?
Why should my judgement give him such offence?
An upright gentleman may write bad verse;
That's not a stain on his integrity.
I think him a fine man in every way,
A man of valour, worth, distinction, what
You will – but as a writer he's no good.
I'll praise his lavish household if you wish,
1150   His skill at riding, fencing and the dance;
But praise his sonnet – there he must excuse me.
A man blessed with so little talent for it
Should vow to keep away from writing verse
Unless condemned to write on pain of death.'
They pleaded, but the most he would concede,
And that with great reluctance, was to say,
As he thought greatly softening his tone,
'I'm sorry, sir, to be so difficult.
Out of regard for you I wish, in earnest,
1160   That I could find more merit in your sonnet.'
And with no more ado they were obliged
To wrap the matter up – in an embrace!

ÉLIANTE

Yes, his behaviour is peculiar, but
I must confess, I do admire him for it:
His passion for sincerity has something
About it that is noble and heroic.
It's a rare virtue nowadays; I wish
That people everywhere were more like him.

PHILINTE

The more I see of him the more I marvel
1170   At this strange love affair that he's pursuing:
Given his native temperament, I fail
To see how he could fall in love at all;

And then that he should pick on Célimène –
Well, it's beyond my powers of comprehension.

ÉLIANTE

It shows that natural affinity
Is not what floods the heart with tender feelings;
Their case demolishes the theory
That love is born of mutual empathy.

PHILINTE

But, from what you've observed, does she love him?

ÉLIANTE

It isn't very easy to be sure.   1180
How can one judge if she does really love him?
Her own heart is uncertain of itself:
Sometimes she's in love without knowing it;
Sometimes she thinks she is when she is not.

PHILINTE

I think our friend's involvement with your cousin
Will give him more distress than he imagines;
And, if his heart were mine, I tell you truly,
He'd aim his hopes at quite a different goal:
He'd choose more wisely, madam, and respond
To those warm feelings that *you* nurture for him.   1190

ÉLIANTE

I make no secret of it; in such matters
It's best, I think, to make one's feelings plain.
I don't resent his love for Célimène;
Quite on the contrary, it has my blessing,
And, if the outcome rested in my hands,
I'd see him married to the one he loves.
But if, as happens with the heart's affections,
His suit were destined to be unsuccessful,
If Célimène inclined to someone else,
He could still turn to me, and I'd accept him: 1200
His having been rejected by his first choice
Would not disqualify him in my eyes.

PHILINTE

And I, for my part, madam, don't resent
The tender feelings in your heart for him;

If he so chooses, he himself can tell you
What clear advice on that he's had from me.
But if those two should marry, and place you
In no position to receive his suit,
I'd strive to win the honour of that love
1210 You now so generously reserve for him,
Content if, when he'd passed it by, it might
Be persuaded to rebound and fall to me.

ÉLIANTE

Philinte, you're making fun of me.

PHILINTE

                                   No, madam,
I'm speaking to you from my very soul;
I'm waiting till I may freely press my claim,
And for that chance I long with all my heart.

[IV.ii]   *Enter* ALCESTE.

ALCESTE

Ah! Madam, give me vengeance for a wrong
So monstrous that I can't control myself!

ÉLIANTE

What is it? What's happened to make you so upset?

ALCESTE

1220 The thought of it alone's enough to kill me!
The unleashed forces of the universe
Could not crush me as cruelly as this!
It's over now . . . my love is . . . I can't say it!

ÉLIANTE

Come now, do try to pull yourself together.

ALCESTE

Just Heaven! Must such a lovely form conceal
A soul infected with such loathsome vice?

ÉLIANTE

But tell us what—

ALCESTE

                        Ah! Everything is ruined!
I've been— I've been betrayed! I've been struck dead!
Célimène – could one credit such a thing?
1230 Célimène is deceiving me; she is unfaithful.

ÉLIANTE

Have you good reason for believing that?

PHILINTE

Perhaps it's an unwarranted suspicion:
Your jealous nature sometimes fancies things—

ALCESTE

Oh, keep your nose out of this, for goodness' sake!
The proof of her betrayal's sure enough
When here, in her own hand, it's in my pocket.
Yes, madam, a letter from her to Oronte
Reveals her shame and my humiliation.
Oronte! I thought she fled from his advances:
The one of all the flock I feared the least!   1240

PHILINTE

Letters can often give a false impression;
Sometimes they're not as guilty as they seem.

ALCESTE

Once more, sir, will you kindly hold your noise
And keep your counsel for your own concerns.

ÉLIANTE

Control your anger: the outrage that you feel—

ALCESTE

Madam, that lies with you. I'm turning now
To you to soothe my anger, to release
Me from the burden of this agony.
Take vengeance on your thankless, faithless cousin
For vilely betraying my devoted love;   1250
Avenge me! Her behaviour must appal you.

ÉLIANTE

Avenge you? I? But how?

ALCESTE

                              Accept my love.
Accept it, madam: take the traitor's place.
That's how I can revenge the wrong she's done me:
Her punishment shall be the true attachment,
The deep love, the solicitous concern,
The keen devotion and the ceaseless service
With which my heart will worship at your shrine.

ÉLIANTE

 Alceste, I feel for you in your distress;
1260 I don't disdain the love you offer me;
 But perhaps the wrong's less serious than you think:
 Your wish to be avenged may be short-lived.
 When we're hurt by the one we love, in haste
 We make great plans which we don't follow through.
 At first we see good reason to break free,
 But soon the loved one's guilt dissolves; the harm
 We wished on him or her melts easily.
 We all know what a lover's anger is.

ALCESTE

 No, madam, no: the wound has cut too deep;
1270 There's no going back, I have to break with her;
 Nothing could make me alter my resolve:
 To love her now would make me loathe myself.
 She's coming. At sight of her my anger swells:
 I'll roundly chide her for her evil ways,
 Confound her utterly, and then bring you
 A heart quite freed from her deceitful charm.

[IV.iii] *Exeunt* ÉLIANTE *and* PHILINTE.

ALCESTE (*alone*)

 O Heaven! Can I control my feelings now?
  Enter CÉLIMÈNE.

CÉLIMÈNE

 Oho! So what's put you in such a state?
 What do you mean by all those sighs you're heaving
1280 And those black looks you're beaming out at me?

ALCESTE

 That all the worst imaginable horrors
 Are not so dire as your disloyalty;
 That Fate, the devil, and the wrath of Heaven
 Have brought forth nothing so depraved as you.

CÉLIMÈNE

 Now that's the kind of compliment I like!

ALCESTE

 Ah! Don't make jokes! This is no time for laughing:
 You should be blushing, you have cause enough.
 I have proof positive of your betrayal.

I sensed it; that is what was troubling me;
My heart had every reason to feel threatened;   1290
All my suspicions, which you found so odious,
Were groping for the sad truth I've now found.
For all your prudence, all your skilled deceit,
My guiding star was telling me what I
Should fear. But don't imagine I shall bear
The pain of being ill-used without revenge.
I know that we can't govern our affections,
That love is born unbidden where it will,
That no heart can be forced to yield itself,
That every soul is free to name its captor;   1300
And so I'd have no reason to complain
If you'd responded to me honestly;
If you'd rejected me when first I spoke,
Then I'd have only destiny to blame.
But to encourage my love with hollow vows,
That's a betrayal, that's duplicity
For which no punishment can be too great,
And I shall give my bitterness full rein;
Yes, after such an outrage fear the worst.
I'm not myself now, I'm possessed by rage: 1310
You've pierced me with a thrust so murderous that
My senses are no longer ruled by reason;
I'm at the mercy of my righteous anger;
I cannot answer for what I may do.

CÉLIMÈNE
What's caused this outburst, will you tell me, please?
What's wrong? Have you entirely lost your wits?

ALCESTE
Yes, yes, I lost them when I first saw you
And took the poison that is killing me;
When I believed there was sincerity
In the false beauty that bewitched my soul.   1320

CÉLIMÈNE
How am I false? What have I said or done?

ALCESTE
Ah! How two-faced you are, my fine dissembler!
But I have all I need to call your bluff:

Look at this note and recognize your hand.
That is enough to damn you; in the face
Of that sure proof there's nothing to be said.

CÉLIMÈNE

So this is what is troubling you so much?

ALCESTE

Does it not make you blush to look at it?

CÉLIMÈNE

Why should the sight of this note make me blush?

ALCESTE

1330   So you pile impudence upon deceit?
Because it isn't signed will you disown it?

CÉLIMÈNE

No: why disown a note in my own hand?

ALCESTE

Well, aren't you mortified to see that by
Its tone you stand condemned of wronging me?

CÉLIMÈNE

You really are an awfully silly man.

ALCESTE

What! Can you brave it out before such proof?
It's full of tender feelings for Oronte!
Doesn't that shame you? And gravely injure me?

CÉLIMÈNE

Oronte? Who said the note was meant for him?

ALCESTE

1340   Those who've just kindly passed it on to me.
But let's suppose it was for someone else,
Would that give me less reason to complain?
Would that allay the wrong you do to me?

CÉLIMÈNE

But, if the note were written to a woman,
How would that injure you? Where lies the guilt?

ALCESTE

Ah! That's a clever dodge, a brilliant ploy!
I wasn't expecting that move, I confess,
And now of course I'm utterly disarmed!
Dare you resort to wiles as crude as that?

Do you really think that people are so stupid?   1350
All right, let's see what shift you'll use, what pose,
To try to prop up such a blatant lie:
Let's see how you can make the warm endearments
This note contains appropriate to a woman.
Whitewash your treachery by reconciling
What I'm about to read you—
CÉLIMÈNE
                                I don't care to.
It's quite absurd of you to be so lordly
And dare to say such rude things to my face.
ALCESTE
No, no; let's not get ruffled: just you try
To make a case for using these expressions.   1360
CÉLIMÈNE
No! I'll do no such thing. Upon this subject
I don't much care what you may choose to think.
ALCESTE
Please! I'll be satisfied: just show me how
This note could be intended for a woman.
CÉLIMÈNE
No. It was to Oronte. Go on, believe it.
I welcome his attentions with delight,
Like what he says, admire his character,
And I agree with everything you say.
Go on, be resolute: break off with me;
But leave me in peace before you drive me mad.   1370
ALCESTE
My God! Could a crueller torment be devised?
Was ever any man's heart treated so?
What? With just cause I'm roused to anger with her;
I come to complain – and I'm the one rebuked!
She whips up my distress and my suspicions,
She lets me think the worst, she revels in it!
And still my heart is so despicable
It cannot break its chains and arm itself
With proud contempt against the thankless object
Of its obsessive, foolish adoration!   1380

You minx! How artfully you turn against
Me my great weakness and exploit the vast
Love that your faithless eyes inspired in me!
At least mount some defence: explain away
This hideous wrong you've done that's crushing me.
Don't just pretend you're guilty: do your best
To make me think this note is innocent.
My love for you will make it easy: try
To make it seem that you are faithful to me,
1390   And I'll try to believe you truly are.

CÉLIMÈNE

Alceste! In these jealous fits you're quite insane;
You don't deserve the love I have for you.
I'd like to know what reason could compel me
To sink so low for you as to pretend;
And why, if someone else had won my heart,
I should not say so in all honesty.
Good heavens! I've told you plainly that I love you!
Shouldn't that free me from your cheap suspicions?
Should they prevail against that warranty?
1400   By heeding them aren't you insulting me?
When the age we live in makes it so hard for
A woman to tell a man directly that
She loves him, since her honour checks her heart
From making such an open declaration,
Shouldn't a man for whom she breaks the rules
Be punished when he dares to doubt her word?
Isn't he in the wrong for not believing
What, after such a struggle, he's been told?
Come, your suspicions rightly rouse my anger;
1410   You're not worth my concern: I've been a fool.
I blame myself for being so naïve
As to have any feelings left for you.
I *should* turn my attentions somewhere else
And give you some just cause for your complaints.

ALCESTE

Ah, serpent! How weakly I give in to you!
I'm sure you play me false with those sweet words;

But be it so, I must accept my fate:
My soul is at your mercy. I must test
Your heart to the bitter end: I have to know
If you will be so base as to betray me.   1420

CÉLIMÈNE

No, you don't love me as a man should love.

ALCESTE

Ah, nothing can compare with my great love.
I long so much to flaunt it to the world,
I even wish disasters would befall you.
Yes, I should like to see you spurned by all,
To see you sunk in direst wretchedness.
I wish that Heaven had brought you forth with nothing,
That you did not have birth, or rank, or wealth,
So that my heart, in shining sacrifice,
Might right the wrong of such injustice, and   1430
Could reap the joy and honour of seeing you
Beholden to my love for everything.

CÉLIMÈNE

Well, that's a charming way to wish me well!
Heaven grant that you may never have the chance—
But here's your man Du Bois – in strange attire!*

    Enter DU BOIS.   [IV.iv]

ALCESTE

Dressed for the road and looking scared to death?
What's wrong?

DU BOIS

                    Sir . . .

ALCESTE

                              Well?

DU BOIS

                                        There are strange things afoot.

ALCESTE

What things?

DU BOIS

                    Sir, our affairs are not going well.

ALCESTE

What?

DU BOIS
    Sir, shall I speak out loud?

ALCESTE
                          Yes, speak, be quick.

DU BOIS
1440 Isn't there someone—

ALCESTE
                  Oh, don't shilly-shally!
Speak, will you.

DU BOIS
            Sir, we must beat a swift retreat.

ALCESTE
    What's that?

DU BOIS
          We must decamp without a fanfare.

ALCESTE
    Well, why?

DU BOIS
          I tell you, we must get away.

ALCESTE
    The reason?

DU BOIS
          We must leave with no farewells.

ALCESTE
    What is the cause of your speaking to me like this?

DU BOIS
    The cause is, sir, that we must pack our traps.

ALCESTE
    Oh, I shall surely break your head, you fool,
    If you don't tell me plainly what you mean.

DU BOIS
    A man, sir, with a black coat and a black look
1450 Came right inside our kitchen to deliver
    A paper scribbled in such a funny way
    The devil's cunning could not make it out.
    It's all about your court case, I know that,
    But not Old Nick himself could understand it.

ALCESTE
    And so? Eh? What's this paper got to do,

You jackass, with what you said about our leaving?
DU BOIS
    I mean, sir, that an hour went by, and then
    Another man, who often calls on you,
    Came hurrying round to find you, and when you
    Could not be found, he asked me, civilly,   1460
    Knowing that I'm your good and faithful servant,
    If I would tell you— Wait now, what's his name?
ALCESTE
    Dolt! Never mind his name: what did he say?
DU BOIS
    Well, he's a friend of yours, that's sure enough.
    He said it's dangerous for you to stay here:
    There's quite a chance that you could be arrested.
ALCESTE
    What! Would he tell you nothing more than that?
DU BOIS
    No: but he asked me for some ink and paper,
    And wrote a note, from which you will be able,
    I think, to fathom out the mystery.   1470
ALCESTE
    Give it me, then!
CÉLIMÈNE
                        What can this mean, do you think?
ALCESTE
    I don't know, but I hope to be enlightened.
    Well, will you soon be done, you stupid clown?
DU BOIS (*after a lengthy search*)
    Oh, deary me! I've left it on the table.
ALCESTE
    I don't know what is stopping me—
CÉLIMÈNE
                                        Keep calm.
    Go quickly and unravel this strange business.
ALCESTE
    It seems that Fate, however hard I try,
    Has sworn to stop me speaking to you, madam,
    But help me to defeat it: let us two
    Speak once again before the day is through.   1480

ACT V

ALCESTE, PHILINTE

ALCESTE
I tell you the decision has been made.
PHILINTE
It's a hard knock, but must you let it drive you—
ALCESTE
No: you can reason to your heart's content;
Nothing you say will make me change my mind.
The age we live in is shot through with vice:
I want no more to do with human beings.
God! Ranged against my adversary stand
Probity, honour, decency and law;
The whole world sees my claim as fair and just;
1490 I trust in equity to vindicate me,
And in the judgement find myself betrayed.
With justice on my side I lose my case!
A scoundrel with a squalid reputation
Emerges with his villainy condoned;
Good faith retreats before his treachery!
He slits my throat and he is innocent!
His foxy tongue's transparent artifice
Twists wrong to right, turns justice inside out,
And crowns his crime with legal sanctity!
1500   Then, still not satisfied with all the wrong
He's done me, there's a book being passed around
So odious that to read it is a sin,
A book whose author should be soundly whipped,
And the vile rogue has the gall to say I wrote it!
On top of that Oronte goes buzzing round
Wickedly propping up the filthy lie!
Oronte, reputedly a man of honour,
To whom I've merely been sincere and frank:
He flings himself upon me uninvited
1510 And asks my views about some verse he's written;
And then, because my honesty will not

Betray him or the truth, he joins in trying
To crush me with a crime I've not committed!
Behold him now my greatest enemy;
Never will he forgive me in his heart
For not considering his sonnet good!
   And that, God help us, sums up human beings:
Those are the things their false pride makes them do;
That's the extent to which integrity,
Justice and honour can be found among them!   1520
No: why endure the torments they inflict?
Out of this cut-throat jungle! Since that's how
You human creatures live, like a pack of wolves,
You scum, my days shall not be spent with you.

PHILINTE

I think you're acting rather hastily:
Matters are not so bad as you suggest.
Your adversary's spiteful imputation
Had insufficient credit to result
In your arrest; his libellous attack
Has fallen flat and may well damage him.   1530

ALCESTE

Him? Wiles like that give him no cause to fear:
He has carte blanche to be a thorough crook.
His credit won't be in the least affected:
Tomorrow you'll see him cockier than before.

PHILINTE

Still, it's a fact that no one has believed
The vicious rumour that he's spread about you,
So from that quarter you can feel secure.
As for the lawsuit, yes, you have a grievance,
But you can easily appeal against
The judgement—

ALCESTE

                No, no, no, I'll let it stand.   1540
Despite the wrong I suffer by that judgement
I will not have it quashed: it's a perfect case
Of justice being turned upon its head.
I want it to remain as testimony,

As glorious proof in all the years to come
Of our contemporaries' beastliness.
It may well cost me twenty thousand francs,
But at that price I'll have acquired the right
To blast the rottenness of human beings
1550   And cherish an undying hatred for them.

PHILINTE
But really—

ALCESTE
                    Yes, but really: save your breath.
What have you got to add, sir, on that score?
You cannot have the nerve to justify
The nastiness that goes on everywhere?

PHILINTE
No, I agree with every word you say:
Intrigues and influence govern everything;
Success is won by guile and fraudulence,
And human beings ought not to be so.
But is their lack of equity a reason
1560   For opting out of their society?
These human frailties offer us the means
Of exercising our philosophy;
Virtue can find no more worthwhile employment.
And, if the world were clothed in honesty,
If everyone were meek, sincere and just,
Most of our virtues would be useless to us,
Since they exist to help us bear with patience
Being unjustly treated when we're right;
And, just as the most virtuous of souls—

ALCESTE
1570   Your eloquence I know, sir, is superb;
You're always ready with sound arguments.
But all your fine words cut no ice with me.
Reason, for my own good, drives me away:
I can't control my tongue; if I remained,
I could not answer for what I might say:
I'd draw a heap of troubles on my head.
        Leave me in peace to wait for Célimène:

She must consent to what I have in mind;
I mean to find out if she really loves me.
This is the moment that will end my doubts.   1580

PHILINTE
Let's wait with Éliante till she returns.

ALCESTE
No, I have too much preying on my mind.
You go and see her; leave me here alone
In this dark corner with my gloomy thoughts.

PHILINTE
That is strange company to leave you with:
I'll go and ask Éliante if she'll come down.
    Exit PHILINTE. *Enter* ORONTE *and* CÉLIMÈNE.   [V.ii]

ORONTE (*not seeing* ALCESTE)
Yes, madam, you must decide if it's your wish
To bind me to you with those tender vows.
I need complete assurance of your feelings:
What suitors can't abide is vacillation.   1590
If my devoted love has touched your heart,
Without dissembling you must tell me so;
And what I'm asking of you now as proof
Is that you cease to allow Alceste to court you,
And sacrifice him to my love: in short,
That from today you ban him from your house.

CÉLIMÈNE
But what has turned you so against him, you,
Whom I have heard so often sing his praise?

ORONTE
Madam, we needn't enter into that;
The point is that I have to know your mind.   1600
Be good enough to make your choice between us:
My own commitment waits only upon yours.

ALCESTE (*emerging from his dark corner*)
Yes, madam, he is right: you must decide.
What he is asking is what I wish too;
The same devotion, the same doubts bring me here:
My love requires clear evidence of yours.
This matter will not suffer more delay:

The time has come: you must unveil your heart.

ORONTE

I've no wish, sir, with untoward affection
1610   In any way to trouble your good fortune.

ALCESTE

Jealous I may be, but I say that too:
I've no wish, sir, to share her heart with you.

ORONTE

If your love conquers my love in her view—

ALCESTE

If she can feel the least regard for you—

ORONTE

I swear henceforward to renounce my claim.

ALCESTE

I swear, by Heaven, I won't see her again.

ORONTE

Madam, it's up to you to speak your mind.

ALCESTE

Madam, you may speak fearlessly, you'll find.

ORONTE

You only have to state your inclination.

ALCESTE

1620   You only have to choose: no hesitation.

ORONTE

What! It seems hard to know which one to favour?

ALCESTE

What! Your heart's doubtful and you seem to waver?

CÉLIMÈNE

Heavens! How unseemly your insistence is,
And how unreasonable you both are!
I know what my decision has to be;
It isn't that my heart is in the balance;
It's certainly not wavering between you;
No choice is sooner made than whom to love.
But truly I do find it much too painful
1630   To make such a confession publicly.
Unpleasant facts should not, it seems to me,
Be blurted out to people face to face;

Our inclinations make themselves quite plain
Without being harshly rammed down suitors' throats.
It's surely enough if an admirer learns
From gentler evidence that he has failed.

ORONTE

No, no, a frank statement holds no fears for me;
I don't object to it.

ALCESTE

                    And I demand it.
A public statement's what I need to hear;
I don't want any mollycoddling from you.   1640
Your aim is to keep strings on everyone!
But no more tantalizing, no more doubt:
You must make clear what your true feelings are;
And, if you won't, I'll take that as a verdict;
I shall know how to understand your silence,
And I shall act as if my fate were sealed.

ORONTE

I'm in your debt, sir, for your angry tone;
What you are saying is what I say too.

CÉLIMÈNE

How tiresome you both are with your bizarre
Demand! Is what you're asking fair and just?   1650
Haven't I told you why I can't comply?
Here's Éliante: now she can arbitrate.

      Enter ÉLIANTE *and* PHILINTE.   [V.iii]

CÉLIMÈNE (*continues*)

Cousin, I'm being persecuted here
By these two, who, it seems, have made a pact:
They both insist with equal urgency
That I declare to which my heart inclines,
And that I ban the other to his face
From coming here and paying court to me.
Tell me if things are ever done like that.

ÉLIANTE

On such a matter don't ask my advice: 1660
You may find you've selected the wrong judge.
I am for those who plainly speak their mind.

ORONTE
  Madam, you face defeat on this occasion.
ALCESTE
  Here you find no support for your evasion.
ORONTE
  Stop wavering; speak out; you must concede.
ALCESTE
  Go on refusing: that is all I need.
ORONTE
  One word I need and all is sealed and signed.
ALCESTE
  If you say nothing, I shall know your mind.

[V.iv]   *Enter* ACASTE, CLITANDRE *and* ARSINOÉ.

ACASTE
  Madam, we've come, the two of us together,
1670 So that you may cast light on a little matter.
CLITANDRE
  Your presence, gentlemen, is apropos:
  You also are involved in this affair.
ARSINOÉ
  Madam, you'll be surprised to see me here:
  I've come because of these two gentlemen.
  They sought me out together, and complained
  Of conduct which I truly cannot credit.
  You stand too high in my esteem for me
  To think you guilty of such infamy;
  My eyes disdained their proofs, strong though they are;
1680 And, since true friendship weathers minor storms,
  I agreed to come here with them to your house
  To see you clear yourself of this vile charge.
ACASTE
  Yes, madam, let's see, quietly and calmly,
  How you will set about explaining this.
  You wrote this letter to Clitandre, I think?
CLITANDRE
  And to Acaste you wrote this billet-doux?
ACASTE
  Gentlemen, this is no strange hand to you:
  I have no doubt that she has kindly made

You only too familiar with her hand.
Her letter to Clitandre will interest you:

1690

> *What a peculiar man you are to blame me for being in high spirits, and complain that I'm happiest when I'm not with you. Nothing could be further from the truth; and, if you don't come running to ask my pardon, I shall never forgive you for as long as I live. Our great lolloping viscount . . .*

It's a shame he's not here—

> *Our great lolloping viscount, the first man you object to, is not at all the kind of man to appeal to me. I've never thought very highly of him since I watched him spend three-quarters of an hour spitting into a well to make rings in the water. As for the little marquess . . .*

That, ladies and gentlemen, is I, without wishing to boast.

> *As for the little marquess, who danced attendance on me for hours yesterday, you could never find a more piffling ninny: he has nothing to offer but his fine feathers. As for the man with green ribbons . . .**

The ball lands in your court, Alceste.

> *As for the man with green ribbons, he does sometimes amuse me with his blunt speaking and his crabby temper, but you'd be surprised how often I find him the most tiresome creature in the world. As for the would-be poet . . .*

Oronte, this is your portion.

> *As for the would-be poet, who has cast himself as a wit and set himself up as an author in defiance of everyone's better judgement, I can't be bothered to listen to him: his prose bores me as much as his verse. So try to understand that I don't have such a jolly time as you think. I miss you horribly at all the diversions I'm dragged to; the pleasures of life are a lot more fun when you can share them with someone you care about.*

CLITANDRE

Now here's what she wrote to *him* about *me*.

> *You mention your chum Clitandre: he's very good at*
> *playing the lovelorn swain, but he's the last man on earth*
> *I could fall for. He must be crazy to think I love him, and*
> *you must be crazy to think I don't love you. Come to*
> *your senses, exchange your beliefs for his, and come and*
> *see me as often as you can to help me put up with the*
> *torture of being pestered by him.*

A charming character is modelled there,
Madam; I think you know the name for it?
Right: we shall both of us exhibit round
The town this glorious portrait of your heart.

ACASTE

There's plenty I could say: the theme is rich;
But I don't think you worthy of my anger;
And you shall see that 'little marquesses'
Can turn to nobler hearts for consolation.

       Exeunt ACASTE *and* CLITANDRE.

ORONTE

So this, I see, is how you vilify me
1700   After you've written to me with such warmth:
Your heart, tricked out with all the marks of love,
Pledges itself to every man in turn!
How green I was! But here's an end to that:
You do me a kindness in showing your true self;
My profit is to have my heart restored:
My revenge to know the worth of what you've lost.
No longer, Alceste, shall I obstruct your courtship:
You're free to clinch your claim to the fair lady.

       Exit ORONTE.

ARSINOÉ

Really! This conduct is despicable;
1710   I can't contain myself, I feel so strongly.
Has anyone seen the like of such behaviour?
The others are of no concern to me,

But he, whom you were lucky to attract,
Alceste, a man like him, of worth and honour,
Who cherished you, who idolized you, should
He be—

ALCESTE

        Permit me, madam, if you please,
To deal in my own way with my own business,
And spare yourself this needless sympathy.
My heart remains unmoved by your support
And can't repay your eager interest;   1720
It's not to you that I shall think of turning,
If by another choice I seek revenge.

ARSINOÉ

Oh! Do you think, sir, I had that in mind?
And that you're really such a splendid catch?
You're certainly not lacking in conceit
If you can flatter yourself with that belief:
This lady's leavings are not merchandise
Precious enough to be so coveted.
Open your eyes, good sir, come down to earth:
A person like myself is not for you.   1730
You'd best go chasing after her again:
I long to witness such a glorious match.
    Exit ARSINOÉ.

ALCESTE

Well, I have held my peace in spite of all,
And suffered all the rest to speak before me.
Have I restrained myself for long enough,
And may I now—

CÉLIMÈNE

            Yes, you may speak your mind;
You will be in the right when you complain;
You may reproach me to your heart's content.
I'm in the wrong, I know, and in my shame
I shall not buy you off with vain excuses.   1740
The anger of the rest aroused my scorn,
But in respect of you I own my guilt.

Of course, you've every reason to feel bitter;
I know how bad I must appear to you,
How everything suggests that I've been faithless;
In short, you have good cause to hate me: do so,
I give you leave.

ALCESTE

                           Ah, can I, little serpent?
Can I just wipe out all the love I feel?
However fiercely I may want to hate you,
1750   Will my poor heart be ready to obey me?
Éliante, Philinte, see my infirmity:
Witness the power of an ignoble love;
And, let me tell you, still I have not done:
Now see me indulge my weakness to the last,
And prove how wrong it is to call us wise,
How no heart is exempt from human frailty.
Yes, faithless creature, I'll forget your sins;
I shall be able truly to forgive them
And see them as wrongdoing into which
1760   The vices of the age seduced your youth,
Provided that your love supports my purpose
Of fleeing the entire human race,
And you resolve at once to come with me
To that retreat where I have vowed to live.
That is the only course which will atone,
In all eyes, for the harm done by your letters,
The only course which, after this vile scandal,
Will enable me to love you as before.

CÉLIMÈNE

I? Turn my back upon the world before
1770   I'm old, and wither in your wilderness?

ALCESTE

Ah! But if you love me as I love you,
Can you not let the rest of the world go hang?
Are all your wishes not fulfilled in me?

CÉLIMÈNE

At twenty I'm afraid of solitude;
I don't feel that my soul is great enough,

Or strong enough, for such a way of life.
But if you'll be contented with my hand,
I can resolve to bind myself to you,
And marriage—

ALCESTE

No. From this moment I detest you:
That answer outdoes all your other wrongs.   1780
Since you are not prepared, in that dear union,
To find your all in me, as I in you,
Go your sweet way: that harsh rejection frees me
For ever from my shameful slavery.
    Exit CÉLIMÈNE.

ALCESTE (*continues*)
Éliante, your beauty is enhanced by virtue,
And only in you have I found sincerity;
I've long regarded you with admiration.
But let me hold you always in the same
Esteem: permit my troubled heart to make
No bid for the great honour of your hand.   1790
I feel unworthy of you, and see now
That Heaven does not intend me to be married.
To offer you a heart that has been spurned
By one so far beneath you would insult
You too—

ÉLIANTE

You may believe so, if you wish;
I have no lack of suitors: your friend Philinte here,
Without my seeking further, if I asked him,
Might bring himself to take me as his wife.

PHILINTE
Ah, madam, that honour is my heart's desire;
I'd sacrifice my life and soul for it.   1800

ALCESTE
May you preserve these feelings for each other,
And so be blessed with everlasting joy.
Betrayed on every side, crushed by injustice,
I leave this foul abyss where vices thrive
To seek upon the earth a place apart

Where one is free to be an honest man.
    Exit ALCESTE.
PHILINTE
    Dear Éliante, let's muster all our art
    To turn him from the purpose in his heart.

RACINE

ANDROMACHE

A Tragedy

ANDROMAQUE

Tragédie

Following the first performance at Court in the Queen's apartment on 17 November 1667, the first public performance took place the next day at the Hôtel de Bourgogne

First Preface

(1668 and 1673)

Virgil, *The Aeneid*, Book III

The speaker is Aeneas.

Littoraque Epiri legimus, portuque subimus
Chaonio, et celsam Buthroti ascendimus urbem . . .
Solemnes tum forte dapes et tristia dona . . .
Libabat cineri Andromache, Manesque vocabat
Hectoreum ad tumulum, viridi quem cespite inanem,
Et geminas, causam lacrymis, sacraverat aras . . .
Dejecit vultum, et demissa voce locuta est:
'O felix una ante alias Priameia virgo,
Hostilem ad tumulum, Trojæ sub mœnibus altis,
Jussa mori! quæ sortitus non pertulit ullos,
Nec victoris heri tetigit captiva cubile.
Nos, patria incensa, diversa per æquora vectæ,
Stirpis Achilleæ fastus, juvenemque superbum,
Servitio enixæ, tulimus, qui deinde secutus
Ledæam Hermionem, Lacedæmoniosque hymenæos . . .
Ast illum, ereptæ magno inflammatus amore
Conjugis, et scelerum Furiis agitatus, Orestes
Excipit incautum, patriasque obtruncat ad aras.'

[We sail along the coast of Epirus, and, having put into the
port of Chaonia, we make our way up to the lofty city of
Buthrotum . . . It happened just then . . . that Andromache
was offering the sacrificial dishes and funereal gifts to Hector's ashes and calling on his shade to come to the empty

tomb of green turf she had raised in front of two fair altars she had consecrated to his eternal memory. Here she would come to weep for him . . . With lowered eyes and in hushed tones she said: 'Polyxena, most blessed of all Priam's daughters, condemned to die on the tomb of an enemy under the soaring walls of Troy: she did not have to submit to being chosen by lot, nor as a captive did she have to lie in the bed of a conqueror, her master. I, from the ashes of my homeland dragged from sea to sea, have suffered the arrogance and youthful insolence of Achilles' son, and brought forth his child in slavery. Then did he turn to Leda's granddaughter, Hermione, and sought a Spartan marriage . . . But Orestes, aflame with love for Hermione stolen from him, and tormented by the Furies for the crime of matricide, fell on Pyrrhus unprepared and slaughtered him before the altar of Achilles.'

(ll. 292–3, 301, 303–5, 320–28, 330–32)]

There, in a few lines, is the entire subject of this tragedy. There are the setting, the action, the four principal participants, and even their characters. Except for that of Hermione, whose jealousy and passionate outbursts are well enough portrayed in the *Andromache* of Euripides.

But truly my characters are so well known that, however slight one's acquaintance with antiquity, it will be clear that I have depicted them just as the ancient poets have handed them down to us. Indeed, I have not considered myself free to modify any element of their manners and customs. The only liberty I have taken is to soften a little Pyrrhus' savagery, which Seneca in his *Troad* and Virgil in Book II of the *Aeneid* made much fiercer than I thought justified.

Even so, there are those who have complained at his raging against Andromache and his determination to marry his captive at whatever cost. I admit that he is not as acquiescent as he might be to the will of his lady, and that Céladon* was better versed than he in the conduct of a perfect lover. But what is one to do? Pyrrhus had not read our novels. He was by nature a violent man. And not every hero is cut out to be a Céladon.

However that may be, the public response to my work has been too favourable for me to be troubled by the carping of two or three individuals who would like to see one reform all the heroes of antiquity so as to make perfect heroes out of them. I understand their wish to see only flawless men put on the stage. But I ask them to remember that it is not my business to rewrite the rules of the theatre. Horace urges us to portray Achilles as savage, remorseless and violent, as he was, and as his son is depicted.

And Aristotle, far from asking of us perfect heroes, on the contrary wants tragic characters, that is to say those whose misfortune constitutes the tragedy's catastrophe, to be neither wholly good nor wholly bad. He does not want them to be completely virtuous, because to see a saintly man punished would arouse indignation rather than pity in the audience; nor should they be excessively wicked, because a scoundrel stirs no pity. They must accordingly be of moderate virtue – that is, virtue prone to weakness – so that they fall into evil ways as the result of some flaw, which causes them to be pitied without being detested.

Second Preface

(1676)

Racine's new preface for his first collected edition begins with the same eighteen lines from Virgil as began the original preface, followed by the first paragraph of that preface (pp. 139–40), and continues:

That is almost the only thing that I borrow from that writer. For, although my tragedy bears the same name as his, the subject is very different. In Euripides' version, Andromache fears for the life of Molossus, a son she has had by Pyrrhus and whom Hermione wishes to see put to death with his mother. But in my play there is no Molossus. Andromache has known no husband other than Hector and no son but Astyanax. In this I thought to make my character conform to the image we now have of that princess. Most of those who have heard of Andromache know her only as Hector's widow and the mother of Astyanax. It is not conceivable that she should love another husband or another son. And I doubt whether Andromache's tears would have moved my audiences as they have if they had flowed for any son other than the one she had by Hector.

It is true that I have had to make Astyanax live rather longer than he did; but I am living in a country where no objection could be raised to my taking that liberty. For – not to mention Ronsard, who chose that same Astyanax as the hero of his *Franciade* – who is not aware that our ancient kings are held to descend from this son of Hector, and that our old chronicles preserve that same young prince's life, after the devastation of his country, to make him the founder of our monarchy?

How much bolder was Euripides in his tragedy *Helen*! He blatantly flies in the face of the belief held by the whole of Greece. In his version, Helen never set foot in Troy, and after the burning of that city Menelaus finds his wife in Egypt where she had been all the time. All this according to a belief held only by the Egyptians, as may be found in Herodotus.

I do not consider that I need have recourse to this example from Euripides to justify the slight liberty I have taken. For there is a great difference between destroying the fundamental bedrock of a legend and modifying a few elements which shift in every version of it. For example, Achilles, according to most writers, can be wounded only in the heel, yet Homer has him wounded in the arm and does not consider him invulnerable in any part of his anatomy. Then Sophocles has Jocasta die immediately after the revelation of Oedipus' true identity, while Euripides prolongs her life until the combat and death of her two sons. And it is in reference to this kind of inconsistency that an ancient commentator on Sophocles* remarks judiciously that 'one should not pounce joyously on some slight changes a writer has made in the legend but rather focus on the excellent use he has made of the changes, and the skilful way he has adapted the legend to his theme'.

CHARACTERS

ANDROMACHE, widow of Hector; captive of Pyrrhus
PYRRHUS, son of Achilles; king of Epirus
ORESTES, son of Agamemnon, the king of Mycenae and of
  Argos
HERMIONE, daughter of Menelaus and Helen, the king and
  queen of Sparta; betrothed to Pyrrhus
PYLADES, friend of Orestes
CLEONE, confidante of Hermione
CEPHISA, confidante of Andromache
PHOENIX, formerly tutor of Achilles, subsequently of
  Pyrrhus
SOLDIERS of the retinue of Orestes as Greek ambassador

The scene is set in Buthrotum, a city of Epirus;
a room in the palace of Pyrrhus*

ACT I

ORESTES, PYLADES

ORESTES

Yes, now that I've found again so true a friend,*
My destiny will take a different turn;
Already it appears less harsh, since it
Contrived to reunite us in this place.
To think a shore so hostile to my love
Should greet me with the sight of Pylades;
That, more than six months after losing you,
At Pyrrhus' court you'd be restored to me!

PYLADES

For that I thank the gods, who seem to have
Prevented me from going home to Greece   10
Since that unhappy day when, in the storm,
Our ships were parted off Epirus' shore.
What fears I've suffered in my banishment!
What tears I've shed to think of your misfortunes,
Always afraid of some new threat to you
That in sad fellowship I could not share!
I dreaded most those bouts of melancholy
Which I have so long seen enshroud your soul:
I feared that Heaven might send you cruel aid
And offer you the death you longed to find.   20
  But here you are, my lord; and it would seem
A happier fate has brought you to Epirus:
Your lavish retinue does not suggest
A miserable man who longs to die.

ORESTES

Ah, who can tell what fate awaits me here?
I'm drawn by love for one who loves me not;
But who knows what that love ordains for me:
Whether I come in search of life or death?

PYLADES

What's this? Can you be so enslaved to love
30   That you entrust it with your very life?
Are you bewitched? Have you forgotten what
You suffered, to let yourself be trapped again?
Hermione in Sparta scorned your suit;
Do you think that in Epirus she will yield?
Shamed by your futile pleas, you loathed her; well,
You spoke no more of her to me. So you,
My lord, deceived me.

ORESTES

I deceived myself.
Bear with a fond friend, who's a wretched fool:
When have I kept my heart's desires from you?
40   You saw my passion born, you saw it grow;
And then, when Menelaus betrothed his daughter
To Pyrrhus, who'd avenged his family,
You saw me in despair; and, since, you've seen
Me drag my painful chain from sea to sea.
You would not leave me in my sorry state;
At every turn I found you by my side,
Checking my headstrong passion constantly,
Protecting me each day from my own hand.
    But when I thought how, while I agonized,
50   Hermione was fawning over Pyrrhus,
You know my angry heart determined to
Forget her, and so punish her contempt.
I thought, and made you think, I'd freed myself;
I took my fury for a furious hate;
I cursed her coldness, belittled her appeal,
And dared her to unsettle me again.
I truly thought I'd choked my love for her.
In that deceptive lull I went to Greece;
And there I found the kings were all assembled,
60   Distressed by some grave danger, so it seemed.
I rushed to help. I thought that war and honour
Would fill my mind with weightier concerns,
That, once my energies had been renewed,

Love finally would vanish from my heart.
But marvel with me at how destiny
Drove me towards the trap I was avoiding.
Pyrrhus, I heard, was under threat: all Greece
Was up in arms, outraged that he, a Greek
Himself, despite his word, was raising in
His court their enemy, Astyanax,   70
The young, ill-fated son of Hector, sole
Survivor of so many kings of Troy.
I learnt that, to preserve his infant life,
Andromache had tricked shrewd Ulysses:
The child torn from her arms was not her son;
Another boy in his name had been killed.*
Pyrrhus, I heard, had snubbed Hermione,
And offered Andromache his heart and crown.
King Menelaus, incredulous and hurt,
Was chafing at the delay to his daughter's wedding.   80
While he was overwhelmed by bitter sorrow,
In me there rose a hidden happiness.
I revelled in my triumph, thinking my
Delight sprang from pure vengefulness; but soon
My unfeeling mistress ruled my heart again.
I felt the warmth of my ill-smothered fire;
I knew my hate for her was fading fast;
Or, rather, that my love had never died.
    And so I begged to come here as the Greek
Ambassador to Pyrrhus. And my mission?   90
To prise away from him the child who, while
He lives, strikes fear in every part of Greece:
Much happier if my passion could deprive him
Not of Astyanax, but my princess!
For I tell you that not the gravest threat
Can daunt the renewed power of my love.
Since all my efforts to resist have failed,
Blindly I yield to the fate that sweeps me on:
I love Hermione; I've come to win her,
Or steal her away, or die before her eyes.   100
You, who know Pyrrhus, what do you think he'll do?

How is it in his court, and in his heart?
Is he still bound to my Hermione?
He stole her from me; will he give her back?

PYLADES

My lord, I should mislead you to suggest
That he will freely give her back to you;
And yet he takes no pride in his possession;
It's Hector's widow he's enslaved to now:
He loves Andromache; but she so far
110   Has given him only hatred for his love;
Each day he either tries to woo his captive,
Or else to make her yield by frightening her.
He hides her infant son, threatens to kill him,
Wrings tears from her, and straightway dries her eyes.
Time and again in fury he's renewed
His former courtship of Hermione,
Offered his baffled vows again to her,
And at her feet sighed less with love than rage.
So don't ask me to answer for a man
120   So ruled by love he can't control himself.
In his disordered state he may be driven
To marry her he hates, and punish her he loves.

ORESTES

What of Hermione? How does she view
Her wedding delayed, her beauty unavailing?

PYLADES

Hermione appears at least to scorn
Her bridegroom's faithlessness, and thinks that Pyrrhus,
Only too happy one day to repent,
Will beg her to accept his heart again.
But I've been privy to her tears: she weeps,
130   In secret, to see her beauty cast aside;
Ever prepared to leave, and never leaving,
Sometimes she calls Orestes to her aid.

ORESTES

Ah! If I thought so, Pylades, I'd go
At once and kneel—

PYLADES

               My lord, fulfil your mission.
Pyrrhus is coming: tell him that the Greeks
Are baying for the blood of Hector's son.
Their hatred won't make him give up the child,
But rather inflame his love for Andromache;
Urge him to leave her, and he'll cleave to her:
Claim everything – to ensure that you gain nothing.   140
He's here.

ORESTES

           Go and prepare my cold princess
To receive a man who's here to win her heart.

     Exit PYLADES. *Enter* PYRRHUS *with* PHOENIX.   [I.ii]

ORESTES (*continues*)

Before the Greeks all speak to you through me,
May I express my pride to be their envoy,
And my great pleasure, sir, to look upon
Achilles' son, the conqueror of Troy.
Yes, we admire your deeds no less than his:
By him was Hector vanquished, Troy by you;
And your triumphant bravery has shown
That Achilles' son alone could take his place.   150
    But Greece is grieved to see you giving aid,
As he would not have done, to Trojan blood,
Letting ill-fated pity move your heart
And succouring a long war's sole survivor.
Have you forgotten, sir, what Hector was?
Our weak and weary people still remember.
Our widows and daughters tremble at his name,
And in all Greece there is no family
Not claiming redress from his luckless son
For father or husband snatched away by Hector.   160
And who knows what that son may do one day?
Perhaps we'll see him fall upon our harbours,
Just as his father did, and fire our ships,
Follow them, flame in hand, across the water.
    My lord, may I tell you what I truly think?

You yourself fear the reward your pains may reap:
The viper you are nursing in your bosom
May one day turn on you for saving it.
So give the Greeks what they all want from you;
170   Secure their vengeance, and secure your life:
Destroy an enemy who's to be feared
The more because he'll strike at them through you.

PYRRHUS
Greece frets herself too much on my behalf:
I thought more serious problems troubled her;
The choice of you as envoy, my good sir,
Led me to look for loftier designs.
Who would have thought, indeed, that such a mission
Would merit sending Agamemnon's son;
That such a race of mighty conquerors
180   Would stoop to plot the murder of a child?
      But to whom am I meant to sacrifice him?
Does Greece still have some claim upon his life?
And may not I alone of all the Greeks
Dispose of a captive Fate has granted me?
Yes, my lord, when beneath Troy's smoking walls
The bleeding victors shared their living spoils,
The lottery on which we all agreed
Bestowed on me Andromache and her son.
Ulysses took the sorrowing Hecuba;
190   Cassandra went to Argos with your father;*
Have I made claims on them or on their captives?
Have I disposed of the rewards they won?
      It's feared that Troy may be reborn with Hector:
His son may take my life for sparing his.
Such extreme prudence, sir, is overcautious;
I can't foresee misfortunes so far off.
I think upon that city as it was,
So proudly ramparted, so rich in heroes,
Mistress of Asia; I think of what befell her,
200   And wonder what her destiny might be.
And all I see are towers cloaked in ashes,

A river red with blood, deserted fields,
A child in chains; and I can't think that Troy,
Reduced to this, can hope to seek revenge.
Why, if we swore that Hector's son must die,
Have we deferred his death for twelve whole months?
Could he not have been killed in Priam's arms?
He should have gone with all the dead, with Troy.
Then everything was just: the old and young
In vain looked to their weakness for defence: 210
Conquest and darkness drove our cruelty,
Spurred us to slaughter, careless whom we killed.
My rage dealt all too fiercely with the fallen.
But that my harshness should outlive my fury!
That I should quell the pity in my heart
And coldly steep myself in a child's blood!
Oh, no: the Greeks can seek some other prey,
Go elsewhere to hunt down what's left of Troy.
My animosity is dead; what was
Preserved at Troy, Epirus will preserve.   220

ORESTES

My lord, you know the trickery by which
A false Astyanax was put to death
When Hector's only son should have been killed;
The Greeks are hunting Hector, not the Trojans.
Yes, through the son, they're tracking down the father.
He bought their anger with the blood he shed:
By his blood only can it be appeased.
And that may draw them even to Epirus.
Forestall them.

PYRRHUS

     No, I welcome them: here in
Epirus let them seek a second Troy,   230
Mistake their enemy, confuse the blood
That made them victors with the vanquished blood.
It will not be the first time that the Greeks
Repay Achilles' service with injustice.*
Hector made deadly use of their misjudgement:

One day his son may do so in his turn.

ORESTES

So Greece finds you rebellious to her will?

PYRRHUS

Did I conquer Troy for her to be her slave?

ORESTES

Hermione, my lord, will stay your hand:
240   Your feelings for her will protect her father.

PYRRHUS

I may still care for Hermione, my lord;
I may love her, and not kneel to her father.
And I have hopes that I may reconcile
The claims of kingship with the claims of love.
    Now you will wish to speak with Helen's daughter:
I know how closely you are bound by blood.*
That done, my lord, you will be free to go;
And you may tell the Greeks that I say no.

[I.iii]   *Exit* ORESTES.

PHOENIX

And so you cast him at Hermione's feet?

PYRRHUS

250   They say that he was long in love with her.

PHOENIX

And if that fire, my lord, should be rekindled?
If he should give his heart and conquer hers?

PYRRHUS

Ah, let him, Phoenix! I say, let her go!
Let them go doting home again to Sparta.
Our harbours are all open to them both.
What anguish, what constraint she'd free me from!

PHOENIX

Sir—

PYRRHUS

    Later I'll confide in you. Here is
Andromache.

[I.iv]   *Enter* ANDROMACHE *with* CEPHISA.

PYRRHUS (*continues*)
                Can you be seeking me,

My lady? Am I permitted that sweet hope?
ANDROMACHE
I'm on my way to where my son is kept.   260
Since once a day you suffer me to see
All I have left of Hector and of Troy,
I meant, my lord, to weep with him awhile:
I have not held him in my arms today.
PYRRHUS
My lady, it seems the Greeks are full of fear:
They'll soon give you another cause for tears.
ANDROMACHE
And what can this fear be that strikes their hearts,
My lord? Can some Trojan have eluded you?
PYRRHUS
Their hatred of Hector is not yet burned out:
They dread his son.
ANDROMACHE
                         He's to be feared indeed!   270
A poor child, not aware as yet that Pyrrhus
Is now his master, and that he's Hector's son!
PYRRHUS
Because he is, the Greeks all want him killed.
Agamemnon's son is here to see it done.
ANDROMACHE
And will you authorize such cruelty?
Is he to be condemned on my account?
Ah! They don't fear that he'll avenge his father:
They fear that he will dry his mother's tears.
He'd have replaced my father and my husband;
But I must lose all, and always by your hand.*   280
PYRRHUS
To forestall your tears, my lady, I've refused.
The Greeks already threaten me with force;
But were they once again to cross the seas
And bring a thousand ships to claim your son,
If it should cost the blood that flowed for Helen,
If in ten years my palace lies in ashes,
I am resolved, I fly to his defence;

I'll save his life at the expense of mine.
   But, while I face these perils for your sake,
290   Will you not be less hard on me? I'm hated
By all the Greeks, attacked on every side;
Must I be wounded by your coldness too?
My arm is yours: may I not hope that you'll
Accept as well a heart that worships you?
In fighting for you, shall I be allowed
Not to count you among my enemies?

ANDROMACHE

Reflect, my lord: the Greeks would marvel that
A mighty heart like yours could be so weak!
Do you want a fine, heroic act of mercy
300   To seem the madness of a lovesick brain?
How can you wish for love from Andromache?
A moping captive, I detest myself.
What charm can you find in these unhappy eyes
That you've condemned to shed eternal tears?
No, no: take pity on your enemy's
Despair, restore a child to his mother's arms,
Defend him from a cruel multitude
Without my heart as payment; shelter him,
Not for me, but, if need be, in spite of me.
310   That course, my lord, befits Achilles' son.

PYRRHUS

Ah! Has your anger not yet run its course?
Can hate be endless, punishment unceasing?
It's true I've caused great sorrow; yes, my hand
Has many times been bathed in Trojan blood.
But how your ruthless eyes have worked on me!
How dear they've sold to me the tears they've shed!
To what remorse they have subjected me!
I'm suffering all the ills I wreaked at Troy:
Defeated, chained, consumed with fierce regret,
320   Burning with more fires than I started there,
Such aching grief, and weeping, restless longing . . .
Ah! Was I ever as harsh as you are now?
But we have caused each other enough pain;

Our common enemies should make us friends.
Just let me hope, and you shall have your son;
I'll be a father to him, I myself
Will teach him to avenge the fall of Troy;
I'll punish Greece for your wrongs and my own.
One look from you and I can do it all:
Your Troy can from its ashes rise again;   330
In less time than the Greeks spent taking it,
Within its new walls I can crown your son.

ANDROMACHE

My lord, such greatness is beyond us now:
I planned it for him while his father lived.
No, you will not see us again, you sacred
Battlements that could not save my Hector!
The wretched sue for lesser favours, sir;
What my tears ask of you is banishment:
Far from the Greeks, and even far from you,
Let me conceal my son and mourn my husband.   340
Your love stirs up against us too much hate:
Go back, go back to Helen's daughter, go.

PYRRHUS

You think I can? Ah, how you torture me!
Can I give her a heart that you hold fast?
I know that she was promised my devotion;
I know that she came here to be my queen;
Destiny willed that both of you should come,
You to be fettered, she to fetter me.
But have I tried in any way to woo her?
Would one not say, to see the contrary,   350
Your charms omnipotent and hers disdained,
That she's the captive here and you the queen?
Ah, if just one of all those sighs you wring
From me could fly to her, what joy she'd know!

ANDROMACHE

And why should your sighs not be welcome to her?
Could she forget what you have done for her?
Does Troy, does Hector make her recoil from you?
Is her love faithful to a husband's ashes?

And such a husband! Ah! Must I remember?
360 Killing him made your father a great hero:
He owes his fame in war to Hector's blood;
You're both renowned for causing me to weep.

PYRRHUS

Well, so be it, I see I must obey you:
I must forget you; or rather I must hate you.
Yes, my desire has grown too violent
To be confined to mere indifference now.
Think on it well: henceforth my heart must feel,
If not ecstatic love, then furious hate.
In my just anger I shall know no mercy:
370 The son shall answer for the mother's scorn;
Greece claims him; and my honour is not served
By saving those who show no gratitude.

ANDROMACHE

Ah! Then he'll die! He has no shield except
His mother's tears and his own innocence.
And it may be that by his death I too
Will find a speedy end to all my sorrows.
For his sake I've dragged out a weary life;
But in his wake I too will join his father.
So all three, reunited, sir, by you—

PYRRHUS

380 My lady, go and see your son. Your love,
On seeing him, may grow more fearful for him
And cease to let your anger be its guide.
I'll come again to hear our fate from you.
Hug him and kiss him: resolve to save him too.

ACT II

[II.i]   HERMIONE, CLEONE

HERMIONE

It's what you want: I've said that he can see me;
I'll once more let him have that pleasure. Soon
He'll be brought here by Pylades. But if
I pleased myself, I would refuse to see him.

CLEONE

   Why should the sight of him be so unwelcome?
   My lady, is he not that same Orestes   390
   Whom you've so often longed to see again,
   Whose love and constancy you've missed so much?

HERMIONE

   That very love, so coldly spurned, is what
   Makes it so hard for me to see him here.
   What shame for me, what a victory for him,
   To see my sorrow equal what he's suffered!
   Is this, he'll say, the proud Hermione?
   She scorned me; now she finds herself rejected.
   So her hard heart that prized itself so highly
   Is learning how it feels to be despised.   400
   Ah, gods!

CLEONE

           No; banish such unworthy fears:
   His feelings for you run too deep. You think
   He comes to jeer at you? He's fought in vain
   Against his love for you: his heart's still yours.
   But you've not told me what your father writes.

HERMIONE

   If Pyrrhus continues to delay, and will
   Not let the Trojan boy be put to death,
   I'm to return home with the Greek legation.

CLEONE

   Well now, my lady, hear Orestes' suit.
   Pyrrhus cooled first: at least conclude the break.   410
   To be correct you ought to have forestalled him.
   Did you not tell me that you hated him?

HERMIONE

   Hate him, Cleone? My honour calls for hate,
   When he forgets how good to him I've been.
   So dear he was to me, and to betray me!
   Ah, yes! I loved him too much not to hate him.

CLEONE

   Then break with him: Orestes worships you—

HERMIONE

   Oh! Give my newborn anger time to breathe!

Let me grow used to hating where I loved.

420   I want to loathe him as I leave him. Ah!
He'll make too sure of that, the faithless brute!

CLEONE

You mean you want some further insult from him?
To fall for a captive, and show his feelings for her
Before your eyes, has that not made him odious
Enough to you? What more is left? If he
Could make you hate him, you would hate him now.

HERMIONE

Why must you probe my wounds so callously?
In this state I'm afraid to know myself.
Try not to credit what you see in me;

430   Believe my love is dead; congratulate me;
Believe that hate has hardened in my heart;
Ah! If you can, make me believe it too.
I ought to leave him? Well, why not? I'll go.
Let him enjoy his squalid conquest; let
His captive wrap her coils more tightly round him;
I'll go . . . But if he should repent? If some
Regard for his sworn word should creep into
His heart? If he should kneel and ask my pardon?
If love should bind him to me, make him mine, if—

440   But all he wants of me is to insult me.
And yet I'll stay to spoil their happiness!
It will amuse me to be in their way;
Or, by compelling him to break his word,
I'll damn him in the eyes of all the Greeks.
I've made them clamour for the son's death: now
They shall demand the mother's death as well.
I'll give her back the pain she's given me.
Let her be killed by him, or cause his death.

CLEONE

You think a woman blinded by her tears

450   Finds joy in luring him from your embrace;
That with a heart oppressed by grief she would
Go touting for the love of her tormentor?
Do you see her any less unhappy for it?

Why is her soul engulfed in sorrow still?
Why is she so cold to him, if she desires him?
HERMIONE
Why, oh why did I put my trust in him?
I made no mystery of what I felt:
I thought it safe to be sincere; not for
A moment did I steel my eyes with scorn;
Each word I spoke to him came from my heart.   460
And who would not, like me, have told her love,
Hearing such sacred vows of deep devotion?
Was I then what I am to him today?
Remember, everything was in his favour:
My family avenged, the Greeks rejoicing,
Our ships all laden with the spoils of Troy,
His father's deeds transcended by his own,
His love, more ardent, so I thought, than mine,
My heart – you too, quite dazzled by his fame:
You all betrayed me, long before he did.   470
    But now I've borne enough; let Pyrrhus go.
I can appreciate Orestes' virtues:
Even unloved, he loves devotedly;
He may yet learn to win love for himself.
So let him come to me.
CLEONE
                        He's here, my lady.
HERMIONE
He's here! I did not think he was so close.
    Enter ORESTES.   [II.ii]
HERMIONE (*continues*)
Am I to think some lingering affection
Draws you, my lord, to this unhappy princess?
Or is it just your duty I must thank
For bringing you so speedily to see me?   480
ORESTES
It's the bleak blindness of my love; you know it,
My lady; you know Orestes' destiny
Is always to come back and worship you,
And always swear that he will not come back.

I know your eyes will open my old wounds;
Each step towards you is a perjury;
I know it, and it shames me. But, by the gods,
Who witnessed my last agonized farewell,
I swear I've been to lands where death was sure
490 To free me from my vows and from my pain.
Where savage men appease their gods with human
Sacrifice I pleaded to be killed;
They closed their temples to me; and the blood
I longed to lavish, those barbarians spared.*
So back I come to you, compelled to search
In your eyes for that death I've failed to find.
Despair makes me look only for indifference:
You only have to tell me not to hope;
To grant the death I crave, you only have
500 To say once more what you have always said.
The last twelve months I've lived for this alone.
My lady, it's left to you to seize a victim
The Scythians would have stolen from your grasp
If they'd been as hard-hearted as you are.

HERMIONE
No more, my lord, no more such morbid talk.
The Greeks have charged you with more urgent matters.
Why speak of Scythia and my hard-heartedness?
Remember all those kings you represent.
Must their revenge depend upon your feelings?
510 Is it Orestes' blood that's asked of you?
Discharge the task you've been entrusted with.

ORESTES
It's been discharged, my lady: Pyrrhus has
Refused; he sends me back; some other power
Makes him embrace the cause of Hector's son.

HERMIONE
So faithless!

ORESTES
                    And so, before I leave, I came
To discover my own destiny from you.
Already I believe I hear your answer

Delivered in the coldness of your tone.

HERMIONE

Oh, will you never cease to utter gloomy,
Unjust reproaches for my coldness to you?   520
What have I done to merit your complaints?
I came here to Epirus out of duty:
My father commanded me. But who can say
That here in secret I've not shared your pain?
Do you think that you alone have had to suffer?
That here in Epirus I have shed no tears?
How can you be so sure that I've not sometimes
Forgotten my duty, and wished that I could see you?

ORESTES

You've wished to see me? Ah! My dear princess—
But, tell me, is it I you're speaking to?   530
Open your eyes: Orestes stands before you,
Orestes, whom you've so long reviled and spurned.

HERMIONE

Yes, it is you, who loved my youthful beauty,
First teaching me the power it could wield;
You, whom a thousand virtues made me prize;
You, whom I pitied, whom I wished to love.

ORESTES

I understand. That's my unhappy lot:
Your heart for Pyrrhus, your good will for me.

HERMIONE

Ah! Do not wish for Pyrrhus' destiny:
I'd hate you.

ORESTES

                    So you'd love me all the more.   540
Ah, then how differently you'd look on me!
You wish to love me now, but you don't want me;
Then, governed by your heart, you'd love me, want me,
And all the while you'd wish that you could hate me.
Ah, gods! Such high regard, such true devotion!
So much speaks for me, if you could but hear!
You alone put the case for Pyrrhus now,
Perhaps against your will, against his surely:

For he hates you; another has his heart,
550 And he won't—

HERMIONE

                    How do you know, sir, that he hates me?
You've learnt that from the way he looks and speaks,
    then,
Have you? You think I'm worthy to be spurned,
To set hearts burning with such short-lived fires?
Others, perhaps, may value me more highly.

ORESTES

Go on, it's fine to hurl abuse at me.
Why attack me? Am I the one who spurns you?
Have I not proved my constancy? Do I
Bear witness that you can't inspire true love?
I've spurned you? Ah! How pleased you'd be if Pyrrhus
560 Spurned you as heartily as I have done!

HERMIONE

What do I care, sir, for his hate or love?
Go and call Greece to arms against a rebel;
Exact from him the price of his revolt,
And let Epirus be a second Troy.
Go. Now will you still tell me that I love him?

ORESTES

Do more, my lady: come with me yourself.
Will you stay here to be a hostage? Come,
And with your presence fire the hearts of all.
Let's fight our common enemy together.

HERMIONE

570 But if, when I'd gone, he should marry Andromache?

ORESTES

Ah, yes!

HERMIONE

                    Just think how shameful it would be
For us if he should take a Trojan wife!

ORESTES

And you say you hate him? Why not confess the truth?
We cannot keep the fires of love concealed:
Our voice, our eyes, our silence all betray us;

And badly smothered fires burn brighter still.

HERMIONE

My lord, I see that your own prejudice
Coats all my words with a destructive poison,
Looks for some twisted motive in my reasons,
And takes my hatred for a proof of love.   580
And so I must explain; then you will act.
You know my duty brought me to Epirus;
My duty keeps me here until my father
Or Pyrrhus bids me leave. Speak for my father:
Tell Pyrrhus that an enemy to Greece
Can never be my father's son-in-law;
Force him to choose the Trojan boy or me.
He must keep one, and let the other go:
Send me away, or let you have the boy.
Farewell. If Pyrrhus consents, I'll leave with you.   590

    Exit HERMIONE *with* CLEONE.   [II.iii]

ORESTES (*alone*)

Yes, yes, you'll come with me, no doubt of that;
I can assure you now, that's what he'll say.
I have no fear that Pyrrhus will detain you:
His sweet Andromache is all he sees;
All else offends his gaze; some pretext may
Be all he needs to free himself of you.
We only have to speak; it's done! What joy
To steal away with such a lovely prey!
Epirus, preserve what's left of Troy and Hector;
Hold fast his son, his widow, whom you will: 600
Suffice it that Hermione comes home
And never sees your shores or king again.
Good fortune brings him here: I'll speak to him.
Love, blind him to the prize that could be his!

    Enter PYRRHUS *with* PHOENIX.   [II.iv]

PYRRHUS

Sir, I was seeking you. I must confess,
My irritation caused me to resist
Your arguments; and, since I parted from you,
I've realized how strong and just they are.

I've seen, like you, that I was combating
610   Greece, and my father, and, indeed, myself;
That I was restoring Troy, and undermining
All that Achilles, all that I, had done.
The anger of the Greeks is justified:
Your victim, sir, will be surrendered to you.

ORESTES

My lord, a wise and harsh resolve: to purchase
Peace with the blood of a luckless innocent.

PYRRHUS

Yes, but I mean to make it more secure:
Hermione's the pledge of lasting peace;
I'll marry her. That happy sight, it seems,
620   Awaited only you to witness it.
You stand for all the Greeks and for her father,
Whose brother Agamemnon lives in you.
Go, then, and tell her that I look for peace
By taking her tomorrow from your hand.

ORESTES

Ah, gods!

[II.v]   *Exit* ORESTES.

PYRRHUS

          Well, Phoenix, am I ruled by love?
Do your eyes still refuse to recognize me?

PHOENIX

I know you now: this just severity
Restores you to the Greeks and to yourself;
Not now the plaything of a slavish passion,
630   But Pyrrhus, son and rival of Achilles,
Bound once again to honour's glorious cause,
Victorious over Troy a second time.

PYRRHUS

Say rather that my triumph starts today:
I have not relished victory till now.
My heart, as proud now as it was debased,
In conquering love sees countless foes destroyed.
Think, Phoenix, of the anguish I'm escaping,

The train of evils love draws in its wake:
Friends, duties sacrificed, the dangers – for
One look I would have wiped them from my mind.   640
The Greeks had mustered to destroy a rebel:
It pleased me to be facing death for her!

PHOENIX

My lord, I bless her stubbornness, that's brought
You to your—

PYRRHUS
                          You saw how she treated me.
I thought that fear for her cherished son would fling her
Defenceless into my protective arms.
I went to see how cuddling him had moved her,
And found no more than tears and frenzied shrieks.
Bitter and shrill with anguish, frantic, wild,
Again and again she cried out Hector's name.   650
My promises to shield the child were futile:
'It's Hector,' she kept saying, and kissed him hard;
'These are his eyes, his lips, his courage too;
It's he, it's you, dear husband, in my arms.'
What is she thinking of? Does she suppose
Her son shall live to feed her love for Hector?

PHOENIX

No doubt that's all the thanks you'd get from her.
Forget her.

PYRRHUS
                        Vain creature, I can read her mind.
She thinks she's irresistible, that I'll
Soon cool, and grovel at her feet again.   660
I'd see her plead at my feet and I'd feel nothing.
She's Hector's widow, I'm Achilles' son:
We two are kept apart by too much hate.

PHOENIX

Then talk to me of something else but her!
Go to Hermione; make up to her,
And at her feet forget your angry mood.
Urge her to marry you; woo her yourself;

Don't leave it to Orestes to persuade her:
He's much too fond of her.

PYRRHUS

                                    If I marry her,
670   Andromache will be jealous, don't you think?

PHOENIX

What! Are you still obsessed by Andromache?
Gods! Why does it matter what she feels? Are you
Bewitched, that against your will she binds you to her?

PYRRHUS

No, I did not say all I should have said;
I gave her only an inkling of my rage;
She's no idea what an enemy
She's made of me. I'll go back. Face to face,
I want to give full rein to my revulsion.
Come, Phoenix, and see me humble that proud beauty.
680   Come.

PHOENIX

                Go, sir, and prostrate yourself before her;
Go, swear undying love for her, and so
Give her the chance to spurn you yet again.

PYRRHUS

I see: you think I'm ready to forgive her,
That my heart longs to be at peace with her.

PHOENIX

You love her: that's enough.

PYRRHUS

                                    I love her? When
The more I cosset her, the more she loathes me?
She has no parents, friends or hope save me;
I can destroy her son, perhaps I should;
An outcast, no, a slave, here in Epirus,
690   I offer her her son, my soul, my throne:
And in her false heart she won't offer me
A worthier place than that of her tormentor?
No, no, I've sworn it, I'll have my revenge;
Her hatred of me shall be justified.
I'll cease to shield her son. What tears will flow!

How she'll revile me in her misery!
The sight she's going to have to face today!
She won't survive it; and I'll be the cause:
As if I'd plunged a sword into her breast!

PHOENIX

Then why must you tell her what you plan to do?   700
Is it not your weakness that is driving you?

PYRRHUS

I know what you're thinking. Indulge my lingering
    fondness.
You've no faith that my anger will prevail?
It's only the final spark of dying love.
Well, Phoenix, I'll do what you think best. The Greeks
Must have her son? Hermione must be seen?

PHOENIX

Yes: see her, sir; swear that in word and deed
You will be true—

PYRRHUS

          Yes, yes, I have agreed.

ACT III

ORESTES, PYLADES   [III.i]

PYLADES

Control this fit of fury, I implore you.
This is not you; I hardly recognize you;   710
Let—

ORESTES

     No: the time for your advice is past.
I'm tired of hearing reason, Pylades.
It's dragging out my tortured life too long.
I'll snatch her away, or die in the attempt.
The plan is laid; I'm going through with it.
It's what I want.

PYLADES

        All right: she must be seized.
We'll do it. But just remember where you are.

What will they think if you behave like this?
Don't give yourself away; restrain yourself;
720 Command your eyes to keep the secret. Here
The guards, the Court, the air you breathe, are ruled
By Pyrrhus; and by Hermione herself.
From her at all costs you must hide your anger.
Gods! Why were you seeking her in such a state?

ORESTES

What can I say? I was beside myself.
Rage swept me on; perhaps I meant to threaten
The pair of them, Hermione and Pyrrhus.

PYLADES

And what would your blind fury have achieved?

ORESTES

Well, tell me, who would not be shattered by
730 The blow that's almost driven me insane?
He'll marry Hermione, he says, tomorrow;
To honour me he'll take her from my hand.
Ah! May this hand in his barbaric blood—

PYLADES

You blame him for this twist of fate, my lord,
But what he's doing may be tormenting him:
Perhaps he's to be pitied, just like you.

ORESTES

No, no; I know him; my despair delights him:
Before he knew I loved her, he ignored her;
Her beauty had not touched him until then.
740 He's taking her to spite me, that's his motive.
Ah, gods! It was all set: Hermione
Was won and would have gone from him for ever;
Half loving and half hating him, her heart
Was mine if he refused. Her eyes were opening,
Pylades; she was listening, speaking to me;
She felt for me. One word was all it needed.

PYLADES

You think so?

ORESTES

              What? She blazed with rage at his
Disdain of—

PYLADES

           He was never loved so much.
If Pyrrhus had let you have her, do you think
She'd not have found some pretext to hold back?   750
Will you believe me? Abandon your delusions.
Instead of seizing her, cut loose from her.
What? Saddle yourself with a fury who'll detest
You all your life and never cease regretting
A marriage that had been so nearly hers,
Who'll—

ORESTES

          That's precisely why I'm going to seize her.
The world would smile on her, and for my part
Should I take with me only futile rage?
Again try to forget her, far away?
No, no: I'll make her share my suffering.   760
To grieve alone's too much. I'm tired of pity.
It's her turn now to be afraid of me;
I want to see those cold eyes filled with tears,
And hear her call me what I've long called her.

PYLADES

So that will be the outcome of your mission:
Orestes, the abductor.

ORESTES

            What of that?
When the Greeks rejoiced that I'd secured their vengeance,
Would her joy be diminished by my tears?
What would it mean to be admired in Greece,
If here I had become a laughing-stock?   770
Do you blame me?

             But, to be quite frank with you,
My innocence begins to weigh me down.
Some unjust power always seems to let
The wicked thrive, and hunt down innocence.
My whole life has been wrecked by undeserved
Misfortunes which shame the justice of the gods.
So let me earn their wrath, deserve their hate,
At least enjoy the sins I'm punished for.
  But, Pylades, why should you also bear

780   A penance that is meant for me alone?
       My friendship has oppressed you for too long:
       I'm luckless, guilty, steer well clear of me.
       Your pity, my dear friend, is your undoing.
       Leave me the peril, since the prize is mine.
       Take home to Greece the child that Pyrrhus yields.
       Away.

PYLADES
                Come, sir, let's seize Hermione.
       In facing danger brave hearts prove their worth.
       What cannot friendship do inspired by love?
       Come, let's enthuse the Greeks in your command;
790   Our ships are standing by, the wind invites us.
       I know the hidden windings of this palace:
       You see the waves beat up against its walls;
       Tonight with ease we'll take your captive by
       A secret passage straight aboard your ship.

ORESTES
       My dear friend, I abuse your loyalty,
       But bear with the weakness in me that you pity;
       Bear with a man who's losing all he loves,
       Who's hated by the world, and hates himself.
       If in my turn a happier fate allowed me—

PYLADES
800   Disguise your feelings, sir, that's all I ask.
       Make sure your plan is not revealed too soon.
       Till then, forget Hermione's indifference;
       Forget your love— But come away: she's here.

ORESTES
       Go. Play your part in this, and I'll play mine.

[III.ii]   *Exit* PYLADES. *Enter* HERMIONE *with* CLEONE.

ORESTES (*continues*)
       So you have Pyrrhus, thanks to me, my lady:
       I spoke to him, and now you're to be married.

HERMIONE
       It seems so; and I've been assured that your
       Sole aim in seeking me was to prepare me.

ORESTES

And can you trust him when he says he loves you?

HERMIONE

Indeed, who would have thought he was still true?   810
That he would take so long to show his feelings?
That he'd come back to me just when I planned
To leave him? I suspect, like you, that he
Fears Greece, that interest, not love, impels him,
That your devotion was more genuine.

ORESTES

No, now I'm sure he loves you. Can your beauty
Fail to obtain for you what you desire?
And you had no desire that he should hate you.

HERMIONE

What choice have I? My hand was promised. Can
I steal from him what was not mine to give?   820
Love does not guide the fate of a princess:
The honour of obeying is our lot.
Yet I was going to leave: you saw how far
For you I was prepared to shirk my duty.

ORESTES

Unfeeling still! You knew that . . . But, my lady,
Our hearts are ours to do with as we will.
Yours was still yours to give. I hoped; but I can't say
You stole it back from me to give away.
It's not you I accuse so much as Fortune.
Why bore you then with wearisome complaint?   830
It is your duty, I confess; and mine
Is not to inflict my sorrow on your joy.

    Exit ORESTES.   [III.iii]

HERMIONE

Did you expect so much restraint, Cleone?

CLEONE

The grief that's silent bodes the greater ill.
I pity him, the source of his own pain;
The blow that crushed him he himself provoked.
Think what it was that sparked your sudden wedding:
He spoke to Pyrrhus, and Pyrrhus proposed at once.

HERMIONE

You think that Pyrrhus is afraid? Of what?

840   Of the Greeks, who spent ten years in flight from Hector?

Who, in their terror when they'd lost Achilles,

Time and again crept home in burning ships?

Who, without him, Achilles' son, would still

Be claiming Helen from a Troy unpunished?

No, no, Cleone: Pyrrhus is his own man.

If he is marrying me, then he must love me.

But let Orestes blame me for his sorrows;

Are we to talk of nothing but his tears?

Pyrrhus is mine again. Ah, dear Cleone,

850   Can you conceive the happiness I feel?

Do you know what kind of man he is? Have you

Heard tell of his great deeds? But who could count them?

A fearless, conquering hero, bewitching, true

Now to his word, his honour quite untarnished.

Think—

CLEONE

                     Hide your joy: Andromache in tears

No doubt comes to you as a supplicant.

HERMIONE

Gods! May I not savour my delight? Let's go.

What should I say to her?

[III.iv]   *Enter* ANDROMACHE *with* CEPHISA.

ANDROMACHE

                                    My lady, stay.

Is it not sweet enough to you, the sight

860   Of Hector's widow weeping at your feet?

I do not come with jealous tears to claim

A heart that's fallen captive to your beauty;

The only heart I've wished to call my own

I saw stabbed by a cruel hand in war.

My love was fired by Hector long ago;

Now it lies buried with him in the tomb.

But yet I have a son. One day you'll know,

My lady, how much we mothers love a son;

But you will never know, I hope indeed,

870   The mortal sorrow that we feel for him

When of the many blessings we enjoyed
He's all that's left, and we're to lose him too.
Ah, when the Trojans, wearied by ten years
Of suffering, turned in fury on your mother,
I made my Hector shield her from their rage.*
As I on him, you can prevail on Pyrrhus.
Hector is dead: why fear his helpless child?
On some deserted island let me hide him;
Your surety is his mother's watchfulness;
With me my son will only learn to weep.   880

HERMIONE

My lady, I understand your grief; but when
My father speaks, stern duty ties my tongue.
It's he, through Pyrrhus, who condemns the child.
Who can sway Pyrrhus more readily than you?
For long enough you ruled his heart. Appeal
To him: what he decides I shall approve.

    Exit HERMIONE *with* CLEONE.   [III.v]

ANDROMACHE

With what cold scorn she spurned my supplication!

CEPHISA

I'd follow her advice and go to Pyrrhus.
With one look you'd put paid to her and Greece.
But here he is.

    Enter PYRRHUS *with* PHOENIX.   [III.vi]

PYRRHUS (*to* PHOENIX)

         So where's Hermione?   890
Did you not tell me I should find her here?

PHOENIX

I thought so.

ANDROMACHE (*to* CEPHISA)

        See the power of my looks!

PYRRHUS

Phoenix, what did she say?

ANDROMACHE

           Ah! There's no hope.

PHOENIX

Come, sir, let's go and find Hermione.

CEPHISA

Why are you waiting? Break this stubborn silence.

ANDROMACHE

He's promised to yield my son.

CEPHISA

                                        He has not done it.

ANDROMACHE

No, no, my tears are vain. My son will die.

PYRRHUS

Will she not deign at least to look at me?
What pride!

ANDROMACHE

                    I only make him angry. Come.

PYRRHUS (*loudly, forcing* ANDROMACHE *to speak*)

900   Fetch Hector's son. I'll give him to the Greeks.

ANDROMACHE

No, don't, my lord! How can you do it? If
You give the son, then give the mother too!
You swore you loved me so devotedly!
Gods! Can I not now at least arouse your pity?
Have you condemned me with no hope of pardon?

PYRRHUS

I've given my word, as Phoenix will confirm.

ANDROMACHE

And you were going to brave such dangers for me.

PYRRHUS

Then I was blind: my eyes are open now.
At your desire he could have been reprieved;
910   You did not even ask that he be saved.
It's too late now.

ANDROMACHE

                        My lord, you understood
The silent pleas I feared to see rejected.
Forgive the lustre of my heritage
This lingering pride that finds it hard to beg.
You know that, but for you, Andromache
Would never have clasped the knee of any master.*

PYRRHUS

No, no, you loathe me; deep down in your soul

You fear to be indebted to my love.
Even the son you cherish so, if I
Had been his saviour, you'd have loved him less.   920
Scorn and abhorrence are what you feel for me;
You hate me more than all the Greeks together.
Well, bask at your leisure in such noble wrath.
Come, Phoenix.

ANDROMACHE
                    Let's go now to my husband's tomb.

CEPHISA
  My lady—

ANDROMACHE
                    What more's to say? Does he, the cause
Of all my sorrows, need to hear them told?
  My lord, see what you have reduced me to.
I've seen my father killed, our walls ablaze;
I've seen the slaughter of my whole family,
My husband dragged still bleeding through the dust,   930
Only my son left with me, spared for chains.
But for a son one can endure: I've lived,
A slave. And more: I've sometimes thanked my fate
That I was exiled here, and not elsewhere,
That, since my royal son must kneel, in his
Misfortune he was blessed to kneel to you.
I thought his prison might become a haven.
When Priam begged, Achilles humoured him;*
His son, I hoped, would show more kindness still.
  Dear Hector, pardon my simplicity!   940
I thought your enemy could do no wrong;
That he could not fail to be generous.
Ah! If he'd only left us by the tomb
I'd raised to house your ashes, there to end
His hatred and our grief, not parting us
From those remains of precious memory!

PYRRHUS
  Wait for me, Phoenix.
      Exit PHOENIX.   [III.vii]

PYRRHUS (*continues*)
                    My lady, do not go.

The son you weep for may yet live. Oh, yes,
In moving you to tears I know I'm only
950   Giving you weapons to deploy against me.
I thought I came here with a harder heart.
My lady, look at me at least, and see
If in my eyes you find a ruthless judge,
An enemy who seeks to earn your hate.
You're forcing me to hurt you: why?
For your son's sake, let's cease to fight each other.
Save him: it's I now who am asking you.
Must I with sobs and sighs beg for his life?
Must I kneel down and clasp your knees for him?
960   For the last time I ask: save him, save us.
I know I'm breaking oaths of steel for you
And kindling fires of hatred for myself.
I'm spurning Hermione, and on her head
Heaping not glory but eternal shame;
I'm leading you to the altar decked for her,
And placing on you the diadem she should wear.
But this is my last offer: weigh it well.
I say: your son shall die, or you shall reign.
For twelve months scorned, my desperate heart can bear
970   No longer not to know its destiny.
I've feared and groaned and threatened for too long.
It's death to lose you, but to wait is death.
Think on it: I shall come and take you to
The temple where your son will be; and there,
Meek lamb or savage tiger, I shall crown you,
Or have him put to death before your eyes.

[III.viii]   *Exit* PYRRHUS.

CEPHISA
       I told you that, despite the threat from Greece,
       You still would be the mistress of your fate.

ANDROMACHE
       Ah, see where your advice has led! I've no
980   Choice now but to condemn my child to death.

CEPHISA
       So loyal to your husband? Think, my lady:

Excessive virtue may be wickedness.
Hector himself would urge you to give way.

CEPHISA

What! After him, let Pyrrhus take his place?

CEPHISA

His son wants that, torn from you by the Greeks.
And do you think his shade would feel dishonoured?
That he would scoff at a victorious king
Who gives you your ancestral rank again,
Tramples on your vindictive conquerors,
Forgets that he's the son of great Achilles   990
And undoes all his father's mighty deeds?

ANDROMACHE

If he thinks not of them, must I forget?
My Hector's body, shorn of funeral rites,
And dragged in shame around our city walls?*
Must I forget his father at my feet,
Clutching the altar spattered with his blood?
Remember, Cephisa, remember that cruel night
That for a whole race meant eternal night;
Remember Pyrrhus coming, eyes ablaze,
Lit by the glare of our burning palaces,   1000
Hacking his way across my brothers' bodies,
Dripping with blood and spurring on the slaughter;
Remember the victors' cries, the cries of death,
By slashing sword, by suffocating fire;
See me in all this horror, dazed and lost.
That is how Pyrrhus first appeared to me;
Those are the deeds which earned him his renown;
And that's the man whom you would have me marry.
No, I will not condone his cruelty:
We'll be his final victims if we must.   1010
I will not bind my bitterness to him.

CEPHISA

Well then! Let's go and see your son die. Only
Your presence is— My lady! Why, you're trembling!

ANDROMACHE

Ah, with what memories you pierce my heart!

Cephisa, shall I see him also die,
My only joy, the image of my Hector,
The son he left me as a pledge of love!
   On that day, I remember, when his valour
Drove him to seek Achilles, and his death,
1020   He called his son and took him in his arms:
'Dear wife,' he said, and wiped away my tears,
'I do not know what Fate has planned for me.
To pledge my love I leave to you my son:
If I should die, let him find me in you.
If you hold dear the memory of our marriage,
Give to my son the love you've given me.'
And I'm to see such precious blood be shed!
And perish with him all his ancestors!
   Barbarous king, for my fault must he pay?
1030   If I can't be your wife, is he to blame?
Has he laid at your door his loved ones' death?
Has he complained of wrongs he does not feel?
   And yet, my son, you die unless I halt
The cruel sword he holds above your head.
When I can stop him, shall I let him strike?
No, no, you shall not die; it must not be.
I'll go to Pyrrhus. No, my dear Cephisa,
You go to him.

CEPHISA
              What shall I say, my lady?

ANDROMACHE
Tell him I love my son so much that I . . .
1040   Do you think he really means to let him die?
Can love so far inflame his barbarousness?

CEPHISA
My lady, he'll soon come raging here again.

ANDROMACHE
Well then . . . Assure him of . . .

CEPHISA
                Of what? Your love?

ANDROMACHE
Ah! Is it still mine to promise it again?

O husband's ashes! Trojans! O my father!
My son, how dearly I must pay to save you!
Come.
CEPHISA
            Where to? What have you decided? Where?
ANDROMACHE
To my husband's tomb. I shall consult him there.

ACT IV

ANDROMACHE, CEPHISA   [IV.i]

CEPHISA
I'm sure of it, my lady: it's your husband.
Hector has worked this miracle in you!   1050
He wants to see Troy rise again by means
Of that blessed child he urges you to save.
Pyrrhus has promised it: you heard him now.
One word from you and he'll restore your son.
He worships you! Your love means more to him
Than father, sceptre, allies, everything!
He and his people are at your command.
Is this the conqueror you hated so?
Fired now by noble anger with the Greeks,
He fears as much as you for your son's life.   1060
He's sent his guards to shield him from their fury,
Leaving himself exposed to keep him safe.
But go now to the temple: you've given your word.
ANDROMACHE
I'll go; but first I want to see my son.
CEPHISA
My lady, why now? In future you will be
At liberty to see him when you please.
Soon you can spoil him to your heart's content,
Hug him and kiss him and play with him all day.
What joy to raise a son, no longer as
A slave to serve his master, but to see   1070
Reborn in him so many noble kings!

ANDROMACHE
   Cephisa, I'm going to see him for the last time.

CEPHISA
   What do you mean? O gods!

ANDROMACHE
                        My dear Cephisa,
From you I cannot hide what's in my heart:
In my distress you've shown me true devotion.
But I felt sure you understood me better.
You thought I could betray my husband, who
Believes that he still lives and breathes in me?
That I could wake the sorrows of the dead
1080   And trouble their peace to secure my own?
Is that the love I promised to his ashes?
And yet I had to save his son. Now Pyrrhus,
By marrying me, becomes his sworn protector.
That's all I need: I trust him. I know Pyrrhus:
He's violent, yes, but he's a man of honour,
And he'll do more than he has promised me.
I trust too that being hated by the Greeks
Will win for Hector's son a second father.
And so, since I must make the sacrifice,
1090   I'll pledge myself to Pyrrhus while I live,
And, by accepting his most holy vows,
I'll bind him to my son with deathless ties.
Then, harming no one else, I shall at once
Cut short my faithless life, and so restore
My honour, while discharging what I owe
To Pyrrhus, my son, my husband, and myself.
This innocent ploy is what my love dictates:
It's what my husband orders me to do.
Alone I shall join Hector and my forebears.
1100   Cephisa, you must close my eyes for me.

CEPHISA
   Ah! Don't expect that I shall live beyond—

ANDROMACHE
   No, no, Cephisa: you must stay behind.
To your care I entrust my only treasure.
You lived for me: live now for Hector's son.

The hope of Troy will rest with you alone;
Think of the kings who will depend on you.
  Keep watch on Pyrrhus: make him keep his word.
If need be, you may speak to him of me.
Make him respect the marriage I'm enduring:
Tell him that I was his before I died;   1110
That he must not be bitter; that my leaving
My son with him shows how much I respect him.
  Acquaint my son with the heroes of his race;
Encourage him to follow in their wake;
Tell him the deeds that blazon forth their names;
Not what they were, but what they did. Each day
Speak of his father's virtues; sometimes too
Tell him about his mother. But, Cephisa,
Let him not harbour any thought of vengeance:
We leave him with a master he must please.   1120
Let him not glory in his ancestors:
He's Hector's blood, but all that remains of it;
Because of that I sacrifice today
At once my life, my hatred, and my love.

CEPHISA
  My lady!

ANDROMACHE
              Do not follow me unless
You're sure your troubled heart can curb your tears.
Someone is coming. Dry your eyes, Cephisa:
Remember that you're entrusted with my fate.
Hermione. Let's escape her fury: come.

  Exit ANDROMACHE *with* CEPHISA. *Enter* HERMIONE
  with CLEONE.   [IV.ii]

CLEONE
  But truly I'm astonished by your silence.   1130
My lady, you say nothing! Are you not
Distressed at being shown such cold contempt?
Can you submit to such an outrage, you,
Who shuddered at the name Andromache?
Who suffered all the anguish of despair
If Pyrrhus honoured her with but a look?
He's marrying her; he'll give her, with his crown,

The vows of love you've just received yourself;
Yet in such agony your lips are sealed,
1140　　Disdaining to protest or to complain?
My lady, such deadly calm fills me with fear:
Better—

HERMIONE
　　　　　　　　Orestes: have you sent for him?

CLEONE
He's coming, my lady: and you'll see that he
Was only too prepared to kneel to you,
Willing to serve you still without reward.
You need not doubt your power over him.
He's here.

[IV.iii]　　　*Enter* ORESTES.

ORESTES
　　　　　　Can it be true, my lady, that
This time I come to you at your command?
Have I been falsely led to raise my hopes,
1150　　Or have you really said you wish to see me?
Dare I believe that you've at last relented,
And want—

HERMIONE
　　　　　　I want to know, sir, if you love me.

ORESTES
If I love you? O gods! The vows I've sworn
And broken, my fleeing, returning, adoring, reviling,
Despairing, my eyes forever bathed in tears;
If all that fails, how can I prove my love?

HERMIONE
Avenge me, and I will believe you love me.

ORESTES
So be it: we'll rouse the Greeks to war again.
With my arm and your name we'll play our parts:
1160　　You the new Helen, I the Agamemnon;
We'll wreak on this land what was wreaked at Troy
And be remembered as our fathers are.
Let's go; I'm ready.

HERMIONE
　　　　　　　No, my lord, we'll stay:

I won't leave bearing such insulting wounds.
What! Crown my enemies' insolence by waiting
So far away for a delayed revenge!
Rely upon the fortunes of a war,
Which might fail to avenge me after all!
I'll leave Epirus weeping when I go.
If you'll avenge me, you must do it now.   1170
As well refuse me as propose delay.
Race to the temple. You must kill . . .

ORESTES

                                    Who?

HERMIONE

                                              Pyrrhus.

ORESTES

Pyrrhus?

HERMIONE

            What's this? Your fury falters? Ah!
Act quickly, lest I call you back. Don't talk
Of rights that I want to forget. It's not
For you to find excuses for him.

ORESTES

                                    I?

Excuse him? All your favours to him make
His baseness all the more repulsive to me.
Let's seek revenge, but not like this. Let's be
His enemies, but not his murderers: 1180
Destroy him, but by just conquest. What! Am I
To take the Greeks his head as his reply?
To come here as their envoy, and discharge
My mission by assassinating him?
By all the gods, let Greece pass judgement on him,
And, branded as a traitor, let him die.
Remember, he's a king, that crowned heads are—

HERMIONE

It's not enough for you that I've condemned him?
It's not enough for you that my stained honour
Demands a victim meant for me alone?   1190
That I'm the prize for slaughtering a tyrant?
That I hate him; and, sir, that once I loved him?

I make no secret of it: I was his,
True to my heart or to my father's will,
No matter which; but take due note of it.
Despite the shame of my deluded hopes,
Despite my just revulsion at his crime,
While he still lives, beware lest I forgive him.
Don't trust my fitful anger: I may love him
1200   Tomorrow if he does not die today.

ORESTES

Then he must die before he is reprieved;
I must— But, even so, what can I do?
How can I give you vengeance with such speed?
Where is my opportunity to strike?
I've scarcely set foot in Epirus, and
You tell me I must overthrow the State,
That I must kill the King, and for the task
You give me just one day, an hour, an instant;
Before his people I must cut him down!
1210   Let me but choose the altar for my victim,
And I won't flinch; I only ask for time
To find the place where I may sacrifice him.
Tonight I'm yours, I'll strike at him tonight.

HERMIONE

But he's to marry Andromache today.
The throne is set already in the temple,
My shame's confirmed, his treachery fulfilled.
And why delay? He's offering you his head:
He's going defenceless to this festival;
He's posted all his guards round Hector's son;
1220   He's bared himself to him who would avenge me.
If he neglects himself, are you to nurse him?
Marshal with your Greeks those who came with me;
Stir up your comrades; mine will follow you.
He's played me false, tricked you, and scorns us all;
Our men all want his blood as much as I.
Marry a Trojan? Let the traitor die.
Rouse them; he can't escape your sword; or, rather,

All you need do is let them strike him down.
Lead their fine fury, or follow in its wake,
And come back drenched in his perfidious blood.   1230
Go: when the deed is done, my heart is yours.

ORESTES
But just consider—

HERMIONE
                                    Ah! No more of that!
So much cold reasoning insults my rage.
I've shown you how to win my favour and
Achieve your heart's desire, but you're still bent
On whining and deserving no reward.
Get out of here with your so-called devotion;
Leave me to manage my revenge myself.
I blush to think how weakly I've indulged you;
This is one snub too many for one day.   1240
I'll go alone to their wedding in the temple,
Where you daren't go to prove you merit me.
I'll draw close to my hated perjurer,
I'll stab the heart I've failed to touch, and then
With bloodstained hand I'll stab my own, and so
Against his will unite our destinies.
Faithless although he is, to me it will
Be sweeter to die with him than live with you.

ORESTES
No, I'll deprive you of that morbid joy,
My lady: no hand but mine shall end his life.   1250
The man who's wronged you I shall sacrifice,
And you'll reward my service, if you wish.

HERMIONE
Go now. Entrust your fate to me. Be sure
Your ships are standing by for our escape.
        Exit ORESTES.   [IV.iv]

CLEONE
You'll die, my lady: think—

HERMIONE
                                    No matter: all

I'm thinking is that I'll have my revenge.
For all his promises I'm still not sure
I should not do myself what must be done.
Pyrrhus to me seems guiltier than to him:
1260   My stabs would be more meaningful than his.
What pleasure to avenge my wrong myself,
To see my arm bathed in his perjured blood,
And, to increase my pleasure and his pain,
To hide that woman from his dying eyes!
    At least Orestes must make sure he dies
Aware that he's my victim. Go, Cleone;
Follow Orestes: Pyrrhus must understand
He's sacrificed, not to the gods, but me.
Cleone, run: my vengeance fails unless
1270   He dies knowing that I am killing him.

CLEONE

I will obey you. But what's this? O gods!
Who'd have believed it, my lady? It's the King.

HERMIONE

Ah! Find Orestes; tell him, dear Cleone,
He must not act without consulting me!

[IV.v]   *Enter* PYRRHUS *with* PHOENIX.

PYRRHUS

You weren't expecting me, my lady, and
I see that I'm intruding. I have not
Come armed with some unworthy trumped-up tale
To whitewash my wrongdoing. In my heart
I stand condemned, and I could not sustain
1280   An argument in which I had no faith.
I'm marrying a Trojan. Yes; I know
I promised you the vows I'll make to her.
Another man might say to you: at Troy
Our fathers bound us in our absence, that,
Without referral to my choice or yours,
We were committed to a loveless match.
But it's enough for me that I agreed.
My heart was promised to you by my envoys;
Far from demurring, I confirmed their word.

With them you came to join me in Epirus;   1290
And, though another's beauty had meanwhile
Forestalled the power of yours to conquer me,
I did not let that new love change my course:
My firm resolve was to be true to you;
I welcomed you as my queen; and till today
I thought my vows could overcome my love.
But this love is too strong; unhappily,
Andromache, who hates me, has my heart.
Dragged by each other, we're racing to the altar
To swear, despite ourselves, undying love.   1300
So now discharge your fury on a turncoat
Who grieves to be one, yet desires it too.
I've no wish to constrain your righteous anger:
It may relieve me just as much as you.
Call me the names that perjurers deserve:
Your silence is what I fear, not your abuse;
The secret testimony of my heart
Will curse me more, the less you say to me.

HERMIONE

My lord, I'm glad your frank confession shows
That you've at least passed judgement on yourself;   1310
That, as you chose to cut a sacred knot,
You knew yourself to be despicable.
Indeed, why should a conqueror obey
The servile law of keeping to his word?
No, no, you relish your perfidiousness,
And you came here to flaunt it in my face.
What? Undeterred by duty or sworn oath,
To pay court to a Greek and love a Trojan?
To leave me, win me back, and then reject
Me, Helen's daughter, and take Hector's widow?   1320
To crown by turns the slave and the princess;
Burn Troy for Greece, spurn Greece for Hector's son?
All that denotes a man who rules himself,
A hero who's no captive to his word.
Perhaps it is to please your bride you bask
In the sweet names of perjuror and traitor.

You came to see how pale I looked, and then
To mock my sorrow lying in her arms.
You'd like to see me weep behind her chariot.*
1330   But for one day that would be too much joy.
And surely you don't need another triumph:
Isn't your record glorious enough?
Hector's old valiant father battered down
Beside his loved ones killed before his eyes,
While, thrusting deep inside his breast, you strove
To find the dregs of blood that age had chilled;
Troy set ablaze and plunged in streams of blood;
Polyxena's throat slit by your hand in front
Of all the Greeks who watched you in disgust:
1340   Who could resist heroic feats like those?

PYRRHUS

My lady, I'm too well aware that avenging
Helen provoked me to excessive rage.
I could begrudge you all the blood I shed;
But I believe the past should be forgotten.
Thank Heaven, I learn from your indifference
That my blessed love hurts no one after all.
Instead of torturing myself I should
Have looked more closely into both our hearts.
My guilty feelings were offensive to you:
1350   To think oneself unfaithful, one must believe
One's loved. But I was not. While fearing to
Betray you, I may be doing you a service.
Our hearts had not been mutually entwined:
My duty guided me, you bowed to yours.
But it was not required of you to love me.

HERMIONE

It wasn't love I felt? What was it, then?*
For you I spurned the hand of all our princes;
I came here to your country to be with you;
I'm with you still, unfaithful though you are,
1360   And though my weakness fills my Greeks with shame.
I asked them to conceal the wrong I've suffered:
I nursed the hope that you'd repent; I thought

That one day duty would prevail, and you'd
Bring back to me a heart that's rightly mine.
I loved you faithless: what if you'd been true?
And even at this moment, when your lips
With such calm cruelty pronounce my death,
I wonder if I do not love you still.

    But, sir, if it must be, if angry Heaven
Grants to another the honour of your love,   1370
Then have your wedding, I consent; but spare
My eyes at least from witnessing the sight.
It may be we shall never meet again;
Wait just one day; tomorrow you'll be free . . .
You make no answer? Viper, I can see
You count the moments that you spend with me.
You're itching to be with your Trojan slave,
And chafe at any other company.
Your heart's with her, your eyes are seeking her.
Well, I won't keep you longer; you can go.   1380
Swear to give her the love you've sworn to me;
Profane the sacred power of the gods:
They will not have forgotten, the just gods,
That those same vows had bound you first to me.
Desert me; race to the altar; but beware:
There you may find that I am with you still.

    Exit HERMIONE *with* CLEONE.   [IV.vi]

PHOENIX
My lord, you heard her: don't ignore the threat
Of a frantic woman scorned who seeks revenge.
She has no lack of strong supporters here:
The grievance of the Greeks is linked with hers.   1390
Orestes loves her; if she can be won—

PYRRHUS
Andromache is waiting. Guard her son.

ACT V

HERMIONE

Where am I? What have I done? What should I do?
Why am I shaking? Why do I ache with grief?
Why am I wandering, restless, aimless? Ah!
Not knowing if it's love or hate I feel?
So hard he was as he sent me away!
No pity, not even feigned regret! Did he
For a single moment feel compassion? Could
1400 I rouse in him a tincture of remorse?
Cold when I sighed, calm when I wept, did he
Seem even conscious that he'd caused my tears?
And still I pity him! And, cruelly,
My shameless heart still pleads that he be spared.
I quake to think what threatens him: already,
About to reap my vengeance, I forgive him!
      No, let the sentence of my anger stand:
Let him be killed! I've no part in his life;
He flaunts his perfidy and mocks my rage;
1410 He thinks this tempest will dissolve in tears;
He thinks that I'm so weak and wavering,
My arm will stop my other hand from striking.
My past indulgence reassures him now.
      But now it's not of me the traitor's thinking:
Triumphant in the temple, he's not brooding
On whether I desire his life or death;
That grim perplexity he leaves to me.
No, no, be firm and let Orestes act.
Death to him, since he courted death, since he
1420 Himself drove me to want to see him dead.
      I want him dead? He dies at my command?
The outcome of my love will be his death?
The prince whose deeds I used to hear retold
In days gone by with so much fond delight,
To whom I'd even bound myself in secret

Before our fatal marriage was arranged:
Have I then crossed so many lands and seas
And only come so far to plot his death,
To kill him? Ah! Before he dies— Cleone!

Enter CLEONE. [V.ii]

HERMIONE (*continues*)

What have I done? What have you come to tell me? 1430
What of Pyrrhus?

CLEONE

He's at the peak of bliss,
The proudest man alive, the most in love.
I saw him go towards the wedding-temple,
A conqueror conducting his new conquest,
His eyes alight with hope and happiness,
Drunk with the joy of looking at his bride.
Andromache, amid the cheering throng,
Takes to the altar memories of Troy;
Unable now to love or hate, she moves
In joyless, mute obedience to her fate. 1440

HERMIONE

And he? He's let the outrage run its course?
But did you closely watch his face, Cleone?
Was his delight untroubled and serene?
Did he not glance at all towards the palace?
Did you make sure that he could see you, and,
When he caught sight of you, did he appear
Guilty, embarrassed and ashamed, or did
He to the last maintain his arrogance?

CLEONE

My lady, he sees nothing: he's oblivious
Of you, of his own safety, and his honour. 1450
Careless if friends or foes press round about him,
His only thought is the pursuit of love.
He's posted all his guards round Hector's son,
Thinking that danger threatens only him.
The child is safe with Phoenix in a fortress
Far from the temple and the palace. That

Is the sole concern of Pyrrhus in his joy.

HERMIONE

The faithless brute! He'll die. But what did Orestes
Say to you?

CLEONE

                      With his Greeks he went inside
1460   The temple.

HERMIONE

                      So he's resolved, then, to avenge me?

CLEONE

I'm not sure.

HERMIONE

                      Not sure? What? Orestes too,
Will he betray me?

CLEONE

                      Orestes worships you;
But he's confused, my lady: torn between
His love for you, and shame at what that love
Demands of him. In Pyrrhus he respects
Achilles, a crowned head, and indeed the man.
He fears Greece, fears the fury of the world,
But most of all, he said, he fears himself.
He'd like to bear the head to you in conquest:
1470   The dreaded name of murderer stays his hand.
He went in still uncertain whether he'd
Emerge a mere spectator or assassin.

HERMIONE

No, no, he'll watch their triumph flow unhindered;
He'll take care not to spoil the spectacle.
I know what dread it is that holds him back:
The coward fears to die, that's all he fears.
To think, my mother had no need to ask:
All Greece rose up in arms to fight for her;
Her beauty caused ten years of war, the death
1480   Of twenty kings she'd never even seen.
And I ask only for one perjurer's death
And charge a lover to redress my wrong;
At that price I will give myself to him:

I'm the reward, and I can't be avenged!
So I myself must settle my account.
Let cries of anguish ring the temple round;
I'll halt their fatal wedding; they'll be joined
No longer than a moment. In the turmoil
I'll make no choice: to me all shall be Pyrrhus,
Even Orestes may it be. I'll die,   1490
But my death will at least avenge me. I'll
Not die alone; someone will die with me.
   Enter ORESTES.   [V.iii]

ORESTES
  It's done! You have your wish: before the altar
  Pyrrhus is yielding up his faithless life.
HERMIONE
  He's dead?
ORESTES
           He's dying now: our outraged Greeks
Have in his own blood washed away his guilt.
I'd given you my word; and though I felt
The plan to be ill-fated in my heart,
I hastened to the temple, where our Greeks,
Scattered among the crowd, stood round the altar.   1500
Pyrrhus observed me, gave no sign, but seemed
To puff himself, as if in me, their envoy,
He threw a challenge out to all the Greeks
And so enhanced the splendour of his wedding.
With great emotion he took up his crown
And placed it on Andromache himself.
'To you,' he said, 'I give my crown and troth;
Reign over Epirus and reign over me.
I promise your son a father's loving care:
Witness the gods, I swear it to his mother.   1510
I have no other enemies but his,
And recognize him as the king of Troy.'
These words, which won his people's acclamation,
Drew from our Greeks a mighty roar of rage;
They wrapped themselves so tightly round the traitor
That I could find no place to strike; they fought

So hard for the renown of killing him.
I watched him struggle with them for a while,
Blood-soaked and trying to escape their swords;
1520   But then at last he fell before the altar.
I battled through the horror-stricken crowds,
And came to take my princess from this place
Out to the harbour where our Greeks will join
Us soon, drenched in the blood I promised you.

HERMIONE
What have they done!

ORESTES
                        Forgive them their impatience:
They spoiled your vengeance, I see that; you wanted
Me to strike first, you wanted him to feel,
As he lay dying, that he died for you.
But it was I who rallied them; it was
1530   For you alone I marched them to the temple,
And you may justly pride yourself upon
A death they merely carried out for you.
You plunged the sword—

HERMIONE
                        Enough, you faithless coward;*
Keep for yourself the credit for your crime.
Go to the Greeks to have your slaughter praised;
Go; I disown it; you fill me with disgust.
What have you done, you beast? What brutal madness
Made you cut short so glorious a life?
Could you all butcher him so heartlessly
1540   Without your own blood rising to defend him?
Say something. Why should you decide his fate?
Why kill him? For what crime? And by what right?
Who told you to?

ORESTES
                        Great gods! What? Did you not
Yourself, a while since, in this very place?

HERMIONE
Ah! Was my lovesick folly to be trusted?
Shouldn't you have divined my deepest thoughts?

Could you not see, in my delirium,
That all the time my heart belied my tongue?
If I demanded it, should you have done it?
Shouldn't you have confirmed it countless times?   1550
Have come to consult me first before you struck?
And come again – or, rather, kept away?
Why could you not leave my revenge to me?
What brought you to this place where you're not wanted?
You see the bitter fruit of your devotion:
You've cursed me with your own unhappy lot.
You and your fatal mission drove him to
That Trojan woman and destroyed us both.
He'd still be torn between us; he might yet
Have loved me; he'd at least have feigned to love me.   1560
Farewell. Go home. I'll stay here in Epirus.
I've done with Greece, with Sparta, all my kin:
It is enough for me, you traitor, that
It can produce the monster that you are.
  Exit HERMIONE *with* CLEONE.   [V.iv]
ORESTES (*alone*)
Was that Hermione? What did she say?
For whom does the blood flow that I have shed?
She says that I'm a treacherous murderer.
Can Pyrrhus be dying? Can I be Orestes?
So: in my heart I snuff the light of reason;
Against my will I kill a king I honour;   1570
In one day I profane the rights of sovereigns,
Envoys, all humankind, and even the altar
Where in my rage I slew him: I commit
Murder and regicide and sacrilege.
For whom? A heartless fury I've sworn to serve,
Who won't see me again unless I kill him,
Whose cause I champion. And when I say he's dying,
She wants his blood unspilled, his life restored!
She loves him! And now I'm a savage monster!
She takes herself for ever from my sight,   1580
And, as she goes, in payment she reviles me
With those cursed names that I have earned for her.

Enter PYLADES *with* ORESTES' SOLDIERS.

PYLADES

Let's go, my lord: we leave this palace now,
Or give up hope of making our escape.
Our Greeks cannot for long defend the gate.
The people are all armed and want our blood.
Andromache is in command here now:
To them she's queen, and we are enemies.
And she herself, who would not yield to Pyrrhus,
1590   Is doing all a faithful widow should,
Calling for his revenge: perhaps she seeks
Revenge from us as well for Troy and Hector.
Let's go: let's not wait here to be surrounded;
Our men will join us. While Hermione
Still holds the people gathered round about her,
This is our way; let's leave in safety now.

ORESTES

No, I must find Hermione, my friends:
Her final judgement spelt my death. You go.
The deed was mine, and I must pay the price.

PYLADES

1600   Hermione, my lord? You must forget her.
What? Still the tool and target of her rage,
Will you seek further shame among the dead?
Because she dies, must you too seek to die?

ORESTES

She's dead? O gods! What's this?

PYLADES

                                        Ah! You've not heard?
As we were coming here, we saw her running
Towards the temple, looking lost and wild.
She met with Pyrrhus, borne by soldiers, spurred
To vengeance by his blood-soaked corpse. That sight
Must have inflamed her frenzy, for, when we looked
1610   Down from the palace gate, we saw her with
A dagger in her hand lean over Pyrrhus,
Look up to Heaven, stab herself, and fall.*

ORESTES

The gods be thanked, my sorrows top the measure!

Yes, Heaven, I praise your tireless perseverance.
Relentlessly determined to torment me,
You've hauled me to the topmost peak of grief.
Your hatred has with pleasure shaped my pain:
I was created to display your wrath,
To be a perfect model of misfortune.
Ah, well, I die content, my fate fulfilled.   1620
Where are those two who loved too well? To crown
My joy I need to drown in blood, theirs joined
With mine. I need to see them as I die:
To see three warring hearts at last made one.
   But why this sudden night that wraps me round?
There's no way out . . . I'm shuddering . . . What horror
Grips me? Heaven be thanked, now I can see . . .
Gods! All around me streams of blood!

PYLADES

                            My lord!

ORESTES

What? Pyrrhus? I meet you again? Am I
To find my hated rival everywhere?   1630
Pierced by so many stabs, how can you live?
Take that now, there's the one I saved for you.
What's this? Hermione is holding him?
She's come to snatch him from my threatening sword.
O gods! What ghastly looks she turns on me!
What snakes, what demons swarm behind her? Ah!
Furies from hell, are your hands raised to strike?*
For whom are those snakes hissing on your heads,
For whom those fiends behind you? Have you come
To take me to eternal night? Come, then: 1640
Orestes will endure your wrath. No, back,
And let Hermione do what she will:
She'll savage me more cruelly than you.
My heart at last I give her to devour.

PYLADES (*kneeling beside Orestes*)

He's not conscious. Time is running out, my friends:
Let's save him while he's powerless to resist.
With speed now, let us carry him aboard,
Before his raging senses are restored.

RACINE

PHAEDRA

A Tragedy

PHÈDRE

Tragédie

First performed on 1 January 1677 in Paris
at the Hôtel de Bourgogne

Preface

(1677)

Here is another tragedy on a subject taken from Euripides.*
Although I have followed a different path from his with respect
to the plot, I have not failed to enrich my play with all the
elements of his version that seemed to me the most impressive.
If I had borrowed from him nothing more than the conception
of Phaedra's character, I might say that I am indebted to him
for perhaps the soundest work that I have written for the
stage. I am not at all surprised that this character won such
high approbation in Euripides' day, and that again in our
own century it has been so successful, since it contains all
the qualities required by Aristotle in a tragic hero, those that
are susceptible of arousing pity and terror. Phaedra is indeed
neither wholly guilty nor wholly innocent; she is embroiled, by
her destiny and the wrath of the gods, in an unlawful passion
which she is the first to view with horror. She does all she
can to overcome it; she would rather die than disclose it to
anyone; and when she is compelled to reveal it, she speaks of
it with a profound sense of shame that leaves no doubt of her
crime being a punishment of the gods rather than an impulse
emanating from her own will.

I have gone so far as to make her somewhat less abhorrent
than she is in the tragedies of the ancients in which she herself
resolves to accuse Hippolytus. I judged the calumny too base
and vile to come from the lips of a princess who otherwise
exhibits such noble and virtuous sentiments. Such baseness
seemed to me more appropriate in a nurse who might have
more slave-like tendencies, but who nevertheless makes the
false accusation only to preserve the life and honour of her

mistress. Phaedra consents to it only because she is beside herself with agitation; and a moment later she appears with the
intention of vindicating innocence and declaring the truth.

Hippolytus is accused in both Euripides and Seneca of actually raping his stepmother: *vim corpus tulit*. But in my play he
is accused of no more than the attempt to do so. I wished to
spare Theseus a degree of mental disturbance that might have
made him less sympathetic to the audience.

As far as the character of Hippolytus is concerned, I had
noted that among the ancients Euripides was taken to task for
portraying him as a man of intellect free of any imperfection;
this resulted in the young prince's death provoking much more
indignation than pity. I thought he should be given some failing which would render him to a degree culpable with respect
to his father, but not detract in any way from the nobility with
which he spares Phaedra's honour and permits himself to be
maltreated without accusing her. I term a failing the passionate
feelings he has despite himself for Aricia, who is the daughter
and sister of his father's mortal enemies.

Aricia herself is by no means an invented character of mine.
According to Virgil, Hippolytus married her and had a son
by her after Aesculapius had brought him back to life. And I
have also read in certain authors that Hippolytus married and
took to Italy a high-born Athenian girl who was called Aricia
and who gave her name to a small Italian town.

I cite these authorities because I have striven hard not to
depart from the ancient legend. I have even remained faithful
to the account of Theseus as it is related in Plutarch.

It was that historian who informed me that what gave occasion to the belief that Theseus had gone down into the Underworld was a journey he made to the source of the Acheron in
Epirus: Pirithoüs* tried to abduct the wife of a king, who in
consequence held Theseus prisoner, having put his companion to death. This enabled me to retain the story's credibility
without losing any of the embellishments of the legend, which
are a rich source of poetic enhancement. And the rumour of
Theseus' death, springing from this legendary journey, gives
rise to Phaedra's declaration of love, which becomes one of the

principal causes of her suffering and is a step she would never have ventured to take as long as she believed her husband was alive.

For the rest, I do not dare assert as yet that this is the finest of my tragedies. Its true worth I leave to the judgement of my readers and to time. What I can claim is that no other work of mine depicts virtue with greater prominence: here the slightest misdemeanour is severely punished; the mere thought of wrongdoing is viewed with as much horror as the enactment of it; lapses that derive from love are treated as absolute failings; the passions are represented only to demonstrate the destructive anarchy to which they give rise; and vice is everywhere portrayed in colours which cause its ugliness to be known for what it is and abhorred. That is the proper objective which every man who writes for the general public should set before himself; and that is what the first tragic poets aimed at above all else. Their theatre was a school where virtue was no less meticulously taught than in the schools of the philosophers. So it was that Aristotle was happy to lay down rules for drama; and Socrates, the wisest of the philosophers, was not above contributing to the creation of Euripides' tragedies. It is to be desired that the works of our age be as soundly principled and replete with useful guidance as those of the ancient poets. If that were so, tragedy might become acceptable to those many people famous for their piety and learning who have recently inveighed against it, and who would doubtless view it more favourably if writers were as concerned with edifying their audiences as with entertaining them, and, having that aim in mind, fulfilled the true purpose of tragedy.

CHARACTERS

THESEUS, son of Aegeus; king of Athens and of Trezene
PHAEDRA, Theseus' wife, daughter of Minos, king of Crete,
  and Pasiphaë
HIPPOLYTUS, son of Theseus and Antiope, queen of the
  Amazons
ARICIA, princess of the blood royal of Athens
OENONE, Phaedra's nurse, now her confidante
THERAMENES, Hippolytus' mentor and confidant
ISMENE, Aricia's confidante
PANOPE, one of Phaedra's waiting women
GUARDS

The scene is set in the royal palace in Trezene,*
a city by the sea in the Peloponnese

ACT I

HIPPOLYTUS

It's all determined. My dear Theramenes,
I go; my stay in sweet Trezene must end.
Tortured by mortal fear as I am now,
I feel ashamed to linger idly here.
For more than six months parted from my father,
So dear to me, I neither know his fate,
Nor even in what land he lies concealed.

THERAMENES

Then where, my lord, do you intend to search?
To satisfy your just fears I myself
Have scoured the seas on either side of Corinth;*   10
I've asked for Theseus where the Acheron
Sinks down into the country of the dead;
I've been to Elis, round Cape Taenarum,
And to that sea where Icarus came down.*
By what new hope, in what more blessèd land,
Do you believe that you will trace his step?
And who can say the King your father wishes
The secret of his absence to be known?
Or if, while we fear for the great man's life,
He's not once more in the pursuit of love,   20
And hiding, safe with some deluded girl—

HIPPOLYTUS

Stop, dear Theramenes: respect the King.
His youthful faults he's put behind him now,
And no unworthy tie keeps him away.
His love for Phaedra curbed his fickle heart
And she long since has feared no rival claim.
At least in seeking him I do my duty,
And flee this place, which I dare see no more.

THERAMENES

    Oh! Since when have you feared the sight, my lord,
30   Of these quiet haunts you so loved as a boy?
    You always wanted to be here; you hated
    The whirling pomp of Athens and the Court.
    What danger, or distress, drives you away?

HIPPOLYTUS

    Those happy times are over. Nothing seems
    The same since to these shores the gods impelled
    The daughter of Minos and Pasiphaë.

THERAMENES

    I understand: I know your sorrow's cause.
    Here Phaedra's presence grieves you, wounds your sight.
    Dangerous stepmother! When she saw you first,
40   Your instant exile testified her power.
    But now the hate for you that gripped her once
    Has either passed away or loosed its hold.
    Besides, what peril do you risk from her,
    A dying woman who desires to die?
    Struck by some ill that she will not disclose,
    Weary of herself and of the light of day,
    Can she contrive the means to harm you now?

HIPPOLYTUS

    It's not her vain hostility I fear.
    I'm fleeing from a different enemy.
50   I will confess: I'm fleeing from young Aricia,
    Last of that fatal blood which would destroy us.*

THERAMENES

    But you do not condemn her? The sons of Pallas
    Were truly vicious, but their gentle sister
    Played no part in their treacherous intrigues.
    Why should you hate her, innocent and fair?

HIPPOLYTUS

    I would not shun her if I hated her.

THERAMENES

    My lord, may I explain your flight? Might you
    No longer be Hippolytus the proud,
    The ruthless enemy of love's decrees,

And of the yoke so often borne by Theseus?   60
Might Venus, so long scorned by your pride, now
Be vindicating Theseus? Ranging you
With other mortals, forcing you to burn
Your incense at her altar? Might you be,
My lord, in love?

HIPPOLYTUS
                    My friend, can you say that?
You, who have known my heart since I drew breath,
Can you expect me basely to betray
That heart's austerity and proud disdain?
An Amazon mother, even with her milk,
Gave me to suck that pride you find so strange;   70
But when in riper years I came to know
My nature, I approved of what I was.
Then you, bound close to me in tender care,*
Would tell the story of my father's life.
You know how my responsive, eager soul
Took fire when you retold his noble deeds,
Painting for me a fearless hero, who
Consoled men for the loss of Hercules
By monsters stifled, brigands swept away:
Procrustes, Sinnis, Sciron, Cercyon,   80
The scattered bones of Epidaurus' giant,*
Crete reeking with the blood of the Minotaur.
   But when you told me of less splendid things,
The vows of love he squandered everywhere:
In Sparta Helen stolen from her parents;
In Salamis the tears of Periboea;*
So many more, whose names he has forgotten,
Too trusting and beguiled by his embrace:
Wronged Ariadne crying to the rocks;
Then Phaedra, taken more auspiciously;   90
You know how loth I was to listen, how
I often begged you not to tell me more,
Wishing that I could steal from memory
That shameful part of such a glorious tale!
Should I then in my turn be shackled so?

Would the gods shame me so? Unmanly sighs
Of love from me would be the more despised,
For Theseus is absolved by his renown,
But I have slain no monsters yet, not earned
100   The right to weakness such as he has shown.
    And even if my pride had been laid low,
Would I have let Aricia conquer me?
Would not my shaken senses still recall
The barrier that must always lie between us?
My father damns her; and by stern decree
Forbids her to bear nephews to her brothers:
He fears an offshoot of their rival branch,
And means to see it wither in her tomb;
Till then to guard her jealously, so that
110   No marriage-torches ever burn for her.
Must I espouse her cause, enrage my father?
Must I provide example for revolt?
And having launched my youth on senseless love—

THERAMENES

Ah, my lord, once your hour has been appointed,
Heaven does not reckon with our reasoning.
Wishing you blind, Theseus has made you see;
His hate has lit in you a rebel flame
And lent his captive girl an added grace.
    But from a love that's pure why shy away?
120   If it is sweet, will you not dare to taste?
Will you mistrust it always, feel such guilt?
Hercules loved: why fear to follow him?
What sturdy heart has Venus failed to tame?
You, who resist her, where would you be if
Antiope had not obeyed her laws
And burned for Theseus with a modest love?
    But why these spurious, lofty protestations?
Nothing is as it was, you must confess:
You're seen less often now, aloof and wild,
130   Making a chariot fly along the shore,
Or, practising the skill that Neptune taught,

Training an untamed steed to heed the rein.*
The forests ring less often with our cries;
Your heavy eyes are weighed with hidden fire.
No question of it: you're in love, you're yearning;
You're wasting from an ill that you're concealing.
Well, has the fair Aricia won your heart?

HIPPOLYTUS

I'm leaving, and I'm going to find my father.

THERAMENES

And will you not see Phaedra before you leave,
My lord?

HIPPOLYTUS

        I mean to do so: you may warn her.   140
Duty demands I see her, and I shall.
But what fresh trouble grieves her dear Oenone?

   Enter OENONE.   [I.ii]

OENONE

What grief, my lord, can be compared with mine?
The Queen has almost reached her destined end.
In vain I watch her night and day. She's dying,
Wrapped in my arms, of an ill she hides from me.
Endless confusion reigns in her frayed mind.
Now restless anguish tears her from her bed.
She longs to see the light, but her distress
Demands that I keep everyone away.   150
She's coming now.

HIPPOLYTUS

           Thank you; then I shall go,
That she may not see my detested face.

   Exeunt HIPPOLYTUS *and* THERAMENES.
   Enter PHAEDRA.   [I.iii]

PHAEDRA

No further. Let me rest, my dear Oenone.
My strength is failing now, deserting me.
My eyes are dazed to see the light again,
And under me my trembling knees give way.
Ah!

(She sits.)

OENONE

    Mighty gods, have pity on our tears!

PHAEDRA

How heavy weigh these robes, these vain adornments!
What tiresome hand entangled all these knots,
And bound my hair so tightly on my brow?
The whole world works to wound and weary me

OENONE

Her wishes always fight against each other!
But you yourself condemned your wicked purpose,
And urged our hands but now to make you fine;
And you yourself, recalling your old strength,
Wished to be seen, to see the light again.
You see it, my lady; will you hide away,
Hating the daylight that you came to find?

PHAEDRA

Sun, glorious founder of a line accursed,
To be whose daughter made my mother proud:
You, who may blush to see me brought so low,
I come to look on you for the last time.

OENONE

What, will you always nurse that cruel desire?
Always am I to see you turn from life
And make grim preparation for your death?

PHAEDRA

Gods! To be in the darkness of the forest!
When shall my eyes, through dust so nobly raised,
Follow a flying chariot in the race?

OENONE

My lady?

PHAEDRA

    I'm mad! Where am I? What did I say?
Can I not curb my longing, or my thoughts?
I've lost my reason, stolen by the gods.
I'm blushing, Oenone: I'm ashamed to let
You see so plainly why I'm in such pain.

My eyes are full of tears I can't hold back.

OENONE

Ah, if you blush, blush for your stubborn silence
That makes your troubles yet more hard to bear.
You fight off help; you're deaf to all our words:
Have you a ruthless urge to end your life?
What madness halts it halfway through its course?
What spell or poison has dried up its spring?   190
The dark three times has overcast the sky
Since sleep invaded last your heavy eyes,
And day three times has chased away the dark
Since last your wasting body tasted food.
By what dread purpose are you tempted? By
What right do you presume to kill yourself?
So you offend the gods, who gave you life;
Betray the husband whom you vowed to love;
And your unhappy children you betray,
By thrusting them beneath a cruel yoke.   200
Remember, that same day that kills their mother
Revives the hopes of the barbarian's son,
Proud enemy to you and to your sons,
That prince born of an Amazon and called
Hippolytus—*

PHAEDRA
                    Ah, gods!

OENONE
                              That rouses you!

PHAEDRA

Misguided soul, what name came from your lips?

OENONE

That's right! Unleash your anger: you've good cause.
I'm glad to see you quake at that dark name.
Live then. Let love, let duty stir you. Live,
And do not let the Scythian woman's son*   210
With hateful power oppress your children, rule
The noblest blood of Greece and of the gods.
But waste no time: each moment speeds your death.

At once restore your ravaged strength, while still
The flickering candle of your life endures,
And still can be revived to shine again.

PHAEDRA

I've let it linger in its guilt too long.

OENONE

What, is it some remorse that tears at you?
What wrong could grieve you so relentlessly?
220 You have not stained your hands with innocent blood?

PHAEDRA

Thanks be to Heaven, my hands have done no wrong.
Would to the gods my heart were pure as they!

OENONE

Then what dread purpose are you nurturing,
The thought of which so terrifies your heart?

PHAEDRA

Enough. Ask me no more. It's to be spared
So shameful a confession that I die.

OENONE

Die then, and keep your brutal silence still;
But find another hand to close your eyes.
Weak though the spark of life that's left to you,
230 My soul will go down first to join the dead.
There lead a thousand ever-open roads,
And my just hurt will choose the shortest one.
Why be so cruel? Have I ever failed you?
When you were born, whose arms received you first?
For you I left my country and my children.*
Is this how you reward my loyalty?

PHAEDRA

You press so hard, what do you hope to gain?
Horror will seize you if I break my silence.

OENONE

What greater horror could there be, great gods,
240 Than watching as you die before my eyes?

PHAEDRA

When you know my offence, my heavy fate,

I still shall die, and die more guilty still.

OENONE

My lady, by the tears I've shed for you,
And by the frailty of these knees I clasp,*
Free me from this tormenting doubt, I pray.

PHAEDRA

You wish it. Rise then.

OENONE

                        Speak. I wait to hear.

PHAEDRA

O Heaven! What shall I say, and where begin?

OENONE

Trust me! Don't leave me fraught with futile fears.

PHAEDRA

Victims of Venus' hate and fatal vengeance!
What strange paths did my mother tread for love!   250

OENONE

Forget, my lady; from the future may
Eternal silence hide the memory.

PHAEDRA

My sister, Ariadne, by love's wound
You died forsaken on an alien shore!

OENONE

Why this? What anguish makes you dwell upon
The unhappy fate of those whose blood you share?

PHAEDRA

Since it is Venus' wish, I die the last
And the most piteous of that grievous blood.

OENONE

Is it, then, love?

PHAEDRA

                        Yes, love: mad, raging love.

OENONE

For whom?

PHAEDRA

                        Hear what o'ertops the height of horror.   260
I love . . . the fatal name fills me with fear.

I love . . .

OENONE

        Yes . . . who?

PHAEDRA

                You know the Amazon's son,
The prince I plagued and made my enemy?

OENONE

Hippolytus! Great gods!

PHAEDRA

                You spoke his name!

OENONE

Just Heaven! My blood is freezing in my veins.
Evil that breeds despair! O piteous race!
Ill-fated journey here! Ill-fated land!
Were we impelled towards your dangerous shore?

PHAEDRA

I was already cursed. By marriage-vows
270   I'd scarcely bound myself to Theseus, when –
My peace, my happiness, it seemed, assured –
Athens revealed my proud, cold conqueror.
I saw him, blushed and blanched at sight of him;
A tumult rose in my bewildered soul;
My eyes forgot to see, I could not speak;
I felt my body burn and freeze at once.
Venus I knew and all her dreaded fires,
The torments borne by those that she hunts down.
By earnest vows I thought to ward them off:
280   I built a temple to her, richly decked;
By day and night I offered sacrifices,
And searched their entrails for my own lost reason.*
Cures futile for a love that could not heal!
In vain my hand burned incense at the altars:
While with my lips I cried upon the goddess,
I worshipped Hippolytus; and, seeing him
Even before the altars that I tended,
I offered all to that god I dared not name.
I fled him everywhere. Most horrible:
290   In looking at his father I found him.*

At last I summoned strength to fight myself;
I steeled my heart to hound him ruthlessly.
To banish the enemy I idolized,
I feigned an unjust stepmother's ill-will.
I urged his exile, and my ceaseless pleas
Wrested him from his father's arms and heart.
I breathed again, Oenone; he away,
My days, less troubled, flowed in innocence.
I yielded to my husband, hid my pain,
And raised the fruit of his ill-fated bed.*   300
    All vain defences! Cruel destiny!
My husband brought me to Trezene himself;
Again I saw the enemy I'd banished.
My still live wound at once began to bleed:
No longer in my veins a hidden fire,
It's Venus clutching, clawing at her prey.
I'm filled with terror by the evil in me;
I hate life, and abhor what I desire.
In death I thought to keep my honour safe,
And hide a flame too dark to meet the day.   310
I could not bear your bitterness, your tears;
I've told you everything. I'm glad I have,
If you will but respect my coming death,
Wound me no more with undeserved reproaches,
And cease your futile efforts to revive
A lingering ember ready to burn out.
    Enter PANOPE.   [I.iv]

PANOPE
I wish that I could keep concealed from you
This sad news, but, my lady, I must speak.
By death your mighty lord is stolen from you;
To all but you is this disaster known.   320

OENONE
What are you saying, Panope?

PANOPE
                            The Queen
In vain asks Heaven for Theseus to return:
From ships just anchored in the port, his son,

Hippolytus, has heard that he is dead.

OENONE

Heaven!

PANOPE

      Athens is uncertain who should rule.
Some give allegiance to the Prince, your son,
My lady; others, who forget the laws,
Dare to support the Amazon woman's son.
It's even said an upstart faction seeks
330 To crown Aricia and the blood of Pallas.*
I thought it right to warn you of this danger.
Hippolytus is set to leave already;
It's feared that if he's seen in this confusion
The fickle mob will try to crown him king.

OENONE

Yes, Panope, the Queen has understood:
Your grave news will be heeded. Leave us now.

[I.v]   *Exit* PANOPE.

OENONE (*continues*)

My lady to your death I was resigned,
And to the tomb I thought to follow you;
To change your purpose I had no more words.
340 But now this new disaster brings new duty;
Your fortune turns, and shows a different view.
The King is dead, and his place must be filled.
His death leaves you a son you must protect:
A slave without you; if you live, a king.
On whom, in his misfortune, should he lean?
There'll be no hand to wipe away his tears;
His innocent cries will rise to Heaven and cause
The gods his forebears to condemn his mother.
Live, for you need reproach yourself no more:
350 Your love is now like any other love.
In dying, Theseus has cut through the knot
Which bound your passion up in hideous wrong.
Hippolytus presents no danger now,
And you can safely see him. He thinks you hate him,*
And means perhaps to lead the lawless rebels

And seize the crown of Athens for himself.
Show your true feelings for him; win his heart.
Here he is king, to him falls fair Trezene;
But he knows that the law gives to your son
The mighty ramparts that Athena built.*   360
You share with him a common enemy:
Unite your forces to defeat Aricia.

PHAEDRA

Ah, well! I will be governed by your words.
I'll live, if I can be restored to life;
If love for a son in this dark time can still
Revive the sickly remnant of my will.

ACT II

ARICIA, ISMENE   [II.i]

ARICIA

Hippolytus is coming here to see me?
Hippolytus wants to say farewell to me?
Ismene, is this true? There's no mistake?

ISMENE

This is the first effect of Theseus' death.   370
My lady, you are going to be besieged
By admirers Theseus kept away from you.
Princess Aricia is uncaged at last,
And soon all Greece will bend the knee to her.

ARICIA

This is no idle rumour, then, Ismene?
I'm free now, and I have no enemy?

ISMENE

The gods no longer frown on you, my lady:
Theseus has joined your brothers' shades below.

ARICIA

And do they say what exploit cost his life?

ISMENE

The tales spread of his death defy belief.   380
Some say that, yet again a faithless husband,

Swallowed by waves, he sank into the sea.
It's even said, and everywhere repeated,
That with Pirithoüs he went down to Hades,
Saw the Cocytus and the dismal strands,*
And walked alive among the shades below;
But that he could not leave that sad abode,
And come back past the bourne of no return.

ARICIA

Shall I believe a mortal can invade
390   The deep home of the dead before his time?
What spell enticed him to those dreaded shores?

ISMENE

Theseus is dead, and all but you believe it.
Athens is grieving, Trezene knows, and already
Has hailed Hippolytus as her new king.
Phaedra, within, is frightened for her son,
And taking counsel from her anxious friends.

ARICIA

And you think that to me Hippolytus
Will be less cruel than his father, ease
My chains, show pity?

ISMENE

                    Yes, I do, my lady.

ARICIA

400   But surely you must know how cold he is?
What vain hope makes you think he'll pity me,
In me alone respect the sex he scorns?
You know how long he has avoided us,
And chosen haunts where we would not be found.

ISMENE

I know how cold they say he is, but I
Have seen the proud Hippolytus near you.
I watched him the more closely, having heard
The tales of his detached, unfeeling heart.
His manner did not match his reputation:
410   At your first glance I saw him grow confused;
His eyes, in vain attempting to avoid you,
Already melting, could not let you be.

The name of lover may offend his pride,
But with his eyes he speaks, if not his tongue.
ARICIA
How eagerly my heart, my dear Ismene,
Seizes upon mere possibility!
O you who know me, did you think that I,
Sad plaything of a ruthless destiny,
A heart forever fed on bitter tears,
Should meet with love and all its foolish pains?   420
   Last blood of Athens' great king, born of Earth,
Alone I escaped the rage of civil war.
Full in the flower of their youth I lost
Six brothers, promise of a glorious house!
All gathered by the sword; and Earth with sorrow
Drank blood sprung from Erechtheus, her own son.*
You know how strictly Theseus, since their death,
Has banned all Greeks from paying court to me:
The sister's flame, he fears, if rashly lit,
May one day bring to life her brothers' ashes.   430
But you know too with what contempt I viewed
That safeguard of a wary conqueror:
You know that, since I disdained love and marriage,
I often blessed the King's unjust decree,
The welcome harshness that upheld my scorn.
My eyes had then . . . I had not seen his son.
Not that I'm weakly held by sight alone,
To love him for his looks, his vaunted grace,
Gifts with which nature chose to honour him,
And he derides, if he's aware of them.   440
I love, I prize in him more noble treasures,
His father's virtues, not his weaknesses.
I love, I will confess, that arrogance
That has not stooped beneath the yoke of love.
Phaedra felt honoured to be Theseus' wife:
I have more pride, and shun the easy fame
Of seizing worship squandered everywhere,
Winning a heart that offers no defence.
But to compel a rigid will to bend,

450   To hurt a soul insensitive to pain,
       To bind a slave amazed to feel his chains,
       Struggling in vain against a tingling yoke:
       That's what I want, that's what excites me most!
       Hercules cost less than Hippolytus
       To conquer: often beaten, sooner straddled,
       He offered less renown to those who tamed him.
          But, dear Ismene – ah, what reckless talk!
       My charms will be resisted all too strongly.
       Perhaps you'll hear me, meekly suffering,
460   Groan for that pride that I admire this day.
       Hippolytus in love! What happiness
       If I had bent that—

ISMENE
                          You shall hear him speak
       To you himself.

[II.ii]   *Enter* HIPPOLYTUS.

HIPPOLYTUS
                          My lady, before I leave,
       I wish to make your new position clear.
       My father is no more. My fears foretold
       Rightly why he did not return to us.
       Nothing but death could end his glorious deeds,
       And keep him so long hidden from the world.
       At last the gods award the murderous Fates
470   Hercules' friend, companion, and successor.
       His virtues, I presume, are spared your hatred,
       And his due titles give you no offence.
       One ray of hope shines through my mortal sorrow:
       I can release you from your bondage; I
       Revoke the ban I always thought too harsh.
       Do as you will with yourself, and with your heart.
       Here in Trezene, my share this day, and once
       The seat of Pittheus, my great ancestor,*
       Where all, with one accord, have made me king,
480   I leave you free as I; and yet more free.

ARICIA
       Your kindness is too much for me to bear.
       Such generous concern for my misfortune

Strengthens my bonds more than you know, my lord,
And curbs the freedom you bestow on me.

HIPPOLYTUS

Who should succeed in Athens is unsure:
I am proposed, and Phaedra's son, and you.

ARICIA

I, my lord?

HIPPOLYTUS

          I confess that I would seem
Excluded by a haughty, pompous law:
My foreign mother rules me out. But if
Only the son of Phaedra barred my way,   490
I have a stronger claim than his, my lady,
That I could rescue from the law's caprice.
A claim still stronger curbs my own ambition:
I yield, or rather, I restore to you
The throne your grandfather inherited
From great Erechtheus, born of Earth herself.
It passed to Aegeus only by adoption,
But under Theseus, his son, Athens prospered,
Proud to acknowledge such a noble king,
And your ill-fated brothers were forgotten.*   500
Now Athens calls you back, her lawful queen.
Enough pain our old enmity has caused her,
Enough your blood has drenched her furrows, making
The very soil reek that engendered it.
Trezene is mine, and Phaedra's son will find
A fertile refuge in the plains of Crete.
Athens is rightly yours. There, in your name,*
I shall unite your followers with mine.

ARICIA

All this amazes and bewilders me;
I almost fear, I fear this is a dream.   510
Am I awake? Do you mean what you are saying?
What god, my lord, what god can have inspired you?
How rightly you are everywhere admired,
And how the truth surpasses your renown!
You mean to sacrifice yourself for me?
Surely it was sufficient not to hate me,

To have so long refused to share your father's
Enmity—
HIPPOLYTUS

      What, I, hate you, my lady?
However garishly they paint my pride,
520 Is it believed a monster gave me birth?
What savage nature, what deep-rooted hate
Could fail to melt and weaken, seeing you?
Could I resist a charm that would beguile . . .
ARICIA

My lord?
HIPPOLYTUS

      I did not mean to say so much.
I see that reason yields to force of feeling.
But since I've now begun to break my silence,
I must go on, my lady; you must know
The secret that is bursting from my heart.
Before you stands a pitiable prince,
530 A fine example of rash arrogance.
I, the vainglorious enemy of love,
Who used to mock at those who wore its chains,
Who pitied weak men shipwrecked in the storm
And thought to watch for ever from the shore,
Enslaved now by the universal law,
I'm borne away in turmoil from myself.
One moment conquered my brash confidence:
This self-sufficient man is filled with need.
For almost six months, desperate with shame,
540 Everywhere bearing the dart that tears at me,
Against you and myself I've fought in vain.
I flee your presence; absent, you are with me;
Deep in the forest your image follows me;
Daylight, night's shadows, everything reflects
The fair enchantment that I'm fleeing from,
Vies to ensnare my rebel heart for you.
All that my futile pains have gained for me
Is now to seek and fail to find myself.
Bow, javelins, chariot, everything repels me;

Even Neptune's horsemanship I have neglected;   550
The woods re-echo only with my groans;
My idle steeds no longer know my voice.
  Perhaps the tale of such barbaric love
Makes you ashamed to hear what you have done.
Crude words with which to offer you my heart!
Strange captive for a chain so finely wrought!
But that should make you prize my offering:
Remember, words like these are foreign to me;
Don't spurn this clumsy declaration that
No one but you could have torn out of me.   560
  Enter THERAMENES.   [II.iii]

THERAMENES
My lord – the Queen! I came in haste to warn you:
She's looking for you.

HIPPOLYTUS
                                    Me?

THERAMENES
                                          I don't know why,
But she sent word to say she wished to see you.
Phaedra would speak with you before you leave.

HIPPOLYTUS
Phaedra? What shall I say? She can't expect—

ARICIA
My lord, you cannot say you will not see her.
Although you know too well how much she hates you,
You owe some grain of pity to her grief.

HIPPOLYTUS
So we must part, and I set sail, not knowing
Whether I have offended where I love;   570
Not knowing if the heart I leave with you—

ARICIA
Go, prince, and carry out your noble purpose;
Fight in my name and make me queen of Athens:
All that you offer me I will accept.
But, great and glorious though that empire is,
To me it's not the dearest of your gifts.
  Exit ARICIA *with* ISMENE.   [II.iv]

HIPPOLYTUS
    My friend, we're ready? But the Queen is coming.
    Go and alert the fleet to sail at once;
    Order the signal; run; and come back here
580   To free me from this awkward interview.
[II.v]   *Exit* THERAMENES. *Enter* PHAEDRA *with* OENONE.
PHAEDRA (*aside to* OENONE)
    He's there. My blood is draining to my heart.
    Seeing him, I can't think what I should say.
OENONE
    Remember your son, who has no hope but you.
PHAEDRA
    I hear you are to take swift leave of us,
    My lord. I come to share your grief with mine.
    I come to tell you of a mother's fears.
    My son is fatherless; and soon enough
    The day of my death too he must endure.
    His childhood is beset by enemies;
590   By you alone his cause can be embraced.
    But secretly my mind is racked by guilt.
    I fear I've made you deaf to his appeals,
    That soon through him your righteous anger will
    Exact revenge upon his hateful mother.
HIPPOLYTUS
    My lady, I have no such base desire.
PHAEDRA
    Your hatred would draw no complaint from me,
    My lord. You've seen me bent on harming you.
    But deep within my heart you could not see.
    I've taken pains to earn your enmity.
600   There where I dwelt I could not let you stay.
    In public, and in private, I condemned you,
    And had you sent from me across the sea.
    I even by express command forbade
    That anyone should speak your name before me.
    But, if the punishment should fit the offence,
    If only hatred should incur your hate,
    Never did woman merit pity more,
    And merit less, my lord, your enmity.

HIPPOLYTUS

A mother jealous of her children's rights
Often resents the son of a former wife.   610
I know, my lady: troublesome mistrust
Is the most common fruit of second marriage.
Another would have borne me the same grudge,
And might have done me graver injury.

PHAEDRA

Ah, no, my lord! High Heaven, I swear, has made
Me an exception to that common rule:
It is not that which grieves and rends my heart.

HIPPOLYTUS

My lady, you may not yet need to grieve.
Your husband may still see the light of day;
Heaven may reward our tears with his return.   620
Neptune is his protector, and my father*
Will not invoke that watchful god in vain.

PHAEDRA

The land of the dead is not seen twice, my lord.
Theseus has looked upon the dismal shores:
No god will bring him back to you; the grasping
Acheron never lets its prey go free.
No: he's not dead, since he still breathes in you.
I seem to see my husband; see and speak
To him; my heart . . . I'm weakening, my lord;
I can't restrain the madness of my longing.   630

HIPPOLYTUS

I see the power of your love at work:
Theseus, though dead, is here before your eyes;
Your soul is burning still with love for him.

PHAEDRA

Yes, prince, I yearn, I'm all on fire for Theseus.
I love him: not as he is seen in Hades,
The fickle worshipper of countless women,
The man who would dishonour Pluto's bed;
But proud and steadfast, shy perhaps, aloof,
Young, captivating, stealing every heart;
As we depict the gods: as I see you.   640
He moved and spoke like you; he had your eyes;

He too would blush with noble virtue, when
He crossed the sea to us in Crete, and in
The hearts of Minos' daughters wakened love.
Where were you then? Why did he gather all
The mightiest Greeks, and not Hippolytus?
Why, still too young, were you not able then
To board the ship that brought him to our shores?
You would have killed the Cretan monster, vast
650   And endless though the windings of its lair.
To unravel its perplexity, my sister
Would with the fatal thread have then armed you.
No: I'd have been too quick for her; my love
Would have inspired me first with that device.
Yes, prince, it's I who would have taught you all
The hidden mysteries of the labyrinth.
How tenderly I would have cherished you!
No thread could have allayed my loving fears:
Sharing the danger that you had to seek,
660   Into the maze I would have led the way,
And, with you deep inside the labyrinth,
With you I'd have been found again, or lost.

HIPPOLYTUS

Gods! What is this? Have you forgotten, my lady,
That I am Theseus' son, and you his wife?

PHAEDRA

And what makes you suppose that I've forgotten,
Prince? Would I be so reckless with my honour?

HIPPOLYTUS

My lady, pardon me. I blush to own
I misinterpreted words spoken in
All innocence. I'll go: I'm too ashamed
670   To look—

PHAEDRA

                You heartless boy! You understood.*
I said enough to leave you in no doubt.
Well then! Know Phaedra and her raging heart.
I love you. But do not believe that I
Regard myself as innocent and good;
Or that with weak indulgence I have fed

The furious poison that infects my mind.
Ill-fated as I am, cursed from on high,
I loathe myself still more than you detest me.
The gods bear witness, they who lit in me
The flame that curses all my family: 680
Those gods, cold boy, who took grim pleasure in
Corrupting my poor mortal heart. Think back
Upon the past yourself: avoiding you
Was not enough; I had you sent away.
I wanted you to think me odious, hard;
To fight you better I provoked your hate.
What good did my vain efforts do for me?
You grew to hate me, and I loved you still.
To see you suffer made me want you more.
I've yearned, I've pined, I've been on fire, in tears.   690
You only need to use your eyes for proof,
If for a moment you could look at me.
    What am I saying? To tell you this, make such
A shameful confession, do you think I meant to do it?
Afraid for a son I did not dare abandon,
I came to beg you not to show him hate.
Frail purpose for a heart too full of love!
To you I could speak of no one else but you.
Take vengeance, punish me for my foul love.
Prove worthy of the hero who begot you,   700
And rid Creation of this galling monster.
The widow of Theseus dares to love his son!
Believe me, this vile monster must not live.
Here is my heart. It's here your hand must strike.
Impatient now to expiate its crime,
I feel it straining forward to your arm.
Strike. If you do not think it worthy, if
Your hatred grudges me such welcome pain,
Or if my base blood would pollute your hand,
Withhold your arm, but lend your sword to me.   710
Give it me—

OENONE
            No, my lady! O just gods!
Someone is coming; you must not be seen;

Away at once; you'll be disgraced, away.

[II.vi]   *Exeunt* PHAEDRA *and* OENONE. *Enter* THERAMENES.

THERAMENES

Phaedra? In haste – or rather, torn away . . .
But what . . . My lord, what's made you so distressed?
Where is your sword? You're pale; you seem struck dumb?

HIPPOLYTUS

Let's get away. I am amazed. To look
At my own body fills me with disgust.
Phaedra— Oh, no, great gods! The truth must be
720   For ever shrouded in oblivion.

THERAMENES

The sails are hoisted, if you wish to leave.
But Athens has already made her choice.
Her leaders have consulted all the tribes:
They've chosen your brother; Phaedra wins the day.*

HIPPOLYTUS

Phaedra?

THERAMENES

From Athens comes an envoy to
Confirm her powers as regent till her son,
The new king, comes of age.

HIPPOLYTUS

You gods, who know her,
Is it her virtue that you so reward?

THERAMENES

Yet there's a rumour that your father lives;
730   That in Epirus Theseus has been seen.
But I went there to search for him; I know—

HIPPOLYTUS

No matter: let's take note of everything.
We'll check this rumour, trace it to its source.
If there's no solid proof, I'll sail to Athens,
And at whatever cost it may demand
I'll place the sceptre in the worthiest hand.*

ACT III

PHAEDRA

Ah! Let them take their titles somewhere else.*
Leave me alone; do you want me to be seen?
Why try to blandish my poor, stricken soul?
Better to hide me: I have said too much.   740
My madness has burst forth and shown itself;
I've uttered what should never have been heard.
Heaven! How he listened! How he dodged and turned,
Coldly evading what my words revealed!
How plainly he was longing to escape,
And how his blushes added to my shame!
Why, why did you not let me kill myself?
Ah, when his sword was raised above my breast,
Did he grow pale for me, or snatch it from me?
It was enough my hand had touched it once: 750
To his inhuman eyes it was defiled;
That wretched blade would desecrate his hands.

OENONE

So, thinking only to bewail your woes,
You feed the fire when you should put it out.
Daughter of Minos, would it not befit you
To seek relief in nobler thoughts: to fight
A thankless love by fleeing from its cause,
To rule, and guide the conduct of the State?

PHAEDRA

I, rule! Impose my will upon a state,
When my weak reason can't rule me, myself!   760
When I have ceased to govern my own senses!
When shame so crushes me I cannot breathe!
When I am dying!

OENONE

　　　　　　Go!

PHAEDRA

　　　　　　　I cannot leave him.

OENONE

   You banished him, and say you cannot leave him?

PHAEDRA

   It's too late now. He knows I'm crazed with longing.
   The bounds of decency have been transgressed;
   I've thrust my shameful feelings in his face;
   And hope, unbidden, has slipped into my heart.
   You it was who recalled my failing strength
770   And my soul poised already on my lips;
   You, with your oily words, restored my life;
   You made me think it possible to love him.

OENONE

   Ah, well, it may be I'm to blame for this:
   What would I not have done to save your life?
   But if barbed insolence has power to rile you,
   Can you forget his arrogant disdain?
   How cold his eyes were when, so stubbornly,
   He left you almost prostrate at his feet!
   How odious he was in his grim pride!
780   If only you had seen with my eyes then!

PHAEDRA

   Oenone, he can shed the pride that galls you.
   He grew up in the forests: he is wild.
   Rough ways have made him hard; Hippolytus
   Has never till this day heard talk of love.
   Perhaps it was amazement silenced him,
   And in our bitterness we are too harsh.

OENONE

   His mother was a barbarian, remember.

PHAEDRA

   Barbarian, Amazon, yes, and yet she loved.

OENONE

   He has a fatal hatred for our sex.

PHAEDRA

790   No rival, then, will ever take my place.
   But your wise words are out of season now:
   Oenone, serve my madness, not my reason.
   His heart is closed to love, you say: then we

Must aim at some more vulnerable mark.
The charms of empire seemed to stir him; Athens
Excited him, for all he tried to hide it.
His prow was turned, already set to leave,
With streaming sails abandoned to the wind.
Go, find him for me. He is young, ambitious:
Dazzle his eyes, Oenone, with the crown.   800
His brow can wear the sacred diadem:
All I want is to place it on his head.
Let him enjoy the power I cannot keep.
He'll teach my son the art of ruling men;
Perhaps he'll want to be a father to him.
Mother and son I place at his command.
Use every means you can to win him for me.
He'll heed your words more readily than mine.
Persuade, weep, groan, lament a dying Phaedra;
Don't be ashamed to plead for me. I'll stand   810
By all you promise; I've no hope but you.
Go: I suspend my life till you return.

    Exit OENONE.   [III.ii]

PHAEDRA (*alone*)

O you, relentless Venus, who can see
My depth of shame, have I not borne enough?
No worse pain could your cruelty devise.
Your triumph stands: your darts have all struck home.
Harsh goddess, if you seek still greater glory,
Attack a more rebellious enemy.
Hippolytus eludes you; he defies you;
Never has he knelt down before your altar.   820
Your very name appears to wound his pride.
Avenge yourself; we have a common cause:
That he should love.

    Enter OENONE.   [III.iii]

PHAEDRA (*continues*)

                  Oenone, here so soon?
He hates me, then; he would not hear you speak.

OENONE

My lady, this hopeless passion must be choked.

You must revive your former purity.
The King, whom we thought dead, will soon be here.
Theseus has landed, Theseus has come home.
The people are all rushing out to see him.
830   As I went out to find Hippolytus,
A thousand voices shot up to the sky—

PHAEDRA

My husband lives, Oenone; that's enough.
I've basely owned to feelings that defile him.
He is alive. I need to know no more.

OENONE

My lady?

PHAEDRA

             I told you, but you would not hear.
Over my just remorse your tears prevailed.
My death this morning would have been lamented:
I heeded you, and die dishonoured now.

OENONE

You die?

PHAEDRA

             Just Heaven! What have I done this day?
840   My husband will be here, his son with him.
The son who saw my adulterous lust unleashed
Will watch to see how I approach his father,
My heart still big with sighs he would not hear,
My eyes still wet with tears he would not heed.
Do you think that his respect for Theseus' honour
Will make him hide the love that burns in me
And see his father and his king betrayed?
Could he suppress the disgust he feels for me?
If he said nothing, I still know my guilt,
850   Oenone; I'm not of that shameless band
Who can rest easy in their wickedness
And show the world a bold, unblushing front.
My fevered madness haunts my memory.
To me these walls, these arches seem about
To speak, all waiting to denounce me to

My husband and reveal the truth to him.
So let me die; from so much horror let
Death free me. Is to end a life so great
An ill? The wretched do not fear to die.
My fear is for the name I leave behind me.   860
A cruel heritage for my poor sons!
Jupiter's blood should swell their confidence,*
But, justly proud though noble blood may make them,
The burden of a mother's guilt weighs hard.
I fear that one day they may be reviled
On my account in words – ah, all too true!
I fear the weight of shame may crush them so
That they will never dare lift up their heads.

OENONE

Believe me, your two children have my pity;
No fear had ever better ground than yours.   870
But why expose them to such injury?
Why should you testify against yourself?
Yes; Phaedra's guilt, they'll say, drove her to flee
The anger of the husband she betrayed.
Happy Hippolytus, that with your life
You will have paid to lend his words support.
When he accuses you, what shall I say?
Before him they will quickly silence me.
So I shall see him vaunt his hideous triumph,
And tell your shame to all who wish to hear.   880
Ah, first let fire from Heaven strike me down!
But tell me, is he still so dear to you?
That insolent prince, how do you see him now?

PHAEDRA

I see him as a monster that appals me.

OENONE

Then why yield him a total victory?
You fear him, why not bring against him first
The accusation he can charge you with?
What can disprove you? Everything condemns him:
His sword by happy chance left in your hand,

890 Your agitation now, your past distress,
His father long forewarned by the complaints
That led you to demand his banishment.

PHAEDRA

I, persecute and blacken innocence!

OENONE

Your silence is the only help I need.
I too am fearful; I feel some remorse.
I'd sooner brave a thousand deaths. But since
I must take this sad remedy or lose you,
I prize your life above all other things.
I shall speak. Theseus, prompted by my words,
900 Will do no more than banish his own son.
A father punishing is still a father,
My lady; a gentle sentence cools his wrath.
But even if innocent blood were to be shed,
What price can be too high to save your honour?
Its treasure is too precious to be risked.
Whatever it demands, you must comply,
My lady; when honour's threatened, everything,
Including virtue, must be sacrificed.
But I see Theseus!

PHAEDRA

                    And I see his son!
910 I read my ruin in his scornful eyes.
You do what you judge best; I can't decide.
I'm too distraught to think what I should do.

[III.iv]   *Enter* THESEUS, HIPPOLYTUS *and* THERAMENES.

THESEUS

Fortune at last has ceased to frown on me,
My lady, and to your arms restores—

PHAEDRA

                                No, Theseus,
No: you must not profane such pure, sweet joy.
I do not now deserve this tender greeting.
My lord, you stand dishonoured. Jealous Fortune
During your absence has not spared your wife.

    Unworthy of your love, unfit to touch you,
    I must for ever hide myself away.   920
       Exit PHAEDRA *with* OENONE.   [III.v]
THESEUS
    My son, why this strange welcome for your father?
HIPPOLYTUS
    Phaedra alone can solve that mystery.
    But if, my lord, you'll hear my urgent plea,
    Grant that I never look on her again.
    Grant that Hippolytus may ever shun,
    In fear, those places where your wife may dwell.
THESEUS
    You'd leave me, you, my son?
HIPPOLYTUS
                I did not seek
    Her out. You brought her to these shores yourself.
    Here in Trezene, my lord, when you departed,
    You deigned to leave Aricia and the Queen,   930
    And I was even charged with their protection.
    But now what charge, what duty keeps me here?
    I've idled my youth in the forests long enough,
    Pitting my skill against unworthy beasts.
    May I not be released from shameful ease,
    And stain my javelin with more glorious blood?
    Before you were as old as I am now,
    There were fierce monsters, there were tyrants, who
    Had felt the mighty power of your arm;
    Already crushing lawless insolence,   940
    You had made safe the coastline of two seas.
    Men travelled without fear of injury;
    Hercules, freed from labour by your deeds,
    Already owed his rest to your renown.*
    And I, the unknown son of such a father,
    I've not yet even reached my mother's mark.
    Let me at last find some use for my valour.
    If still some monster has eluded you,
    Let me bring home the honourable spoils,

950   Or let the memory of a glorious death
       Immortalize a life so nobly ended,
       And show the world that I was your true son.
THESEUS
       What is this? What strange horror haunts this place,
       Frightening my family away from me?
       If I return so feared, and so unwanted,
       O Heaven, why did you free me from my prison?
           One friend I had: Pirithoüs. Crazed by love,
       He planned to steal the King's wife in Epirus.
       I aided him, although unwillingly.
960   But angry Fate thought fit to blind us both:
       The King surprised me helpless and unarmed.
       Pirithoüs I saw thrown – and wept for him –
       By that barbarian brute to cruel monsters
       He fed upon ill-fated human flesh.*
       Me he immured in caves where darkness dwells,
       Deep down beside the empire of the dead.
       Six months. At last the gods took heed of me:
       I tricked the eyes that watched me, and I purged
       The world of a perfidious enemy:
970   Himself he served as fodder to his monsters.
           And when I joyfully return to all
       The gods have left me that I hold most dear;
       What? When my newly liberated soul
       Comes home to feast itself on tender scenes,
       The only welcome I receive is fear;
       I am avoided, my embrace is shunned.
       I feel myself the terror that I rouse,
       And wish Epirus' prison held me still.
           Speak. Phaedra says that I have been dishonoured.
980   Who is the traitor? Why am I not avenged?
       Can Greece, that owes so much to my strong arm,
       Be sheltering the one who has betrayed me?
       You do not answer. Can my son, my own
       Son, be conspiring with my enemies?
       I'll go in. This uncertainty torments me.
       Both crime and culprit I must know at once:

Phaedra shall tell the cause of her distress.
    Exit THESEUS.   [III.vi]

HIPPOLYTUS

What did she mean? Her words froze me with fear.
Is Phaedra still so preyed on by her passion
That she'll confess, and so destroy herself?   990
Gods! What will Theseus say? What deadly poison
Has been diffused by love throughout his house!
I myself, loving where his hate forbids,
What I was once, and what he finds me now!
Black, menacing forebodings crowd my mind.
But innocence can have no cause to fear.
   Come, I must find some happy means to wake
My father's tender feelings, then confess
A bond of love which he may try to break,
But which his mighty empire could not shake.   1000

ACT IV

THESEUS, OENONE   [IV.i]

THESEUS

What are you saying to me? The reckless traitor
Meant so to violate his father's honour?*
Cruel destiny, you hunt me hard! I do
Not know where I am going, where I am.
My love, my kindness he repays with this!
An insolent assault! O loathsome thought!
To gain the object of his dark desire
He was resorting brazenly to force.
I know that sword he drew to appease his lust:
The sword I armed him with for nobler use.   1010
The ties of blood were powerless to restrain him?
And Phaedra made no demand that he be punished?
Her silence would have spared the criminal?

OENONE

No: Phaedra meant to spare his wounded father.
Shamed by her would-be lover's frenzied purpose,

And by the evil lust her eyes had kindled,
She was about to die; by her own hand
The pure light of those eyes would have been dimmed.
I saw her raise her arm, I ran to stop her.
1020   I it was who preserved her for your love;
And, pitying your fears and her distress,
Unwillingly, I have explained her tears.

THESEUS

Such a betrayal! He could not help but blench:
I saw him quake with fear while greeting me.
I marvelled that he showed so little joy;
His cold embraces froze the warmth of mine.
But this forbidden love that now consumes him,
Had it revealed itself before, in Athens?

OENONE

Remember Phaedra's grievances, my lord.
1030   Her hatred sprang from unpermitted love.

THESEUS

And in Trezene this fire blazed up again?

OENONE

My lord, I've told you all that passed. The Queen
Should not be left alone in her great sorrow.
Give me your leave, my lord, to go to her.

[IV.ii]   *Exit* OENONE. *Enter* HIPPOLYTUS.

THESEUS

Ah, there he is. Great gods! That noble bearing
Surely deceives all eyes, as it did mine?
Must the adulterer's ungodly brow
Shine with the holy print of innocence?
And should we not by sure marks recognize
1040   The hearts of men disposed to treachery?

HIPPOLYTUS

My royal father, may I ask what cloud
Has cast its troubled shadow on your face?
Will you not trust me with your confidence?

THESEUS

My false son! Dare you show yourself to me?*
Monster the wrath of Heaven has spared too long,
Corrupted vestige of the human scum

Of which I've purged the earth, your foul desire
Thrusts you to your own father's bed, and you
Still dare confront me, my worst enemy,
You stay where your abomination reeks,   1050
Instead of seeking out some alien sky,
Some land where men have never heard my name.
Flee, traitor! Do not come to brave my hate
And tempt the anger I can scarce restrain.
It is eternal shame enough for me
To have begotten such an evil son;
By killing you let me not further soil
The glorious record of my noble deeds.
Flee; and unless you wish swift vengeance to
Add you to all the vermin I've destroyed,   1060
Take care the sun that lights us never sees
You set a rebel foot upon this soil.
Flee, I say, never to return: away,
And purge my empire of your loathsome sight.
   O Neptune, hear me now: if my endeavours
Once cleansed your shores of dreaded murderers,
Remember that in payment for my deeds
You promised to accede to my first prayer.
In the long hardship of a cruel prison
I did not sue to your immortal power;   1070
Saving the sure support of your protection,
I held you in reserve for greater need.
I beg you now: avenge an ill-used father.
This traitor I abandon to your wrath;
Smother in his own blood his shameless lust.
Your favour I shall measure by your rage.

HIPPOLYTUS

I'm charged by Phaedra with unlawful love?
Such mounting horror stuns my soul; so many
Unexpected blows crush me at once,
My tongue is stifled, I can hardly speak.   1080

THESEUS

Traitor, in craven silence, so you thought,
Phaedra would shroud your brutal insolence.
You should not, when you ran away, have left

Your sword, which in her hand confirms your guilt.
Or rather, with one last perfidious stroke,
You should have robbed her of both speech and life.

HIPPOLYTUS

In my just anger at so black a lie,
I should declare the truth, my lord; but I
Must keep a secret touching you. Commend
1090 The deep respect for you that locks my tongue;
And do not seek to add to your own pain,
But look into my life, think what I am.
Great crimes are always heralded by small.
A man who once has crossed the bounds of right
In time may violate the holiest laws.
As virtue is progressive, so is vice;
Never has timid innocence been known
Suddenly to become depravity.
A virtuous man does not in one day take
1100 To murderous treachery and vile incest.
My mother was both valiant and chaste,
And I have not belied her noble blood.
Pittheus, of all men judged the wisest, took
Me from her arms himself, and tutored me.
I have no wish to paint myself too fair,
But if some virtue is granted me, my lord,
I think it is to have proclaimed a loathing
Of such vile filth as that ascribed to me.
For this I'm known throughout all Greece. My zeal
1110 For chastity has made me cold and coarse;
I'm famed for rigid, harsh austerity.
My heart shines pure, as clear and clean as light.
And, burning with ungodly lust, I'm said to—

THESEUS

Yes, by that very pride you stand condemned.
The foul cause of your coldness I can see:
Phaedra alone charmed your lascivious gaze,
And, blind to other women, you disdained
To give your heart where love was innocent.

HIPPOLYTUS

No, father, I must tell you that my heart
Has not disdained to burn with honest love.   1120
At your feet I confess my real offence:
I am in love, it's true against your wish.
Aricia has my heart at her command;
Your son has been enslaved by Pallas' daughter.
I worship her; my soul, defying you,
Can burn and ache for nobody but her.

THESEUS

You love her? Heaven! No. A crude device:
To mask your guilt you feign a different crime.

HIPPOLYTUS

For six whole months I've fled from her and loved her.
I came here now in fear to tell you so.   1130
What, then, will nothing make you see the truth?
By what dread oath will you be satisfied?
I swear by Earth, by Heaven, by all Creation—

THESEUS

All criminals resort to perjury.
Stop, spare me further tedious argument
If your false virtue has no other aid.

HIPPOLYTUS

To you it must seem false and full of guile.
Phaedra does me more justice in her heart.

THESEUS

Take care! Such insolence will stoke my rage.

HIPPOLYTUS

How long, and where, do you decree my exile?   1140

THESEUS

Were you beyond the pillars of Hercules,*
I still should feel too close to treachery.

HIPPOLYTUS

What friends will pity me, cast out by you,
Smeared with the vileness you ascribe to me?

THESEUS

Go and find those with values black enough

    To honour adultery, prize incestuous lust,
    Thankless, perfidious, lawless, shameless villains,
    Fit friends and guardians for such filth as you.

HIPPOLYTUS

    You talk of incest and adultery still?
1150 I will not speak. But Phaedra, sir, springs from
    A mother – Phaedra's blood, as well you know,
    Reeks more than mine of horrors such as those.

THESEUS

    You dare unleash your anger to my face?
    For the last time, I say, out of my sight!
    Go, traitor, do not let a father's fury
    Command that you be shamefully thrust out.

[IV.iii]   *Exit* HIPPOLYTUS.

THESEUS (*alone*)

    Damned soul, your death is certain. Neptune swore
    To grant my wish upon that river dreaded
    Even by the gods: he'll keep his word.*
1160 A god seeks vengeance: you will not escape.
    I loved you; and despite the wrong you've done me,
    My heart bleeds for you, knowing what must come.
    But you yourself compelled me to condemn you:
    Was ever any father injured so?
    Just gods, who see the grief that crushes me,
    Can I have fathered such an evil child?

[IV.iv]   *Enter* PHAEDRA.

PHAEDRA

    My lord, I'm frightened, and I have good cause.
    I heard the mounting danger in your voice;
    I fear swift execution of your threats.
1170 If there's still time, have mercy on your son;
    Spare your own blood, I make bold to implore you.
    Let me not quake to hear its tortured cry;
    Do not store up for me the endless pain
    Of causing it to spill by a father's hand.

THESEUS

    No, my own hand is not stained with my blood;
    And yet the culprit is not free of me.

The hand of an Immortal will destroy him:
Neptune owes me a debt; you'll be avenged.

PHAEDRA

Neptune owes— What? You prayed to him in anger?

THESEUS

What's this? You're frightened lest my prayer be heard?   1180
Join with me rather in my just demand;
Impress on me the blackness of his guilt;
Inflame my too restrained and sluggish rage.
You don't yet know the full range of his baseness:
His anger with you vents itself in insults:
Your mouth, he says, is full of twisted lies;
Aricia, so he claims, has won his heart:
He loves her.

PHAEDRA
                        What, my lord?

THESEUS
                                        That's what he said.
But such a feeble ruse I cast aside.
So let us hope from Neptune speedy justice.   1190
I'll go myself and kneel before his altar:
I'll urge him to fulfil his sacred oath.

        Exit THESEUS.   [IV.v]

PHAEDRA (*alone*)

With that he leaves me. What dread news is this?
And what ill-smothered flame leaps in my breast?
O Heaven! A thunderbolt to strike my heart!
I flew here to the rescue of his son;
I tore myself from a terrified Oenone,
Yielding to the remorse that racks me. Who
Can say where my repentance would have led?
Perhaps I'd have confessed my guilt; if I   1200
Had been allowed to speak, the truth perhaps,
The ugly truth would have escaped my lips.
Hippolytus can love, and he does not
Love me! Aricia has his heart! Aricia!
Gods! When he coldly armed himself against me
With such proud eyes, with such a threatening brow,

I thought his heart was still unknown to love
And armed against all women equally.
And all the time another had enslaved him;
His cruel eyes had melted for another!
Perhaps his heart grows tender easily?
I am the only one he can't endure!
And I was going to rush to his defence!

[IV.vi]   *Enter* OENONE.

PHAEDRA (*continues*)
My dear Oenone, have you heard?

OENONE

                                        No, but
I come here trembling for you, that's the truth.
I blenched at your intention when you left me.
I feared the King would kill you in his rage.

PHAEDRA
Oenone, who'd have thought there was another?

OENONE
Another . . . ?

PHAEDRA
                        Hippolytus is in love. It's true.
That fierce opponent who could not be won,
Who spurned praise and resented pleading tears,
That tiger I was frightened to approach:
He's beaten, tamed, he's been brought to his knees.
Aricia's found the way into his heart.

OENONE
Aricia?

PHAEDRA
                Ah! What pain unknown till now!
For what fresh torment I preserved my life!
All I have suffered, all my fears and fevers,
The rage of love, the horror of remorse,
The bitter insult of a cold rebuff
Were only preludes to this agony.
They are in love! How did they blind my eyes?
How have they been together? Where? Since when?
You knew. Why did you let me be deluded?

Could you not tell me of their stolen passion?
Have they been often seen, whispering, gazing?
Deep in the forest did they hide away?
Ah, they were free to be together. In
The sight of Heaven their love was innocent;
Remorse did not restrain their longing hearts;
For them the days dawned cloudless and serene.   1240
And I, poor castaway disowned by nature,
I hid myself from day, I fled from light:
Death was the only god I dared implore;
I waited for the time when I should die.
Wormwood I had for food, and tears to drink;
In my misfortune still too closely watched,
I dared not drown myself at will in weeping;
In fear I tasted that grim joy; and often
I had to mask my anguish with a brow
Serene, and to deprive myself of tears.   1250

OENONE

And what fruit will their futile love afford them?
They'll never meet again.

PHAEDRA

                                 They'll love for ever.
Now as I speak – ah, how the thought torments me! –
They're braving the dangerous rage of my revenge.
They are defying the exile that should part them,
And swearing always to remain together.
No! They shall not be happy and mock me!
Oenone, take pity on my jealous fury:
Aricia must be destroyed. I must rekindle
My husband's anger with her hateful blood.   1260
Let him not be content with mild reprisals:
The sister's crime is blacker than her brothers';
My jealous fever drives me to implore him . . .
     What am I saying? Where will my madness take me?
I'm jealous, and it's Theseus' help I beg!
My husband is alive, and still I'm yearning!
For whom? The man I long for is his son!
Each word I utter makes my hair stand up.

My foul offences top the measure now:
1270 In me breathe incest and false witness, while
My murderous hands, impatient for revenge,
Are burning to be plunged in guiltless blood.
Vile wretch! And I still live, endure the gaze
Of the sacred Sun from whom I am descended?
My forebear is the master of the gods;
The skies are all thronged with my ancestors.
Where shall I hide? Down in infernal night.
No: there my father holds the urn of Fate,
Which has been placed, they say, in his stern hands;
1280 Minos in Hades judges human souls.
Ah, how his shade will tremble with dismay
To see his daughter brought before his eyes
And forced to own so many hideous crimes,
Iniquities perhaps unknown in Hades!
    Father, how will you greet that fearsome sight?
I see the urn slip from your grasp; I see
You search for some new penance, and become
Yourself the torturer of your own child.
Forgive! A cruel goddess has destroyed
1290 Your family: in my folly see her vengeance.
Ah! My poor heart bears all the shame of sin,
And yet I've never tasted its sweet fruit.*
Hounded to my last breath by evil chance,
In torment I yield up a life of pain.

OENONE

Oh, no, my lady! Fight your groundless fears.
Look differently upon a fault that is
Excusable. You love. We cannot change
Our destiny: you were fatally possessed.
Among us is that such a rarity?
1300 Has love to this day conquered only you?
To humans weakness is but natural;
Mortal you are, submit to mortal fate.
The curse that you complain of is not new.
The gods themselves, the gods on high Olympus,
Who shatter evil-doers with outraged wrath,
Have sometimes burned with a forbidden fire.

PHAEDRA

What now? What counsel dare you offer me?
So to the last you mean to poison me,
You wicked soul? See how you have destroyed me:
Fleeing from life, I was turned back by you;   1310
When you entreated, I forgot my duty;
I shunned Hippolytus, you made me see him.
Why did you meddle? How could your impious tongue
Dare slander him and darken all his days?
Perhaps he'll die: the sacrilegious prayer
Of a distracted father may be answered.
I will hear you no more. Go, loathsome monster;
Go; leave to me the care of my sad fate.
May Heaven's justice pay you worthily!
And may your punishment appal for ever   1320
All those like you, who by vile stratagems
Feed the infirmities of luckless princes,
Urge them to follow where their heart would lead
And smooth for them the path to deadly sin.
Odious flatterers, worst of all the gifts
The wrath of Heaven can bestow on kings!
    Exit PHAEDRA.

OENONE (*alone*)

Ah, gods! To serve her I betrayed all trust!
And this is my reward? It is most just.

ACT V

HIPPOLYTUS, ARICIA, ISMENE   [V.i]

ARICIA

So in such peril you can still be silent
And leave your loving father still deceived?   1330
If my poor tears are powerless to move you,
And you can bear to see me nevermore,
Then go, and leave me desolate; but first
At least ensure the safety of your life.
Defend your honour from a shameful charge,
And force your father to revoke his prayer.

There is still time: why not? What senseless whim
Drives you to give free rein to your accuser?
Enlighten Theseus.

HIPPOLYTUS

                              What is left to tell?
1340   The tale of his dishonoured marriage-bed?
Was I, by my too candid words, to make
My father's face ignobly blush with shame?
The hideous secret you alone have learnt.
My heart speaks only to the gods and you.
All that I would have hidden from myself
I could not hide from you: is that not love?
But under seal of silence it was told.
Forget, if you can do so, that I spoke,
And never may these pure lips part to breathe
1350   So horrible a story. Rather let us
Trust that high Heaven will see justice done:
My vindication matters to the gods.
Phaedra must some day bear her punishment
And all the public shame that is her due.
On you this is the only curb I set;
In all the rest I leave my anger free:
Renounce the slavery that is your lot;
Be brave and join me, come away with me;
Break free from this unholy place of darkness
1360   Where virtue breathes corrupt and poisoned air.
Steal away soon, while the confusion my
Disgrace has stirred will cover your departure.
I can provide the means for your escape:
No other guards but mine attend you still.
Our cause will be maintained by strong defenders:
Argos invites us, Sparta calls to us.
Let us appeal for justice to our friends;
Do not let Phaedra seize our scattered fortunes,
Deprive us both of our paternal throne
1370   And claim our due as spoils to give her son.*
This is our chance and we must grasp it now.
          What fear restrains you? Why do you hesitate?
Your cause alone it is that spurs me on.

When I am fire, how is it you are ice?
Are you afraid to join a banished man?

ARICIA

How dear, my lord, would such an exile be!
Once wedded to your destiny, in what
Delight I'd live, forgotten by the world!
But, not united by that perfect bond,
Can I with honour steal away with you?*   1380
I know the strictest code of honour will
Permit me to escape your father's grasp:
To me he is no parent, this no home;
To those who run from tyrants flight is free.
But you love me, my lord; I fear the shame—

HIPPOLYTUS

No, no: your honour is too precious to me.
A nobler plan I have to offer you.
Escape your persecutors as my bride.
Orphaned as we both are, the will of Heaven
Frees us to wed with no consent but ours.   1390
True marriage does not need the blaze of torches.*
Beside the city gates, among those tombs,
The ancient graves of princes of my race,
A temple stands, the dread of perjurers.
There mortal men take care to swear the truth:
The faithless suffer sudden punishment;
And fearing there to meet a certain death,
The liar knows no curb more terrible.
There, if you trust me, we shall meet and make
A solemn oath to love for evermore.   1400
The god who is honoured there shall be our witness;
We both shall pray to him to be our father.
I'll call on the most holy gods to hear me;
And chaste Diana, gracious Juno, all
The gods shall witness my true love affirmed,
And stand as surety of my sacred vows.

ARICIA

The King is coming. Go at once, my prince,
I'll wait a little to conceal my flight.
Go now; but leave with me some trusted guide

1410   To help me find my fearful way to you.

[V.ii]   *Exit* HIPPOLYTUS. *Enter* THESEUS.

THESEUS

O gods! Cast light on my confusion: deign
To help me recognize the truth I seek.

ARICIA (*aside*)

Go, dear Ismene, and prepare to leave.

[V.iii]   *Exit* ISMENE.

THESEUS

You've lost your colour, my lady, and, it seems,
Your tongue. Why did Hippolytus come here?

ARICIA

My lord, to say farewell to me for ever.

THESEUS

So your eyes tamed that rebel spirit: his
First sighs of love are your successful work?

ARICIA

My lord, I can't deny the truth to you:
1420   Your unjust hatred has not passed to him;
He did not use me as a criminal.

THESEUS

I understand: he swore eternal love.
But do not trust to his inconstant heart:
He swore as much to others as to you.

ARICIA

Did he?

THESEUS

You should have taught him to be true.
How could you bear so loathsomely to share him?

ARICIA

And how can you bear loathsome slandering
To dim the course of such a glorious life?
Have you so little knowledge of his heart?
1430   Are you so poor at telling good from evil?
Must from your eyes alone an odious cloud
Conceal his virtue bright for all to see?
Oh, don't abandon him to lying tongues.
Stop. Ask forgiveness for your murderous prayer.

Beware, my lord, beware: the angry gods
May so hate you that they will grant your wish.
They often take our victims in their wrath:
Their gifts to us are often penances.

THESEUS

No, you shan't mask his foul depravity.
You're blinded in his favour by your love.   1440
But I've sure witnesses that I can trust:
Their tears, true tears, I've seen with my own eyes.

ARICIA

Take care, my lord. Your mighty arm has slain
Innumerable monsters for mankind.
But not all: there is one you still permit
To live . . . But your son forbids me to go on.
Knowing his wish to shield your dignity,
I'd grieve him if I dared to tell you more.
I must respect his scruples; let me leave you
Before I break the silence he imposed.   1450

    Exit ARICIA.   [V.iv]

THESEUS (*alone*)

What's in her mind? What can her words conceal,
Starting to tell, and always breaking off?
Have they devised some trickery to blind me?
Have they conspired to torture me with doubt?
But deep in my own heart, for all my stubborn
Harshness, what plaintive voice cries out to me?
A secret, gnawing pity saps my spirit.
    Oenone: I must question her again.
I must have more light thrown on what took place.
Guards: have Oenone come to me alone.   1460

    Enter PANOPE.   [V.v]

PANOPE

My lord, I cannot say just what the Queen
Intends, but her distress fills me with fear.
Mortal despair is written on her face,
And on her cheeks already lies pale death.
Oenone, driven from her in disgrace,
Has hurled herself deep down into the sea.

What caused her desperation is not known:
The waves have swept her from our sight for ever.

THESEUS
What is—

PANOPE
                    Her death has not appeased the Queen.
1470   In her divided soul her anguish swells.
Sometimes, to soothe the pain of secret sorrow,
She clasps her children, bathes them in her tears;
Then suddenly all mother-love forsakes her,
And, horror-struck, she pushes them away.
No firm direction guides her faltering steps;
Her wild eyes see us now unknowingly.
Three times she has begun to write; and then
Three times, with altered mind, destroyed her words.
See her, my lord; see her, and ease her pain.

THESEUS
1480   Oenone dead, and Phaedra longs to die?
Call back my son; let him defend himself!
Bring him to me: I'll listen to him now.
    O Neptune, do not speed your deadly gift;
Rather may it for ever be denied.
I may have trusted doubtful witnesses,
And raised my cruel hands to you too soon.
Ah, what despair would flow from my own prayer!

[V.vi]   *Enter* THERAMENES.

THESEUS (*continues*)
Theramenes, it's you? Where is my son?
To you I entrusted him when he was but
1490   A little boy. But why these tears? What of
My son?

THERAMENES
                    You care too late. Your love for him
Is futile now. Hippolytus is dead.

THESEUS
Gods!

THERAMENES
        I've seen die the kindest of mankind,
And, I swear, the most innocent, my lord.

THESEUS

My son dead? Just when I hold out my arms
To him, the gods have struck him down?
What tore him from me, what swift thunderbolt?

THERAMENES

The city gates were scarcely left behind us;
His chariot bore him up; his grieving guards,
Silent in sympathy, were drawn around him.   1500
Pensive, he took the road towards Mycenae;
His hand let drift the reins upon his horses.
His noble steeds, in former days so proud
And full of eagerness to heed his voice,
With drooping eye today and lowered head
Seemed in accord with his sad thoughtfulness.

A fearsome roar, from deep down in the sea,
Broke forth just then to wake the sleeping air;
And from within the earth a mighty voice
Groaned in reply to that appalling roar.   1510
Our very heart's blood froze in sudden fear;
The bristling horses pricked attentive ears.
Then on the surface of the watery plain
Rears up in seething whirls a liquid mountain.
The wave comes in, it breaks, and at our feet
In floods of foam it spews a raging monster.
Its massive brow is armed with threatening horns,
Its body overlaid with yellowing scales:
A fierce wild bull, a fiery-tempered dragon,
Behind it twists and curves a thrashing tail.   1520
Its roaring echoes round the trembling shore.
This savage monster horrifies the heavens,
Astounds the earth, pollutes the air; the wave
That bore it to the shore draws back, aghast.

All flee; and, armed with no vain bravery,
Seek refuge in the temple close at hand.
Hippolytus alone, true hero's son,
Restrains his horses, grasps his javelins,
Aims at the monster, hurls with steady hand,
And in its side inflicts a spreading wound.   1530
Leaping with pain and rage, the monster comes

Bellowing up to the horses' hooves, falls down,
And rolls, to show them blazing jaws that wrap
Them utterly in fire, and blood, and smoke.
Terror sweeps them away and, deafened now,
They will not answer to the rein or voice;
Their struggling master tires himself in vain;
The bits turn crimson with their blood-flecked foam.
Some even say that in the hideous tumult
1540   A god was seen to goad their dusty flanks.
Forced on by fear, they trample over rocks:
The axle shrieks and snaps. The brave prince sees
His shattered chariot split and fly apart;
He falls – and he's entangled in the reins.
     Forgive my grief. For me that cruel sight
Will be an everlasting source of tears.
My lord, I saw your poor ill-fated son
Dragged by the horses he himself had fed.
He calls them back; they panic at his voice;
1550   They gallop. His body soon becomes one wound.
Our cries of anguish ring throughout the plain.
At last their headlong flight begins to slacken;
They stop, just by those ancient tombs where lie
The cold remains of kings, his ancestors.
I race to him in tears, his guard behind me.
We're guided by the trail of his brave blood:
The rocks are red with it; the dripping thorns
Are hung with blood-stained spoils that were his hair.
I reach him, call him; giving me his hand,
1560   He opens dying eyes that close at once,
And says: 'Heaven tears from me a blameless life.
Care for Aricia, forsaken by my death.
Dear friend, my father may be undeceived
One day, and sorry for his son accused
Unjustly. Say my blood and mournful shade
Will be appeased if he is gentle with
His captive, and restores to her . . .' He died,
And in my arms I held a shapeless corpse:
A sorry triumph of the angry gods
1570   That his own father would not recognize.

THESEUS
>My son! Dear hope that I have cast away!
>Relentless gods, too well you have served me!
>What dread remorse must fill my mortal days!

THERAMENES
>Then came Aricia, anxious and afraid.
>She meant, my lord, escaping from your wrath,
>To pledge herself his wife before the gods.
>She draws near, sees the red and smoking grass,
>And sees – a sight to greet his bride indeed –
>A grey and crumpled heap: Hippolytus.
>At first she struggles to evade her sorrow: 1580
>Not knowing now the hero that she loves,
>She sees Hippolytus, yet asks for him.
>At last, too sure that he is there before her,
>With sad reproach she lifts her eyes to Heaven;
>Then, cold and groaning, scarcely drawing breath,
>She swoons and sinks down at her lover's feet.
>Ismene is there: Ismene, bathed in tears,
>Summons her back to life, or, rather, grief.
>   And I have come, abhorring light itself,
>To tell you of a hero's dying wish,   1590
>So to discharge, my lord, the unhappy task
>That his departing spirit laid on me.
>But see: his mortal enemy is here.

>>*Enter* PHAEDRA *with* PANOPE.   [V.vii]

THESEUS
>So you're victorious, and my son is dead.
>Ah, yes! I'm right to fear! A cruel doubt
>Acquits him in my heart and makes me tremble!
>But he is dead, my lady: take your victim;
>Relish his fall, unjust or merited.
>If I've been blinded, do not make me see:
>Since you accuse him, I believe him guilty.   1600
>His death gives me sufficient cause for weeping
>Without my seeking fearsome knowledge, which
>Could not restore him to my grieving heart,
>And might perhaps increase my wretchedness.
>Far from these shores, and you, let me escape

The torn and bleeding image of my son.
Crazed, racked by that grim memory, I crave
For exile from the universe. The whole
World seems to rise and censure my injustice.
1610   My very fame inflates my penance. If
Men did not know me, I could hide myself.
I even hate to be the favoured of
The gods; their murderous gifts I shall lament,
And no more weary them with my vain prayers.
Grant what they might to me, their deadly blessing
Could not repay what they have taken from me.

PHAEDRA

No, Theseus, I must break my unjust silence;
Your son must be restored to innocence.
He did no wrong.

THESEUS

                    Cursed father that I am!
1620   My faith in you compelled me to condemn him!
You cannot justify such cruelty—

PHAEDRA

Each moment is precious to me, Theseus, hear me.
It's I who looked upon your dutiful,
Chaste son with ungodly and incestuous eyes.
Heaven lit a deadly passion in my breast.
What followed was the vile Oenone's work.
Hippolytus, she feared, would tell you of
My raging love, which filled him with disgust.
Falsely abusing my weak state, she rushed
1630   To blacken him in your eyes with my guilt.
She fled my anger, chose her punishment,
And in the sea found death too easily.
I would by now have perished by the sword,
But your son's virtue would be left in pain.
To show you my remorse I'm following
A slower road to join the dead below.
I've taken, poured along my burning veins,
A poison that Medea brought to Athens.*
Already I can feel the venom strike,

Casting strange coldness round my dying heart. 1640
Now through a mist I see the heavens and
The husband whom by my presence I defile.
Death steals the brightness from my eyes to make
The sunlight, that they sullied, pure again.

PANOPE

My lord, she's dead.

THESEUS

Would that the memory
Of such a deed of darkness died with her!
Come, since my error now is all too plain,
Let my tears mingle with my poor son's blood;
Let me hold in my arms his dear remains,
And expiate my loathsome angry prayer. 1650
I'll honour him as he too well deserves;
And to appease his injured shade the more,
Despite the scheming of her treacherous race,
For me his bride shall take a daughter's place.*

Notes

Scene changes and stage directions

In accordance with French practice, the original texts of these plays do not explicitly indicate entrances and exits, but deem a new scene to begin almost always when characters enter or leave the stage. To avoid confusion, in this volume the normal English practice is followed and entrances and exits are marked. There are no 'scene' headings, but to facilitate cross-reference the French scene divisions within each act are noted in brackets in the margin – given as act and scene number in each case.

For this volume, stage directions (given in italics) and background detail in the lists of characters have been edited at the translator's discretion and presented as they would be printed in an English play, with the intention of creating scripts that are easy for non-specialists to follow and for potential actors to perform.

Line numbering and asterisks

French plays of this period, when written in verse, are line numbered, and this numbering is constant (as opposed to editions of Shakespeare, for example), so the numbering here is the same as the reader will find in any edition of the original French text. However, passages in prose – such as that beginning at line 1690 of *The Misanthrope* in which Célimène's letters are read out – are not included in the numbering, presumably because the number of lines taken by prose will vary from edition to edition, unlike lines of verse.

An asterisk at the end of a line indicates that the line, or range of lines, is annotated in the Notes below, each note being preceded by the line number(s) in question. Notes on the prefaces or scene-setting details are also flagged by an asterisk, placed after the word or phrase in question.

CINNA

Historical background

From the founding of the city in 753 BC until 509 BC, Rome was ruled by kings. After the overthrow of the last king, Tarquin the Proud, and the establishment of the Republic, the very word 'king' was anathema. From 107 BC Rome was beset by power struggles, culminating in 82 BC, when Sulla defeated Marius and had himself appointed dictator. His rule was notoriously cruel, but he abdicated in 79 BC, died the following year and was given an elaborate funeral. The power struggles resumed, and from 49 BC resulted in civil wars. Cinna's grandfather, the republican Pompey the Great, was defeated by Julius Caesar, who in 44 BC made himself 'dictator for life'. In that same year he was assassinated by Brutus and Cassius, who were attempting to restore the old Republic. In the ensuing civil strife, they were defeated by Octavius and Mark Antony and died on the battlefield at Philippi in Macedonia in 42 BC. Their failure led to the Triumvirate of Mark Antony, Lepidus and Octavius Caesar, the conflict between Octavius and Mark Antony, and the latter's defeat at Actium in 31 BC followed by his self-inflicted death a year later which left Octavius sole ruler of the Roman world. In 27 BC the Senate gave him the splendid title *Augustus* – 'majestic' or 'venerable'; the word 'king' remained unacceptable, but he was in effect an absolute monarch. The title *imperator*, which translates literally as 'emperor', meant 'commander of the armed forces'. Augustus died in AD 14 and was given honours appropriate to a god.

Corneille drew on an account of Cinna's conspiracy written by Seneca for the benefit of Nero (AD 37–68) and published in translation by the sixteenth-century French essayist Michel de Montaigne in Book I of his *Essays*. He was perhaps drawn to the subject by perceived similarities between the reign of Augustus and Cardinal Richelieu's rule in France (1624–42). Gnaeus Cornelius Cinna Magnus was born between 47 and 35 BC. Emilia and Maximus are fictional characters.

Setting

The play conforms to the neo-classical unities of time and action (see the Introduction, p. xvii), having a single plot worked out within twenty-four hours, and somewhat loosely resolves the problem presented by the stricture of the unity of place by having the stage represent two locations, both within Augustus' palace. In his 'Critique' Corneille explains why he needed to stretch the dramatic convention of his day.

1–52. *[I.i]*: This scene, comprising Emilia's demanding opening soliloquy, has sometimes been cut in performance.

11. *raised him to his throne*: Roman emperors did not wear crowns (l. 480), sit on thrones or execute using scaffolds (l. 197): their mention in historical drama either is intended to suggest parallels with seventeenth-century France, or results from ignorance.

72. *a man proscribed*: To be proscribed meant losing one's possessions, one's citizenship and the protection of the law: a proscribed man could be killed with impunity, and indeed was. His name would be advertised on posters, as the word (from the Latin *proscribere*, 'publish in writing') implies.

179. *eagle mowed down eagle*: The eagle was the symbol carried by the Roman legions, who in civil wars fought each other.

261. *The outcome cannot soil your memory*: In the French, from this point onwards, Emilia addresses Cinna as *tu*, but for him she is always *vous*. This signifies how much he respects her; perhaps is in awe of her.

394. *Agrippa and Maecenas*: Marcus Vipsanius Agrippa (*c.* 63 BC–12 BC), the Roman statesman and general, had been Augustus' military companion and counsellor. He commanded Octavius' fleet at the defeat of Mark Antony in the battle of Actium (see 'Historical background'), so winning the campaign for him; he married Julia, the daughter of Octavius, then emperor, in 21 BC. Gaius Cilnius Maecenas (70 BC–*c.* 8 BC), the patron of writers including Horace and Virgil, was also a close friend and political adviser. The arguments for and against democracy put forward by Cinna and Maximus were taken in part by Corneille from a debate between Agrippa and Maecenas recorded by Dio Cassius (AD 150–235) in Book 52 of his history of Rome, written in Greek.

550. *She owes to consuls her great power and glory*: Under the Republic, two elected consuls held the supreme executive power.

554–6. *You've closed the Janus-gates . . . second of her kings achieved*: Janus, after whom the month of January is named, was the Roman god of beginnings and transitions, hence of gates and doorways. Looking to both the past and the future, he is represented with two faces. The doors of his temple in

Rome were closed only in peacetime. This happened under the consuls after the successful outcome of the First Punic War, when Carthage was defeated (241 BC), and under the pious and peace-loving King Numa (753–673 BC), who succeeded the warlike Romulus, founder of the city.

561. *Even the Tarquins' exile cost us blood*: In 509 BC an ancestor of the Brutus who assassinated Julius Caesar exiled from Rome the last king, Tarquin the Proud, who was of Etruscan origin; this led to war with the Etruscans.

583. *So jealousy made Sulla turn on Marius*: Sulla defeated Marius in 82 BC (see 'Historical background').

638. *she takes my daughter Julia's place*: See note on l. 1589.

669. *Cassius it was who failed: his panicking*: At the battle of Philippi in 42 BC (see 'Historical background'), Cassius had himself killed, thinking all was lost, unaware that Brutus had defeated Octavius during the first engagement. The Republic might have been restored after the assassination of Julius Caesar if Cassius had kept his head.

993. *Antony loved a queen: that stained his honour*: Mark Antony's entanglement with Cleopatra, queen of Egypt, was largely responsible for his military decline (see 'Historical background').

994–6. *If great Attalus . . . A freedman of the Romans*: Attalus III (*c.* 170 BC–133 BC), king of Pergamum, left his kingdom to Rome in his will. It was Prusias II (*c.* 220 BC–149 BC), king of Bithynia, who appeared before the Romans in the dress of a freedman when he was forced to make peace. (Prusias is the king in the tragedy *Nicomède*, which Corneille was to write subsequently.)

1097. *Perfidy nurtured in a Fury's breast*: It is hardly appropriate to refer to Cinna as one of the vengeful Furies of Greek mythology, but perfectly applicable to Emilia, if Augustus but knew it.

1133–6. *The streams . . . Perugia and her people*: After their victory at Philippi, Octavius and Mark Antony had all their prisoners slaughtered; Octavius defeated Mark Antony at Actium (see 'Historical background'); Sextus Pompey, younger son of Pompey the Great, was defeated by Agrippa in a naval battle off Sicily in 36 BC; Mark Antony's brother, Lucius, sought refuge in Perugia in 41–40 BC: Octavius massacred the inhabitants and set fire to the city.

1165–6. *Rome is a hydra . . . hundreds more*: Killing the Lernian hydra was one of Hercules' twelve labours. Every time one of the heads of the enormous serpent was cut off, two more grew in its place.

1193. *Livia, I've been betrayed*: The role of Livia has been cut more often than played, it being judged that Augustus appeared a greater man having made up his own mind than having been influenced by his wife.

1202–5. *Lepidus rose ... Egnatius' fury*: Quintus Salvidienus Rufus was executed by Octavius (or committed suicide) in 40 BC for switching his allegiance to Mark Antony. Marcus Aemilius Lepidus, son of Lepidus the triumvir, planned to kill Octavius after the battle of Actium and was executed with his wife in 30 BC. Murena and Cepio led conspiracies after Octavius became emperor and were killed in 22 BC. Rufus Egnatius, a candidate for the consulship in 20 BC, was accused of conspiring against Augustus and executed.

1248. *After twenty years of rule*: This makes Augustus fifty-seven and places the conspiracy in 7–6 BC. The episode actually occurred in AD 4, when Augustus was sixty-seven. Either Corneille was mistaken (see note on ll. 1710–12) or he had his reasons as a dramatist for making his characters ten years younger. Strictly speaking, the fifty-seven-year-old Augustus cannot refer to his daughter's banishment (ll. 638 and 1589), because she was not exiled until 2 BC, when he was sixty-one. But Corneille is writing a play, not a historical documentary.

1266. *Exit LIVIA*: In his 'Critique' of the play (p. 61), Corneille explains why he felt compelled to break with the convention of 'scene-linking' in Act IV. The convention enforced the unity of place by forbidding that the stage should ever be left vacant during an act: succeeding scenes should be linked by at least one character from the preceding scene remaining present at the beginning of the following one. Here the stage is momentarily left empty following Livia's departure and the setting switches from Augustus' apartment to Emilia's.

1435–6. *you spring from ... my father's enemies and mine*: Augustus is referring to his adoptive father, Julius Caesar. Cinna's father, Lucius Cornelius Cinna, was Pompey's son-in-law. He fought against Julius Caesar and approved of his assassination in 44 BC, although he was not a participant in the conspiracy.

1453. *The dignities and honours you've requested*: Notably membership of the priesthood, which explains how Cinna could plan to give Augustus 'a dagger in his breast' instead of incense at the sacrifice (ll. 235–6).

1462–3. *snatched Maecenas ... By untimely death*: Maecenas had died in 8 BC (see note on l. 394).

1535–6. *the Servilii ... the Fabii*: Names of the great Roman families from whom the majority of the Republic's magistrates were drawn.

1546–7. *Pompey's blood ... and his two sons*: Pompey the Great was killed in 48 BC, on the orders of King Ptolemy XIII of Egypt, who wished to ingratiate himself with Julius Caesar, conqueror of Pharsalus. (Corneille's tragedy *The Death of Pompey*, 1643, treats this subject.) Pompey's two sons, Gnaeus and Sextus, were killed in 45 and 35 BC respectively. (See note on ll. 1133–6 and 'Historical background'.)

1564. *You too, my child*: Augustus echoes Julius Caesar's legendary dying words: 'You too, Brutus!'

1589. *I had to banish Julia in disgrace*: As a consequence of her scandalously lewd behaviour, Augustus exiled his daughter Julia for life in 2 BC. Born in 39 BC, she was forced into political marriages three times, the second time to Agrippa (see note on l. 394), who was her senior by nearly twenty-five years. She was made to commit suicide by her third husband, Tiberius, soon after his accession in AD 14.

1710–12. *rank of consul ... Prefer its crimson*: Cinna was in fact a consul in the year AD 5. There has been a mistaken belief that his consulship was in 5 BC, which has caused French editors to date the conspiracy in the previous year, 6 BC. This misguided reasoning is spelt out, for example, in the 1910 Hachette selection of Corneille's plays, *Théâtre choisi de Corneille* (p. 400), and the erroneous dates are repeated as recently as the 2010 Larousse edition of *Cinna* (p. 222), in contradiction of the correct statement (p. 8) that the conspiracy took place in AD 4.

The holder of a consulship wore a toga with a blood-coloured border. Under the Republic two consuls were elected together to serve for a one-year term, and had some power and authority, but with the establishment of the Empire the title was merely honorary, the Emperor acting as supreme leader.

1719–20. *my soul ... surrenders silently*: The soul represented the moral and intellectual faculties while the heart was considered to be the seat of the emotions. In Emilia both reason and sentiment unite in her miraculous enlightenment. She now accepts that Heaven willed the deaths of all those, including her father, who opposed the change in Rome's form of government from democracy to absolute rule.

1777–8. *redoubled sacrifices ... happier auspices*: The next day's sacrifices at which Augustus was to have been assassinated will be held under more favourable omens as a result of his spiritual rebirth.

1780. *Augustus all has learnt and learnt all to forget*: The play's subtitle, *The Clemency of Augustus*, was suppressed after the first edition, presumably because it gave away the ending and destroyed suspense.

THE MISANTHROPE

100. *The School for Husbands*: An in-joke, referring to another comedy by Molière, dating from 1661, in which the overbearing Sganarelle puts down the tolerant Ariste.

165–6. *my phlegm . . . than your bile*: In June 1666, Molière obtained permission to publish a comedy entitled *The Misanthrope, or, The Atrabilious Lover*. The alternative title was never printed but reveals that the dramatist conceived Alceste as a man whose temperament was dictated by a predominance of 'black bile' in his constitution. This, according to seventeenth-century medical theory, would cause him to be gloomy, irritable and even weirdly irrational. Philinte, on the other hand, having a liberal dose of 'phlegm' in his make-up, is controlled, sociable and serious, but lacking in passion.

186. *what canvassers will speak for you*: It was customary in seventeenth-century France to lobby judges either in person or by hiring a professional pleader. It was legal even to sweeten them with gifts, provided they were perishable.

568. *At the levée*: The levée was the ceremonial rising of the King, always attended by a group of privileged nobility. At the King's 'retiring' (l. 739) the ceremony was reversed.

711–30. *That's not the usual . . . her he loves*: Éliante's speech is derived from Lucretius, *De rerum natura*, IV.1149–65.

756–7. *The Marshals . . . patch it up and avoid a duel*: The function of this court was to resolve affairs of honour without resort to the duel, which was forbidden by edict in 1651.

795. *Up on the stage I lead the claps and boos*: The stage was cluttered with chairs for fashionable spectators. Voltaire was instrumental in ending the practice in 1759.

1435. *Du Bois – in strange attire*: We learn from theatre records of the staging that Du Bois appeared disguised as a courier and wearing boots in readiness for the flight he has come urgently to propose.

1690. *As for the man with green ribbons*: The contemporary list of production requirements for the play (*Mémoire de décorations*) mentions green ribbons as a feature of Alceste's costume.

ANDROMACHE

First Preface

p. 140. *Céladon*: The chivalrous but insipid 'precious' hero of the pastoral romance *L'Astrée* (1607–27) by Honoré d'Urfé.

Second Preface

p. 144. *an ancient commentator on Sophocles*: Racine himself notes that the remark was made by a Greek scholar commentating on Sophocles' *Electra*.

Mythological background

Racine supposes his tragedy to take place a year after the end of the Trojan War, the subject of Homer's *Iliad* and Book II of Virgil's *Aeneid*. Paris, son of Priam the Trojan king, had abducted Helen, the wife of Menelaus, king of Sparta. This outrage to Greek honour sparked the ten-year war with Troy which culminated in the destruction and sack of the great Asian city. During the combat Achilles, the mightiest Greek warrior, killed his counterpart, Hector, heir to the Trojan throne; Pyrrhus, son of Achilles, killed Priam and his daughter Polyxena. The surviving female members of the Trojan royal family were shared out by lot among the victorious Greek kings. Andromache, Hector's widow, with her infant son Astyanax, fell to Pyrrhus and was taken home with him to Epirus as his captive.

Setting

p. 145. *The scene is set in Buthrotum*: Buthrotum was situated on the Adriatic coast opposite the island of Corfu. The stage-manager's note for the 1680 production at the Hôtel de Bourgogne describes the stage set as 'a palace with columns and in the background a sea with ships'.

1.   *so true a friend*: Pylades appears in four Greek tragedies as the faithful companion of Orestes.

73–6. *to preserve his infant life . . . had been killed*: Ulysses (this name the Roman form of the Greek 'Odysseus'), a leading figure on the Greek side in the Trojan War and the hero of Homer's *Odyssey*, was noted for his astuteness. In most versions of the legend, Astyanax is killed immediately after the sack of Troy.

189–90. *the sorrowing Hecuba; / Cassandra*: Hecuba was Priam's wife and Cassandra their daughter.

233–4. *It will not be ... with injustice*: Achilles angrily withdrew for a time from the combat because Agamemnon, the Greek leader, took from him his captive, Briseis.

246. *how closely you are bound by blood*: Orestes and Hermione were first cousins since their fathers, Agamemnon and Menelaus, were brothers.

279–80. *He'd have replaced my father ... always by your hand*: Andromache's father, Eëtion, king of Cilician Thebe, was killed by Achilles, as was Hector.

489–94. *I swear ... those barbarians spared*: This is a reminiscence of Euripides' *Iphigenia in Tauris*.

873–5. *Ah, when ... shield her from their rage*: In the *Iliad* Helen expresses her gratitude to Hector over his pyre for defending her against the reproaches of his family.

916. *clasped the knee of any master*: For the Greeks and Romans the ancient custom was for a suppliant to clasp the knees of the person from whom a favour was entreated. In *Phaedra* (l. 244) Oenone clasps Phaedra's knees to force her to reveal her secret.

938. *When Priam begged, Achilles humoured him*: When Priam begged Achilles for his son Hector's body, Achilles released it to him.

993–4. *My Hector's body ... around our city walls*: Achilles attached Hector's corpse to his chariot and dragged it round the walls of Troy.

1329. *You'd like to see me weep behind her chariot*: A captive, as a prisoner of war, would follow the victor's chariot. Cassandra was tied to Agamemnon's chariot. Hermione is alluding bitterly to the reversal of the roles being played by her and Andromache as a result of Pyrrhus' betrayal.

1356. *It wasn't love ... then*: In the French text, Hermione's fluctuating attitude is reflected in her switching from formal *vous* to *tu* from here, reverting to *vous* at line 1369, and employing *tu* again from halfway through line 1375 to her exit.

1533. *Enough, you faithless coward*: Hermione addresses Orestes as *tu* from this point to her exit.

1612. *stab herself, and fall*: In the Greek legend, Hermione survived Pyrrhus and married Orestes.

1637. *Furies from hell, are your hands raised to strike*: The Furies,
      depicted with snakes for hair, pursued those guilty of especially
      heinous murders, in this case regicide. In two plays by Euripides,
      Orestes and *Iphigenia in Tauris*, Orestes has fits of delirium
      accompanied by visions of the Furies because he has killed his
      mother, Clytemnestra. Although Racine presents Orestes as a
      doom-laden figure in the play, he does not mention his most
      heinous crime, matricide.

PHAEDRA

Preface

p. 203. *Here is another tragedy on a subject taken from Euripides*:
        See the First Preface to *Andromache* (p. 140). Racine modelled
        certain scenes on the *Hippolytus* of Euripides (428 BC) and the
        Phaedra of Seneca (*c.* AD 60). He initially called the play *Hip-
        polytus*, but it was first printed and performed with the title
        Phaedra and Hippolytus. Ultimately, he settled for *Phaedra*.
p. 204. *Pirithoüs*: King of the Lapiths, the legendary companion of
        Theseus.

Mythological background

Because Sol, the Sun, had thrown light on her adultery with Mars,
Venus, the goddess of love, willed that all his female descendants
should be cursed with forbidden sexual desire.

Phaedra's mother, Pasiphaë, daughter of the Sun, lusted after a bull
and gave birth to the Minotaur, a monster half-bull, half-man. King
Minos of Crete, her husband, had Daedalus construct a labyrinth in
which the creature lived, feeding off young Greek men and maidens
sent annually as tribute to Crete. One year Theseus accompanied the
chosen unfortunates and slew the monster with the aid of Phaedra's
sister, Ariadne, who provided him with a thread so that he could find
his way out of the maze. Having betrayed her father through her
love for Theseus, Ariadne eloped with him, but he abandoned her
on the rocky isle of Naxos. So did she suffer the curse of Venus.

Theseus returned to Crete, married Phaedra and took her back to
Athens, where he was now king. The curse of Venus at once began
to take its toll on her.

Setting

p. 207. *The scene is set . . . in Trezene*: The spelling 'Trezene' (based on the French 'Trézène') is used here, to rhyme with 'serene', in order to avoid confusion in performance with 'treason', which is how 'Troezen' is pronounced. The city lay on the Saronic Gulf opposite Athens. The theatre records state that for the first production of the play the scene was 'a vaulted palace. A chair at the beginning'.

10. *the seas on either side of Corinth*: The Aegean and Ionian seas, separated by the isthmus on which Corinth stood.

11–14. *the Acheron . . . where Icarus came down*: In Epirus, on the north-west coast of Greece, lay the source of the river Acheron, believed to flow down to Hades (see the Preface, p. 204). Elis was on the west coast of the Peloponnese, and Taenarum a promontory on the most southern point. Icarus flew too near the sun on wings fastened to his shoulders with wax: he came down into the Icarian Sea, off Asia Minor.

50–51. *young Aricia . . . would destroy us*: By introducing Aricia to the story, Racine provides his audience with both a romantic and a political element. He supposes her to be the sister of the Pallantides, the six sons of Pallas who believed they had a more legitimate claim to the throne of Athens than Theseus, since his claim depended on adoption (see the Genealogical Table for *Phaedra*, p. 280). When they stirred up a revolt, Theseus killed them all and forbade Aricia to marry so that their line would die out.

69–73. *An Amazon mother . . . in tender care*: The Amazons were a race of warrior women who normally made use of men only to produce the girl-children they needed, which explains why Hippolytus, once weaned, was brought up by his wise great-grandfather, Pittheus (ll. 1103–4), and, when he was a small boy, placed by his father under the tutorship of Theramenes (ll. 1489–90).

78–81. *Consoled men . . . Epidaurus' giant*: When Hercules was captive to Omphale, queen of Lydia, Theseus took over his mission of destroying giants and brigands who preyed on luckless wayfarers. Procrustes shortened or stretched his victims to fit his bed of torture; Sinnis, Sciron and Cercyon were also

murderous waylayers of passersby; the giant of Epidaurus was
Periphetes, who, though lame, battered travellers with a brazen
club.

85–6. *In Sparta Helen . . . tears of Periboea*: Theseus abducted Helen
before she married Menelaus and was abducted by Paris to
become 'Helen of Troy'. Periboea was abandoned by Theseus.

131–2. *practising the skill . . . heed the rein*: Neptune was the god of
horsemanship as well as the sea. 'Hippolytus' means 'unleasher
of horses' in Greek.

199–205. *your unhappy children . . . Hippolytus*: Oenone means
that Phaedra's suicide would cast disgrace on her children and
disinherit them, leaving the succession open to Hippolytus.

210. *Sythian woman's*: The Amazons were thought to have origin-
ated in Scythia, the reputed home of barbarian hordes around
the Black Sea.

234–5. *When you were born . . . and my children*: Oenone had
delivered Phaedra and been her wet-nurse; she left her homeland, Crete, to accompany Phaedra to Athens when she married Theseus.

244. *these knees I clasp*: Oenone resorts to the traditional action of
a suppliant; see note on l. 916 of *Andromache*.

282. *searched their entrails for my own lost reason*: Phaedra inspected
the victims' entrails to see whether the goddess would be merci-
ful and allow her to overcome her passion.

290. *In looking at his father I found him*: This line forcibly expresses
the horror of experiencing incestuous desire.

300. *the fruit of his ill-fated bed*: Her two sons by Theseus, Demophon and Acamas – not named in the text.

325–30. *Athens is uncertain . . . blood of Pallas*: The three pretend-
ers to the Athenian throne were: Phaedra's elder son, Demophon, which is what Theseus would expect; Hippolytus, in
theory barred by his having a non-Greek mother; and Aricia
as a blood descendant of Pallas. Hippolytus would without
obstacle become king of Trezene, his father's other kingdom,
as Oenone points out in l. 358.

349–54. *Live, for you need . . . you can safely see him*: This is not
so: Phaedra's love might no longer be adulterous, but it was
still incestuous and forbidden by French civil and canon law. In
the eyes of the Church, marriage made a man and woman 'one
flesh'; this makes Hippolytus virtually Phaedra's own son. Racine's audience would know it, and ll. 702, 1270 and 1624 make
clear that Phaedra is only too well aware of it. Both Theseus
and Hippolytus refer to Phaedra's declaration as incestuous

(ll. 1011, 1100 and 1146–9): it accounts for the young man's extreme revulsion (ll. 663–4). Hamlet is similarly revolted by his mother's 'incestuous' marriage to her brother-in-law. In Euripides' version of the Phaedra story, incest is not an issue, since such a liaison was not considered incestuous in ancient Greece, but Racine's play reflects the culture of his day.

360. *The mighty ramparts that Athena built*: The goddess Athena was the founder of Athens.

384–5. *Pirithoüs . . . Cocytus*: For Pirithoüs, see note on the Preface. The Cocytus was one of the four rivers of the Underworld.

421–6. *Athens' great king . . . Erechtheus, her own son*: Erechtheus was the son of Earth (Gaia) and, according to legend, the first king of Athens (see the Genealogical Table for *Phaedra*, p. 280). See also note on ll. 50–51.

478. *Pittheus, my great ancestor*: Pittheus was Theseus' maternal grandfather, and king of Trezene (see the Genealogical Table for *Phaedra*, p. 280).

494–500. *I yield . . . ill-fated brothers were forgotten*: Since Theseus' father Aegeus was only an adopted son of Pandion, his right and that of his descendants to the throne of Athens had been dubious. Hippolytus justifies his father's kingship by the brilliance of his rule, but asserts that with the death of Theseus the crown should revert to the true blood line represented by Aricia.

505–7. *Trezene is mine . . . Athens is rightly yours*: Hippolytus' political vision contrasts with Oenone's (ll. 358–62). He expects to rule Trezene by right, win the throne of Athens for Aricia and have Phaedra's sons withdraw to their mother's homeland, Crete.

621. *Neptune is his protector*: According to another Greek legend, Theseus was the son of Neptune.

670. *You heartless boy! You understood*: During the scene Phaedra's mode of address to Hippolytus becomes progressively less formal. She begins with 'my lord', switches to 'prince' (l. 634) and now uses *tu*, which indicates both intimacy and lack of respect. The principal characters normally address each other as *vous*; they use *tu* to confidants (including Oenone and Theramenes), servants and the gods or abstract concepts such as Destiny.

724. *They've chosen your brother*: Actually Hippolytus' half-brother Demophon, Phaedra's elder son by Theseus (see note on l. 300).

736. *I'll place the sceptre in the worthiest hand*: That is to say, Aricia's hand (see ll. 507–8).

737. *Let them take their titles somewhere else*: Because Phaedra has shut herself away, the Athenian envoy will have charged Oenone with the duty of informing her that the crown has been offered to her son, and that she is expected to act as regent until the boy comes of age.

862. *Jupiter's blood should swell their confidence*: Jupiter was Phaedra's paternal grandfather (see the Genealogical Table for *Phaedra*, p. 280).

943–4. *Hercules ... owed his rest to your renown*: See note on ll. 78–81.

962–4. *Pirithoüs I saw thrown ... human flesh*: According to the legend, Pirithoüs was devoured by a fierce dog that fed on human flesh, but Racine's use of the word 'monster' is carefully calculated throughout the play.

1001–2. *What are you saying ... his father's honour*: Oenone has told her lie during the act-break, producing Hippolytus' sword as supposed evidence.

1044. *Dare you show yourself to me*: In III.v, Theseus had spoken to the Prince with formal respect, using *vous*. He now uses *tu*.

1141. *the pillars of Hercules*: The Straits of Gibraltar, for the ancient Greeks the limit of the inhabited world.

1157–9. *Neptune swore ... dreaded / Even by the gods*: Even the gods feared dire punishment if they broke an oath sworn by the Styx, the greatest river in Hades.

1291–2. *Ah! My poor heart ... its sweet fruit*: These lines have been interpreted as vulgar regret that her love for her stepson had never been consummated, but they surely constitute a plea for clemency on the grounds that the desire has given her nothing but suffering.

1364–70. *No other guards ... to give her son*: Theseus had left Hippolytus in charge of the captive Aricia (ll. 929–31). Unjustly banished by Theseus, Hippolytus feels at liberty to rebel against his father and claim the throne of Athens for himself and Aricia, since both have in his view a stronger right to it than Phaedra's sons.

1380. *Can I with honour steal away with you*: To a modern audience Aricia's prudishness seems ridiculous and out of character, but the convention of 'decorum' was strict in Racine's day. Besides, her hesitation gives Hippolytus the opportunity to make a passionate declaration of his devotion, which leaves us with an impression of noble purity. We shall not see him again.

1391. *True marriage does not need the blaze of torches*: A Greek wedding concluded with a procession to the married couple's new home lit by torches with which their first fire was kindled.

1638. *A poison that Medea brought to Athens*: Medea was a granddaughter of the Sun, just like Phaedra. A sorceress, she tried to kill Theseus by poisoning him.

1653-4. *Despite the scheming ... daughter's place*: Theseus cannot forgive the rebellious Pallantides (see note on ll. 50–51), but the implication is that their sister Aricia will now be Theseus' acknowledged heir to the kingdoms of Athens and Trezene. Following their mother's disgrace, Phaedra's sons may well be sent to her family in Crete (cf. ll. 505–6).

Appendix I
Genealogical Table for *Phaedra*

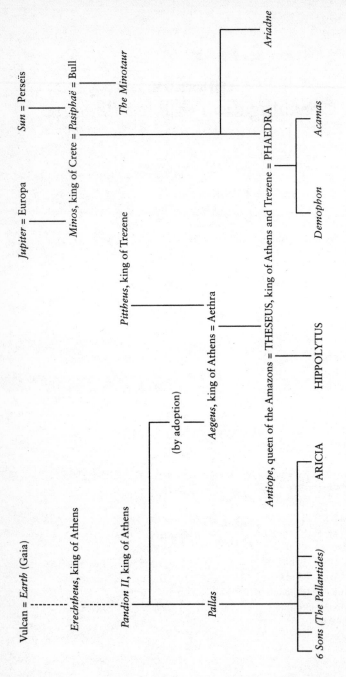

NB: Names in capitals are characters in *Phaedra*; names in italics are referred to in the play

Appendix II
Pronunciation of Proper Names in
Andromache and *Phaedra*

The list below comprises only those names that may be less familiar to readers or actors and potentially trickier to pronounce. Addi-
tional names cited in the prefaces to the plays are not included. The
stress mark ' comes after the stressed syllable, while long 'a' and 'i'
sounds (as in 'fate' and 'high') are indicated by a bar over the letter
(ā and ī).

ACHERON A'keron
AEGEUS Eej'oos (2 syllables)
ANDROMACHE Andro'makee
ANTIOPE Antī'opee
ARIADNE Ariad'nee
ARICIA Ari'cia
ASTYANAX Astī'anax
CEPHISA Sefee'sa
CERCYON Ser'syon
CLEONE Cleo'nee
COCYTUS Kosī'tus
ELIS Ee'lis
EPIRUS Eepī'rus
ERECHTHEUS Erek'thyoos
(3 syllables)
HADES Hā'deez
HYMEN Hī'men
ICARUS I'karus
ISMENE Ismā'nee
MEDEA Medee'a
MENELAUS Menelā'us
MINOS Mī'nos

MINOTAUR Mī'notor
MYCENAE Mīsee'nee
OENONE Eeno'nee
PANOPE Pan'opee
PASIPHAË Pasi'faee
(4 syllables)
PERIBOEA Peribee'a
PHAEDRA Fee'dra
PIRITHOÜS Piri'tho-us
(4 syllables)
PITTHEUS Pith'yoos
(2 syllables)
POLYXENA Poli'xena
PYLADES Pī'ladeez
SALAMIS Sa'lamis
SCIRON Sī'ron
SINNIS Sin'nis
TAENARUM Tee'narum
THERAMENES Thera'meneez
THESEUS Thees'yoos
(2 syllables)
TREZENE Trezeen'

THE STORY OF PENGUIN CLASSICS

Before 1946 ... 'Classics' are mainly the domain of academics and students; readable editions for everyone else are almost unheard of. This all changes when a little-known classicist, E. V. Rieu, presents Penguin founder Allen Lane with the translation of Homer's *Odyssey* that he has been working on in his spare time.

1946 Penguin Classics debuts with *The Odyssey*, which promptly sells three million copies. Suddenly, classics are no longer for the privileged few.

1950s Rieu, now series editor, turns to professional writers for the best modern, readable translations, including Dorothy L. Sayers's *Inferno* and Robert Graves's unexpurgated *Twelve Caesars*.

1960s The Classics are given the distinctive black covers that have remained a constant throughout the life of the series. Rieu retires in 1964, hailing the Penguin Classics list as 'the greatest educative force of the twentieth century.'

1970s A new generation of translators swells the Penguin Classics ranks, introducing readers of English to classics of world literature from more than twenty languages. The list grows to encompass more history, philosophy, science, religion and politics.

1980s The Penguin American Library launches with titles such as *Uncle Tom's Cabin*, and joins forces with Penguin Classics to provide the most comprehensive library of world literature available from any paperback publisher.

1990s The launch of Penguin Audiobooks brings the classics to a listening audience for the first time, and in 1999 the worldwide launch of the Penguin Classics website extends their reach to the global online community.

The 21st Century Penguin Classics are completely redesigned for the first time in nearly twenty years. This world-famous series now consists of more than 1300 titles, making the widest range of the best books ever written available to millions – and constantly redefining what makes a 'classic'.

The Odyssey continues ...

The best books ever written

PENGUIN (🐧) CLASSICS

SINCE 1946

Find out more at www.penguinclassics.com